S0-BSI-202

THE BUSINESS-ORIENTED CIO

A Guide to Market-Driven Management

George Tillmann

WILEY

John Wiley & Sons, Inc.

This book is printed on acid-free paper. ∞

Copyright © 2008 by George Tillmann. All rights reserved.
Published by John Wiley & Sons, Inc., Hoboken, New Jersey.
Published simultaneously in Canada.

No part of this publication may be reproduced, stored in a retrieval system, or
transmitted in any form or by any means, electronic, mechanical, photocopying,
recording, scanning, or otherwise, except as permitted under Section 107 or 108 of
the 1976 United States Copyright Act, without either the prior written permission
of the Publisher, or authorization through payment of the appropriate per-copy fee
to the Copyright Clearance Center, Inc., 222 Rosewood Drive, Danvers, MA 01923,
978-750-8400, fax 978-646-8600, or on the web at www.copyright.com. Requests to
the Publisher for permission should be addressed to the Permissions Department,
John Wiley & Sons, Inc., 111 River Street, Hoboken, NJ 07030, 201-748-6011,
fax 201-748-6008, or online at http://www.wiley.com/go/permissions.

Limit of Liability/Disclaimer of Warranty: While the publisher and author have
used their best efforts in preparing this book, they make no representations
or warranties with respect to the accuracy or completeness of the contents of
this book and specifically disclaim any implied warranties of merchantability
or fitness for a particular purpose. No warranty may be created or extended
by sales representatives or written sales materials. The advice and strategies
contained herein may not be suitable for your situation. You should consult with
a professional where appropriate. Neither the publisher nor author shall be liable
for any loss of profit or any other commercial damages, including but not limited
to special, incidental, consequential, or other damages.

For general information on our other products and services, or technical support,
please contact our Customer Care Department within the United States at
800-762-2974, outside the United States at 317-572-3993, or fax 317-572-4002.

Wiley also publishes its books in a variety of electronic formats. Some content that
appears in print may not be available in electronic books.

For more information about Wiley products, visit our Web site at
http://www.wiley.com.

Library of Congress Cataloging-in-Publication Data:

Tillmann, George.
 The business-oriented CIO : a guide to market-driven management / George
Tillmann.
  p. cm.
 Includes bibliographical references and index.
 ISBN 978-0-470-27812-3 (cloth)
  1. Chief information officers. 2. Information technology—Management.
3. Business planning. 4. Information technology—Economic aspects.
5. Consumer satisfaction—Economic aspects. I. Title. II. Title:
Market-driven management.
 HD30.2.T496 2008
 658.4'038—dc22

                                                              2008002760

Printed in the United States of America

10 9 8 7 6 5 4 3 2 1

For Gloria

Contents

Preface

The common knowledge of a profession often goes
unrecorded in technical literature for two reasons:
one need not preach commonplaces to the initiated,
and one should not attempt to inform the uninitiated
in publications they do not read.
—*Stephen Jay Gould*

Learning is not compulsory . . . neither is survival.
—*W. Edwards Deming*

Imagine that you are sitting across from a medical specialist who tells you that you have a rare and serious condition, the name of which you have never heard, and that you must undergo a dangerous operation, soon, if you are to survive. The rational patient would seek a second opinion, and perhaps even a third. The patient is not necessarily questioning the skill of the original physician. Rather, it is just good judgment to seek the opinion of and advice from more than one expert, especially when it concerns an area with which you are unfamiliar. Getting a second opinion can decrease nagging doubts.

Chief executive officers (CEOs) and business unit leaders rarely have the same option when it comes to information technology (IT). They can ask the opinion and advice of the head of IT, but they rarely have the opportunity to get a second opinion to decrease their nagging doubts. If IT were an unimportant backwater, then there would be little at stake. However, IT is becoming increasingly important to running a business. As the IT department increases in importance to the organization (be it a corporation, a nonprofit, or a government agency), the comfort level of senior management decreases in an inverse relationship.

Corporate and business unit executives live in a competitive world, where success or failure can be just a quarterly report to the shareholders away. Similar schedules and tensions exist in many nonprofit and government posts. As stressful as these senior positions might be, the angst associated with them is increased by their reliance on a function that is vital to their existence; expensive, and growing more costly each year; run by people of questionable education, ability, and business acumen; and involving a modern-day alchemy about which they have little knowledge and, perhaps, less interest. The result is a love-hate relationship that has nothing to do with technology or the people who manage it, but everything to do with an existential dependence on a function over which they have limited real power.

IT's status is rarely affirmed by the company's public displays of approval. There are parties when the sales department makes their quarterly numbers. Meeting or beating a production schedule can be a call for celebration for a manufacturer. Successfully running a disaster recovery test is not only a matter ignored by the business managers, but it might be one they never even knew occurred.

At times, IT seems to be a Cinderella-like stepdaughter: ignored when things go right, called on the carpet when they do not, always on the wrong end of the comment, "You should be more business-like." In fact, this seems to be the senior business manager's mantra regarding IT: Things not going well? Work on the technology. Things going well? Work on being more business-like.

Luckily, IT seems to be doing better on the technology front. Most IT organizations are getting a handle on the technology problems that disrupt service. With improved service, senior IT managers can focus on other issues. As technical staff and junior IT managers are left to keep the servers humming, senior IT managers are free to look more closely at that business-like thing.

How should IT act more business-like? What does that even mean? Where does one start? What, in fact, is wrong with what IT does now? Questions like these need professional help. Luckily, professional help is just a short drive away. One need only stroll into the mall or college bookstore to conclude that, if God had had an eight-day week, on the seventh day he would have created business self-help books. Bookstore shelves are awash with volumes of books telling businesspeople how to run successful and profitable enterprises. Not surprisingly, the business world is avidly reading these books. Forget that many of the authors are academics, who have never worked for a revenue-generating enterprise. Forget that the best companies to emulate in one decade are too often out of business in the next.

Moreover, these business knowledge pilgrims are right. There is good advice on those shelves. If managers are willing to invest a few evenings and Saturdays reading, they can obtain a wealth of knowledge that can help them manufacture their products, move their inventory, and sell their goods, all while keeping staff and stakeholders happy. It is truly an intellectual gold mine.

However, it is not a very useful gold mine for IT. Those rows of business books are 99.9 percent for-profit oriented. The academics, the celebrity CEOs, the business talk show hosts, are writing for revenue-generating organizations, not for cost centers. Unfortunately, very little has been written on managing an overhead function. A few areas receive some attention. There are materials on chief financial officer (CFO) issues, but not nearly as much on running a finance organization. Call centers are popular in the literature, but not the staffing and the day-to-day problems you might encounter in running such a department.

There is really only one thing to do: If one is going to get some expert help on running a cost center, then overhead managers have to adapt the advice given to revenue generators. The chief information officer (CIO) will need to take the for-profit concept of customer satisfaction and fit it into IT's internal context of user satisfaction. Senior IT managers will need to modify supply chain management to accommodate IT's technology procurement. IT will have to take the best thinking, of the best minds, about running a for-profit business and apply it to a cost center.

FIRSTHAND EXPERIENCE

I know, firsthand, the problems IT managers face. I worked as a programmer, a systems analyst, a programming manager, a technical consultant, and, for two decades, as a management consultant for Booz Allen Hamilton Inc., the international management and technology consulting firm, before becoming Booz Allen's CIO. Over the years, I have visited or worked for nearly 100 IT organizations on five continents. I have seen the good, the bad, and the truly dreadful. One of my early consulting goals was to bring the best current business thinking to my clients. As mentioned earlier, I discovered that while there was considerable literature published on how to run a for-profit business, advice for the cost center manager was meager at best. To help my clients, I had to modify the best for-profit business thinking to make it relevant for my overhead clients.

After years of telling CIOs how to manage their organizations, I was asked to lead Booz Allen's internal IT group. Because the firm had more than 19,000 employees, in 100 offices on six continents, my very first overhead job was a challenge. I quickly became a consumer of my own consulting advice. Being a CIO also gave me an opportunity not only to apply what I had preached to others, but also to add, modify, and hone my message.

My contribution to this book is not brains, but experience, and not always my own experience, but information passed to me by dozens of

CIOs and senior IT managers on what has worked for them. What I present I know works because either I tried it, or I have seen others try it, and it worked. Although much of the advice is referenced and footnoted, this is far from an academic text. It is not a work for the ivory tower, but rather for the corporate trenches. It is also not for the hopeless or desperate. If an IT shop is a language translator away from being offshored, then this book will not help.

This book is written for the CIOs and senior IT managers who are doing an acceptable to decent job running an IT organization, but would like to do a little better. Most IT shops that I have encountered are in the middle state of doing well at providing infrastructure, fair at providing end-user services, and somewhere between less than stellar and miserable at customer service. My hope is to help the 80 percent of the shops where the computers hum, the lights blink, but the users, while not terribly unhappy, are nonetheless underwhelmed by IT.

This is a guide for the CIO who is seen by senior business managers (CEO, business unit leaders, etc.) as a nice guy or gal, but not necessarily one of them. They might call on the CIO to attend an executive commit-tee meeting on budgeting, but would not think of calling him or her for a competitive strategy meeting.

The following should be thought of as a notebook of practical techniques that will help the moderately successful CIO improve (1) the services his or her shop offers; (2) the perception of IT, by the rest of the enterprise, as a valued member of the corporate family; and (3) the acceptance of IT managers and IT staff as valuable, and valued, corporate managers and staff.

DIVERSE IT AUDIENCE

CIOs are a diverse group. Aside from their short tenure, averaging between 24 and 30 months,[1] their backgrounds are quite different. Most CIOs come from the technology organization, although a growing minority come from the business side of the enterprise.[2] A few even come from legal, consult-ing, or academic backgrounds. An increasing number of technically trained senior IT managers have MBAs. Writing for such a varied group presents some fundamental problems, not the least of which is finding a common level of understanding of business concepts. As the quote from Stephen Jay Gould at the start of this preface states, "one need not preach common-places to the initiated, and one should not attempt to inform the uniniti-ated."[3] Gould's warning is clear: Do not talk down to the knowledgeable in order to inform the neophyte, and do not try to educate the uninformed. Then again, Gould never had to write for CIOs. At the risk of satisfying nobody, this book attempts to inform the uninformed while engaging the engaged. Certainly an IT challenge all its own.

This book is divided into 11 chapters. It starts with the areas most comfortable to IT, and then goes into what will be, for most IT organizations, new territory.

Part One The Fundamentals

The first chapter examines the relationship between IT and the business—the good as well as the challenges. Subsequent chapters focus on how for-profit experience can supplement some of IT's current best practices.

Chapter 1: In Search of Overhead Heroes   The CIO and the IT management team run a complex organization that, although it is an overhead function, is expected to perform like a business. Most CIOs successfully struggle to decrease the friction caused by the interaction between humans and machines, but many forget, or do not know how to deal with, the more destructive grating caused by trying to run an internal support function as a business.

Chapter 1 examines the end users' perception of IT and IT's perceptions of its internal customers. It also sets the stage for market-driven management, the approach of adapting for-profit best business practices for IT.

Chapter 2: IT Governance   IT's users are confused about how IT decisions are made, who makes them, and how they can be influenced. IT governance is a program to make the major IT decision process transparent and responsive to IT's user base. The IT industry has made significant strides in governance over the past few years, but the for-profits can still help. Examining how business governance bodies, such as the board of directors, function can improve IT's governance effectiveness.

Chapter 3: IT Strategy and Planning   IT needs to be keenly aware of where the business is going. It must also understand what IT needs to do in response to that business direction. Finally, IT has to ensure that all IT stakeholders know of, and are on board with, IT's approach. An IT strategy is an articulation of IT's response to the business strategy. It lays out what IT has to do, what it has to change, and what it should no longer do—to ensure that IT is ready when and where it is needed to support the business. The ancillary multiyear and annual plans and budgets fill out the IT strategy, providing the steps IT and the business need to take to realize both the business and IT strategies.

Chapter 4: Portfolio Management   Projects are the result of the business deciding to invest in itself. However, in most organizations, the resources needed for the investments exceed the resources available. Portfolio management should be an open and equitable process that allows the business to evaluate and decide which investments to fund and which to reject.

IT might be the steward of portfolio management, but it is owned and executed by, and for, the business. Some business world techniques, such as investment selection, funding, and planning, can make portfolio management less onerous and more productive.

Part Two Learning from the Best

Proven business best practices, some familiar to IT, others completely new, can be successfully applied to IT organizations, resulting in both better services for IT's end users and better relations with senior business management.

Chapter 5: Customer Management   IT is effective at managing assets and adequate at managing its own internal staff and processes, but disappointing when managing its internal customers. Yet, the for-profits consider customer management more important than the other two factors combined. This chapter presents some current business best-practice thinking on how to better understand customer needs, interpret their implications, and respond to them within the parameters established in IT's charter.

Chapter 6: Market Intelligence   Given a choice between knowing all about employees or knowing all about competitors, the for-profit manager would always choose the latter. Being aware of customer expectations and how vendors respond to those expectations is worth its weight in gold. IT has some advantages over its for-profit peers because it can gain the information it needs from sources other than competitors. This chapter examines how IT can implement a simple program to learn what other IT organizations are doing, including competitors, and how well what they are doing works.

Chapter 7: Service-Offering Management   In most IT organizations, users sit down with IT technicians to tell them what they need. Technology vendors employ product managers to tell their technical staff what customers need. Why the difference? Technology vendors are convinced that customers do not always know what they need. Customers might have an excellent understanding of the problem, but that does not mean that they are the best ones to define the solution. Product managers are used by vendors to represent the interests of the customer, examine and evaluate proposed solutions by technology staff, decide on how and who should provide the solution, and then measure its success. IT, with some effort, can do the same, creating service-offering managers whose job it is to determine customer need, analyze that need to understand its core components, request solutions from internal and/or external sources, and then pick the best provider to produce the solution.

Chapter 8: Performance Management   IT does an excellent job of measuring the performance of its technology. It does a considerably less effective job of measuring how well that same technology is meeting customer demand. Ask any for-profit manager, and he or she will say that one of the most important pieces of information a business manager can have is an understanding of how satisfied the customer is with the product or service offered. If satisfaction is not stellar, then the manager needs to know why and from where the dissatisfaction comes. IT collects considerable performance data about its technology, but very little about the end-user experience, yet the end-user experience ultimately determines IT's success or failure.

Part Three Pushing the Envelope

The for-profit world is no less dynamic than IT is. Some well-established concepts are just working their way into the business world. Other innovative business issues are just being investigated by academics and industry. All can have profound implications for IT.

Chapter 9: Organizational Competencies   Knowing how to use the information gained from the for-profits is not always easy. Some for-profit techniques are invaluable, whereas others can lead IT in the wrong direction. This chapter examines how IT can understand its core competencies and use them to develop the core services that are critical to the enterprise, while differentiating itself from third-party competitors.

Chapter 10: In Search of Customer Service   What is customer service? How do you measure it? What role does it play in the end-user experience? This chapter looks closely at service as understood and used by the academics, by business, and by customers. Weaving in the lessons gleaned from the previous chapters, service is reexamined, and the conclusions reapplied to explain some of the discrepancies and much of the disappointment surrounding customer service. Finally, its place in IT and the world of the for-profits is analyzed.

Chapter 11: Local Heroes   The problems with fitting the lessons from this book and other IT self-help concepts, such as *running IT like a business*, into an IT organization are not new. This chapter presents best practices from IT organizations that have successfully implemented these or similar programs.

THE DESIRED RESULT

The goal of this book is not to make the IT department into a for-profit business. It is, however, to borrow from the for-profits all of the knowledge, lessons learned, techniques, and tricks that have made them successful and that should help the average IT cost center run more effectively. The model is the successful technology vendor, which understands who its customers are, can articulate its customers' needs, and can provide the product or services to fulfill those needs.

George Tillmann
georgetillman@optonline.net

NOTES

1. Paul Strassmann, "The Cost of Short-Term CIOs," *ComputerWorld*, May 5, 2004. www.strassmann.com/pubs/cw/short-term-cios.shtml; and Allen Bernard. CIO Tenure Improving. *CIO Update*, July 8, 2005. www. cioupdate.com/career/article.php/3518821.
2. Edward Prewitt and Lorraine Cosgrove Ware, "The State of the CIO 2006," *CIO Magazine*, January 1, 2006. http://www.cio.com/ archive/010106/JAN1SOC.pdf; and Lorraine Cosgrove Ware, "The State of the CIO 2003," *CIO Magazine*, March 23, 2003, http://www2. cio.com/research/surveyreport.cfm?=54.
3. Stephen Jay Gould, *The Structure of Evolutionary Theory*, Belknap Press of Harvard University Press, 2002, pp. 749–750.

Acknowledgments

Many individuals contributed their time and brainpower to this undertaking. Daniel Gasparro and Rick Boulin, of Booz Allen Hamilton Inc., were invaluable in solidifying and testing some of the concepts in this book. Chris Verhoef, a professor in the Department of Computer Science at VU Amsterdam, provided guidance and advice concerning the analytical subjects in the text, although I know I have not done justice to either his work or his help. Joe Simon, CIO of Viacom Inc., provided valuable insight into the content of the book. Linda Billard and Theresa Meola helped make the manuscript readable. At John Wiley & Sons, Sheck Cho and Natasha Wolfe oversaw the magic that turns a manuscript into a finished work.

I also want to thank the many IT managers and staff (both client and nonclient professionals) I interviewed over the years as part of my consulting assignments. Although I hope I helped them, they also helped me. Sometimes their assistance came as information about their successes. Sometimes it was sharing with me their failures. Their hard lessons learned are in this book.

Last, but certainly not least, I want to thank my wife, Gloria, who provided the quiet encouragement that kept me going on what sometimes seemed a quixotic journey. Thanks to all of you.

PART ONE

THE FUNDAMENTALS

1

In Search of Overhead Heroes

A customer is the most important visitor in our premises. He is not dependent on us, we are dependent on him. He is not an interruption in our work, he is the purpose of it. He is not an outsider to our business, he is part of it. We are not doing him a favour by serving him, he is doing us a favour by giving us an opportunity to do so.

—*Mahatma Gandhi*

Politics would be a helluva good business if it weren't for the goddamned people.

—*Richard M. Nixon*

"Build a better mousetrap and the world will beat a path to your door," is the often-quoted advice from the American man of letters and philosophy, Ralph Waldo Emerson. The message is that ingenuity and hard work are all one needs to succeed. Unfortunately, Emerson never said it, or at least never wrote it. It is reported that the closest Emerson ever came to the statement was in his *Journal*, published in 1855, where he said, "I trust a good deal to common fame, as we all must. If a man has good corn, or wood, or boards, or pigs to sell, or can make better chairs or knives, crucibles, or church organs, than anybody else, you will find a broad, hard-beaten road to his house, though it be in the woods."[1]

It was only years later, after Emerson's death, that Sarah Yule reported that she heard Emerson say, "If a man can write a better book, preach a better sermon, or make a better mousetrap, than his neighbor, though he builds his house in the woods, the world will make a beaten path to his door."

Regardless of its origin, it is one of those culturally iconic quotes that define a country, a time, and a generation and then inspires other countries, future times, and newer generations. It is a truth that all people who admire resourcefulness and persistence hold dear. Whether Emerson said it or not is unimportant. It is the message that is momentous. Except the message isn't true.

More than 4,400 mousetraps have been patented in the United States alone. There are no accurate figures for the number of patent requests rejected by the patent office or the number of devices never submitted for patent protection in the first place. One can easily imagine U.S. inventors creating 10,000 or more *Mus musculus* death machines during the past 150 years. Of those 4,400 patents granted, fewer than two dozen have ever earned their creators any money.[2]

Why? Well, there are two possible reasons. One, none of them was any good. The U.S. Patent Office has received patent requests for some very strange devices for exterminating mice. Most of them would eliminate mice, but the methods were often clumsy, complicated, or very, very messy. Even so, it is hard to believe that none of those thousands of devices were as good as the current snap trap created in 1899 by John Mast and patented in 1903.

The second, and more probable, reason why so few mousetrap inventors have been rewarded is that doing something better is not necessarily a formula for success. The 1970s saw the VHS/Betamax wars, where the two standards contended for the lion's share of the videocassette market. Technical experts agree that Betamax had the better technology, but VHS took the prize. Many software experts argue that over the past 20 years, the various versions of the Apple Macintosh operating system have been superior to those offered by Microsoft, but Microsoft's share of the personal computer operating system market is more than 20 times that of Apple. Being better does not mean you win. Put another way, having a better mousetrap might be a necessary condition for success, but it is not a sufficient condition. To succeed, you have to be more than good. You have to actively reach out and grab the market.

THE PROBLEM

From a corporate history perspective, information technology (IT) is relatively new. Accounting goes back more than 4,000 years, with modern accounting tracing its roots to the sixteenth century. Human resources (HR) had to exist in ancient times in order to entice freemen to work as rowers on the early Roman galley ships. Considerable recruiting skills would be needed to convince people to sign up for the job. (Slaves as rowers were introduced later when the job required less skill, and multiple rowers pulled oars.) IT's start is more modest, and whether you trace it to the 1950s, with the introduction of the first business computer, or go back a few decades to the first tabulating machines, it is still the new kid on the block.

However, IT is more than just new, it is also different—very different. In the early days of IT, the computer room was often behind floor-to-ceiling glass walls, just outside the corporate headquarters lobby, attended by a priesthood in white lab coats. IT was a symbol of the mystery and magic of the future—certainly not a compatriot of the eye-shaded office workers of the nineteenth century.

The irony is that the corporations IT was mesmerizing were run by those same nineteenth-century eye-shaded office workers, from the lowest clerks right up to the CEO. While they enjoyed taking off their eyeshades to gaze into the future, they just as quickly put them back on to get down to work. IT, while providing a captivating glimpse of tomorrow, was needed to work in the present, a challenge IT struggled to fulfill.

IT's story is one of success and disappointment. No other organization has brought so much change to the enterprise in so short a period of time. Its tale is not just one of efficiency and effectiveness, but one of possibility. Without IT, businesses would be limited in the number of customers they could serve, the number of transactions they could process, and the number and breadth of products and services they could offer. The modern corporation would not only be less efficient without IT, it could not exist. One would think that being the catalyst for all this change, IT would be a corporate hero. Unfortunately, too often, IT is seen unkindly by both its owners and its users.

Exactly how good or bad is IT? No one really knows. Trying to find an assessment of the state of the IT industry is difficult. A search of the academic literature is disappointing. Although there are many articles in scholarly journals about how to measure end-user satisfaction, few of them have done it. What has been studied is limited in geography or type of technology use (i.e., satisfaction with data warehouses, enterprise information systems, web searches, end-user computing interfaces). Even less attention has been paid to changes (positive or negative) over time, giving little indication as to whether things are getting better or worse. The trade press is no better at clearing up the confusion, because reports of IT's successes and failures are anecdotal, providing little data for any scientific analysis.

Vendors also are of little help in clarifying the situation. They readily cite improvements that can be attained if you use their product, but the numbers are often extravagant and unbelievable. Even credible numbers are rarely backed up by standard statistical methods. Longitudinal studies are either unobtainable or limited to before-and-after comparisons.

Surprisingly, the best source of available information about end-user satisfaction with IT comes from IT, and the story is not good. IT staff report that users are dissatisfied with IT, feeling that its services underperform, are overpriced, and are poorly supported. Development projects come in for even harsher criticism: They are viewed as consistently late, exorbitantly expensive, and functionally poor.

Business Concerns about IT

Chief information officers (CIOs), and other senior IT managers, have had a tough time over the past 40 years. Business expectations are high, while praise is low. In the late 1970s and early 1980s, IT was seen as the force that would radically change business for the better. E-commerce followed with an almost euphoric view of technology that bulged university computer science departments and sent IT wages soaring. In reality, if there has been any significant change over the past four decades, it is that user expectation is rising while user satisfaction is dropping. CIOs and industry analysts can legitimately argue that service is actually better than it was 20 years ago. Uptime is better, response time is shorter, and unexpected results are on the decline. Yet, if anything, users are less satisfied now than they were two decades ago. Why? Well the only potential reason can be creeping expectation. While IT might have been viewed as a novelty in 1970, it is now a critical component of the average business process. Outages that were understandable in 1980 are intolerable now. While a machine down for two hours in 1980 might cost the business little, a machine down for a similar amount of time now could result in the loss of millions of dollars in revenue.

There is another change between then and now. While IT was viewed as a laboratory science then, it is a business tool now. IT's elevation from lab experiment to business component is not without its downside. As white coats gave way to pinstripes, IT staff were expected to shift from being technologists to businesspeople. This transition is not without its difficulties. First, the chief executive officer (CEO) and the business unit heads are not of one mind on the transition. While they *want* IT to be a business component, in reality, they are still unsure and uncomfortable with its magic status. Despite the laptop on their desk or the family personal computer at home, many have little knowledge of, and less interest in, IT. Worse, as technology shifts from a business nice-to-have to a must-have, executives are uncomfortable understanding so little about something so pivotal. Most would rather wrestle with hostile takeovers than sit through a meeting on software installation.

Thus, the IT conundrum—IT, the unwanted and misunderstood stepchild, holds the future of the enterprise in its hands. But how can senior business managers allow the future of the company to fall into the hands of IT people, particularly when they have some serious concerns about IT? High costs and the realization that IT can make or break a business have led business managers to bring IT under greater scrutiny. Frequently, business managers feel that IT is:

- *Too expensive.* Whether IT is *too* expensive is debatable. What is not debatable is that IT *is* expensive. The average $3 billion company will spend more than $100 million annually on IT.[3] At such levels, it is unthinkable that IT would escape scrutiny in normal times and not be the subject of additional oversight in bad times, when corporate revenues are under pressure.

- *Not working on the right things.* Business managers have concerns about the quality of IT decision making. Are the right projects being funded? Why were some projects rejected? How are these decisions made? Who makes them? What can be done if a business unit feels that it is not getting its due?

- *Distributes services inequitably.* One of the most common criticisms of IT is that users feel that they pay and pay, but get little in return. They feel that IT is not fairly distributing resources to the business units commensurate with business need or contributions. Making matters worse, they suspect that competitors are getting more from their internal IT organizations for equal or less money. In short, they are convinced that IT resources are not equitably distributed throughout the organization.

- *Slow, expensive, and underperforming.* Users feel that IT projects are too expensive, functionally poor, and take longer than they should. Many feel that outside vendors could probably do a better job than the internal IT organization. There is data to support this belief. According to the Standish Group, more than half of the IT projects undertaken will experience cost overruns in excess of 180 percent. They also report that more than 30 percent of the projects will be cancelled before completion, while completed projects will only include about 42 percent of their proposed functionality.[4] This is a dismal picture at best.

- *Poorly managed.* In the 1960s, senior managers were comfortable leaving IT to the technically inclined, for several reasons. First, it was not that expensive. IT cost, as a percentage of revenue, was relatively small. Second, the impact of IT on the business was minimal. For the most part, IT produced reports on work done, but did not do the work itself. If the machine failed, humans could usually take up the slack. Third, IT was usually under the direct control of the chief financial officer (CFO), a business unit leader, or some similar senior business manager. This gave corporate management the comfort of knowing that someone who knew the business and how to manage was in charge.

Today, this is often not the case. IT is now quite expensive and is routinely critical to the delivery of the enterprise's primary products and services. Another difference is that now, a technically trained CIO usually leads IT. Because of the cost and importance of IT, CIOs frequently sit at the executive table and are witnesses of, if not parties to, the most senior business issues and decisions. In this exclusive club, the criterion for membership is not knowledge about technology, but business acumen. Many CIOs do not possess this quality. This shortfall is obvious to the other members of the management team and undercuts their confidence in the CIO. While some CEOs and management team members are willing, or at least resolved, to allow IT personnel to make some technical decisions, they are very uncomfortable with having the IT department affect the course of the business.

- *Out of touch with the business/market.* Although the phrase, "They just don't understand the business," has been used to describe virtually everyone outside of the business unit, IT has come under more than its share of criticism. There is often a level of truth to the charge. Many IT professionals work more for the IT profession than they do for their employer. You can see this in company hiring practices. If a manufacturing firm needs a network specialist, it is often comfortable hiring one who had previously worked at a bank or for a retailer. Even senior managers, such as CIOs, have been known to cross industries with ease. In the 1970s and 1980s, many firms were more comfortable

---

Why Do They Think Such Terrible Things About IT?

The ancient Greeks believed that the heavens were made of water. The water was kept from flooding the earth by a giant transparent sphere that covered the planet. Where do they come up with these ideas? Well, when people are trying to understand something, and real information about it is scarce or nonexistent, they tend to fill in the gaps with all sorts of strange explanations. Sea monsters devouring ships, witches casting spells to bring plagues down upon towns, people being sacrificed for rain or fertility, and a host of other strong-on-emotion and short-on-data interpretations of natural events come about.

The remedy is information. Discovering that the heavens are not made of water, that vermin and poor sanitation cause plague and disease, and that sacrificing children has no effect on the weather or fertility, brings about, if not more satisfying results, at least better-understood ones. The same is true for IT.

When even the brightest business managers are kept in the dark about the facts of a situation, their imaginations start churning. Why does IT cost so much? Why can't we have our customer relationship application this year? Why did that other division get its supply chain management system when it contributes less to IT than we do? In almost all cases, the imaginings of end users are more dramatic than the realities of IT. Angst can be reduced by making a few facts available.

hiring CIOs from their hardware vendors than they were acquiring them from within or from competitors. This has led to a belief that the people making IT decisions for the business really do not understand the business. So how good could those decisions be?

- *A risk to the business.* From the enterprise perspective, there are two types of risks: loss of service and loss of a positive face to the market. The first risk is the rather traditional system-is-down syndrome, which has been known to cost companies millions of dollars in lost revenue and market capitalization. Fortunately, the loss is usually restricted to the time the system was not operating.

  Loss of a positive face to the market, such as bad publicity or lost customer loyalty, can drive down sales for a protracted period of time. An example would be the damage to corporate reputations from the loss or theft of customer data. This latter type of risk could prove more expensive because it can have negative effects far into the future.

Business concerns about IT can be summarized into four areas:

1. *Efficiency.* Efficiency is typically defined as doing things in a way that minimizes the expenditure of time, resources, or effort.

   IT's customers are concerned about IT's ability to manage corporate assets (technology), business investments (projects), and operations (processes). They point to rising operating costs without the associated rise in benefits, projects that cost more than planned, or projects that are delivered late while not providing the anticipated functionality.

2. *Effectiveness.* Effectiveness is usually defined as doing the right things to gain the right results.

   Users are unsure that IT is heading in the right direction or in a direction congruent with corporate and business unit goals. They also question whether IT can perform the correct actions to produce the desired results. Ineffectiveness can sometimes be masked by efficiency, presenting the business with a false indicator that things are going well. The confusion can be summed up by Yogi Berra's quip, "We're lost, but we're making great time."

3. *Transparency.* Transparency is the level of openness of an organization. It is characterized by full and accurate disclosure of the policies, processes, participants, facts, issues, and decisions made by an organization.

   Business managers are unsure of what IT is doing, why they are doing it, and how they are going about it. They do not know who is making the decisions that could significantly affect the business, or the data and steps used in the decision process. Users want to be a part of the IT decision process or at least be adequately informed about it.

4. *Safe hands.* Safe hands involves the positive feeling people have when a function is under the leadership of a competent individual or team that can be counted on to do the right thing. Safe hands are the people who can be trusted to look out for others' interests without being micromanaged or constantly monitored. When things occasionally go wrong, they can be counted on to inform the appropriate parties and take corrective action in a timely manner.

Business management is unsure that IT staff are safe hands. They question whether the IT team has the knowledge, experience, and wherewithal to make the right decisions, carry them out, and report progress to stakeholders in a timely manner.

Oddly, many IT staff would agree with their end users' assessment and criticisms of IT. They see themselves doing a good job, but not a great job. They recognize that most of what they do is invisible to users, and that what is visible is often not their strength.

IT's Frustrations with the Business

IT has its own frustrations with the business. They often feel that:

- *Business is not engaged.* The most common complaint from IT planners is that they cannot get the time and attention of business managers to discuss business needs and IT services. Steering committees, planning boards, and customer councils have difficulty getting business staff to join, attend, and engage in the discussions. Both the users and IT staff too often see involvement in these organizations as a waste of their professional time. They feel that topics are uninteresting, that discussions are either endless or filled with partisan fighting, that decisions are not made, or, if made, are ignored, and that the impact on one's career is questionable.

- *Business is poor at saying what it wants.* When business staff members do engage, they are often incapable of articulating what the business is doing in the present, where it plans to be in the future, and what role IT should play in either case. The problem often stems from poor business plans or occurs because the staff members who represent the business are too junior to be adequately aware of business direction and needs.

  Not all businesses publish or widely distribute business plans. Often considered confidential documents, these plans are rarely shared with middle or junior management, and certainly not with the IT staff. The result is that middle or junior management staff are not able to answer the questions IT asks about business direction. Sometimes business plans are well known but not recorded in a single document. The business strategy might be spread across numerous memos and meeting minutes. These documents might be available for IT staff if they know where to look for them.

Finally, business staff might know where the business is heading but are unable to articulate the most technology-relevant points to technical staff. Their lack of even fundamental IT knowledge can impede their ability to express the role technology can play in satisfying business needs or exploiting opportunities.

- *Business is dismissive of IT's concerns.* IT often feels ignored by senior business managers. There was a case of two IT directors who flew to Tokyo at the request of the Asia business unit leader. When they got there, they were kept waiting for two days. After finally being ushered into the business unit leader's office, they were asked what *they* wanted. The two IT directors sat there stunned and did not know what to say. After a short and unproductive meeting, they flew back to the United States.

  Less dramatic are the reports by IT staff, including the CIO of senior business managers, repeatedly scheduling and rescheduling meetings. When the meetings finally took place, IT staff were given only an inadequate 15 or 20 minutes to discuss business direction and needs.

  Problems are exacerbated if IT is seen by the business as coming from a different culture or from an oversight organization. One CIO reported that no one from the Latin America region would talk to her or anybody on her staff. They simply did not trust a corporate-run IT team.

- *User expectation is often unrealistic.* IT staff complain that users expect a level of service from IT that matches the service they get from the electric company. Users want and expect that all IT services will be available at peak performance all the time at a relatively inexpensive price.

The fundamental issues facing IT can be summed up as follows: IT has a serious problem if senior business management does not understand how IT decisions are made, the types and costs of the services IT provides, or the investments IT makes.

THE IT SOLUTION

IT, by and large, is sensitive to the criticisms of its users and has been working to alleviate them. Its response tends to center on four areas: new technology, monitoring tools, standardized processes, and running IT like a business.

New Technology

Most in IT see their primary mission as evaluating, procuring, distributing, and supporting technology for their user base. Technology, and knowledge about technology, is what distinguishes IT from the rest of the enterprise. Capitalizing on this difference, IT tries to keep up on the latest technology, looking for that new widget that will help the business.

Monitoring Tools

Recent years have seen the monitoring tool market explode. Mainframes allowed most system-monitoring tools to run within the mainframe itself. The vendor-supplied software and vendor-generated data allowed IT to have a decent picture of the service the machine provided and to diagnose problems when they arose. Vendors supporting early midrange servers offered limited tools to help understand what the hardware and software were doing, and when they did provide information, it was usually limited to the machine on which the monitoring software was running.

With the new millennium, that limitation is changing. Data center managers can now purchase monitoring and diagnostic tools that can peek into data packets, view queues, and understand the load differences across multiple servers, all in real time. These tools are a significant leap in understanding what the technology is doing and help in the diagnosis and remediation of problems.

Standardized Processes

As the size of IT has grown, so has its need for new processes and procedures to ensure that all of the components of IT are working together. Organizations that have well-defined processes and procedures can discover that they are no longer suitable. What worked so well for a $1 billion company can be woefully inadequate when revenue tops $4 billion. Business growth and new technology can render once-excellent processes obsolete.

Rather than creating new processes from scratch, there is a trend to apply tried-and-true standardized procedures. Popular sources of models for new processes include the Capability Maturity Model Integration (CMMI) from the Software Engineering Institute, the Information Technology Infrastructure Library (ITIL) from the Central Computer and Telecommunications Agency of the UK Government, Six Sigma from Motorola, and Control Objects for Information and Related Technology (COBIT) from the IT Governance Institute, part of the former Information Systems Audit and Control Association (ISACA).

Running IT Like a Business

One of the more popular CIO-level self-help trends is *running IT like a business*. It is everywhere in magazines and in newspapers. Virtually every

IT journal published has something to say about *running IT like a business* (RITLAB). Because RITLAB is not attributable to a single source or its popularization to a single author, exactly what it entails can be elusive. However, two themes appear in almost all discussions of the topic: (1) aligning IT with the business and (2) cost management.

Aligning IT with the Business   Business alignment is the effort to ensure that the business and IT—its goals, direction, and timetables—are synchronized. The phraseology is unfortunate—How can IT *align* with the business? Isn't IT *part* of the business?—but the sentiment is clear and on target. A lack of business–IT congruence can result in several mismatches or cross-purpose activities. The most obvious is a strategy mismatch, such as the business focusing on becoming a low-cost provider while IT is providing premium services. Poor alignment can lead to directionality problems. For example, the business is planning to significantly shrink its operation in Asia while doubling it in Europe, just as IT is preparing for slight growth in both geographies. There can also be misalignments related to business model decisions, such as a senior business management decision to distribute business authority and responsibility while IT is still centralized.

Awareness of business–IT alignment problems is not new to *running IT like a business*. Sources report that it has been a top CIO concern for a number of years.[5] The problem probably persists because no single solution will resolve it. Rather, it will require action on multiple fronts. Companies that have achieved some level of recognized alignment have focused on IT governance, IT strategy, portfolio management, customer management, and a few other programs to solve the problem.

Cost Management   The 1990s and the first few years of the new millennium were times of significant corporate cost cutting. When business took an axe to its cost structure, IT was required to do the same. IT was a significant target because, for more than a decade, it was growing at a rate greater than the businesses themselves. Senior management became engaged when it realized that the small report printing organization in the basement of the finance department was suddenly costing the company $100 million per year.

For many organizations, the drastic cost-cutting days are over. However, prudence dictates that IT monitor its costs or, once again, it will get help from corporate in managing its expenses. Cost management can help avoid the necessity of cost cutting by ensuring that costs are justifiable and within acceptable limits.

User Reaction

Senior business management is more hopeful than pleased with IT's approach. Rather than viewing IT's pursuit of *new technology* as a strength, some senior business managers (e.g., CEO, corporate, business unit leaders, etc.) see IT as a toy store filled with the latest gizmos and digital trinkets. Only occasionally do they note some genuine new service to the enterprise. If asked, many senior business managers would rather have IT forgo the new toys and focus on making the existing ones work properly.

Running IT like a business has been well received by business managers as an approach, and they are waiting for some payoff, which seems a long time in coming. So far, neither the business nor IT has been willing to declare RITLAB a success.

There is little reaction to, and less understanding of, IT's other initiatives. Opinions about *standardized processes* and *monitoring tools* are rare because they are largely hidden from IT's customers.

Problem with Running IT Like a Business

IT's current approach is not wrong, it just doesn't go far enough. Keeping up on the latest *new technology* trends allows IT to acquire *monitoring tools* or provide better and/or cheaper services to its users. *Standardized processes*, whether adopted unchanged or used as a model for more customized processes, are also a good idea. *Running IT like a business* is, without a doubt, an excellent strategy. However, if IT and the business aren't headed in the same direction, then results will be unpredictable.

New governance models, better planning and budgeting, and business participation in portfolio management are all individually excellent ideas that every IT shop should employ. Collectively, they point out something critical that is missing.

All of these concepts will work to gain the support and trust of senior business management, but what will they do for the little guy? How does an IT strategy help the average clerk working to process orders or the salesperson on the road trying to access customer information? Planning, budgeting, and managing costs are all activities senior business managers want to hear about, and all are activities the average company employee, working day after day in the corporate trenches, couldn't care less about.

Shifting from calling them end users to calling them customers, as some IT organizations are starting to do, is a good move. It better reflects the nature of the relationship between IT and the user and is a good everyday reminder for IT staff. However, it does not go far enough. IT has two very different customers. There are the senior business managers—the CEO, corporate managers, and business unit leaders—who want accountability from IT. Given their ongoing relationship with IT, a more suitable name for this group would be clients. There are also the day-to-day workers, whose concerns center on application availability, good response times, and easy-to-use interfaces. They want quick response when there is a problem, and they do not want to see or hear from IT at other times. A better name for this group would be technology consumers.

Customers: Clients or Consumers?

For most people, customers, clients, and consumers all describe the same population. The business world is a little different, and although there are no standard definitions, there is a common usage. Customer is most often a generic term for anyone who buys or acquires a product or service from a vendor.

Clients are customers who have an ongoing relationship with a business. A business might not see a client every day or even every year, but when it does, the current relationship is based on past relationships. Lawyers, accountants, and investment bankers tend to refer to their customers as clients.

Consumers are customers who have a transactional relationship with the vendor. The customer might visit a business every day, but each transaction with the vendor is independent of every other transaction. Retail stores and restaurants tend to have a consumer relationship with their customers.

IT's relationship with senior business managers, who might be on IT committees, involved with IT budgets, or responsible for the oversight of IT's functions, is a vendor–client relationship. End users, who might rely on IT's services every day, but who only interact with the IT organization occasionally, and those interactions are episodic, have a more consumer-type relationship with IT.

If we look at the current strategy followed by many IT shops, we see that there has been considerable effort over the last few years to please IT's clients: the senior business managers who approve budgets and fire CIOs. But what about the technology consumers? What has IT done for them lately? IT's treatment of the technology consumer—the part of IT's

Exhibit 1.1   IT Clients versus IT Consumers

IT CLIENTS	IT CONSUMERS
• *Who*: Senior business managers (CEO, senior corporate staff, business unit leaders)	• *Who*: Basic IT users (clerks, salesmen, professional staff, managers)
• *Interaction with IT*: Ongoing through meetings, planning sessions, budgeting, etc.	• *Interaction with IT*: Transactional, when something breaks or does't work properly
• *Concerns*: Alignment with the business and costs	• *Concerns*: Availability and performance
• *Likely topic for next interaction*: Strategy or budget	• *Likely topic for next interaction*: Something that doesn't work properly

customer base that generates the revenue that supports the large paychecks for both senior business managers and IT staff—has changed little over the last decade.

Who—clients or consumers—does IT need to satisfy? The answer is both. Catering to one and ignoring the other is a no-win strategy. The consumers generate the revenue IT likes to spend. Ignoring this group is a nonstarter. However, IT is not going to get the chance to satisfy the consumers unless the clients say so. Client approval is needed for IT to do its job.

As Exhibit 1.1 shows, the challenge for IT is adequately serving all of its customers—clients and consumers. To do this, IT needs to recognize that clients and consumers have different needs and different criteria for IT success.

WHAT THE FOR-PROFITS CAN TEACH IT

Without a doubt, IT needs to be faster in developing new service offerings, it needs to focus more on customer service, and it must be more conscious of the image it projects to its customer base. The first two needs are probably obvious to most readers, and certainly areas where the advice created for the for-profits can be adapted for IT use. The third need, that IT tell its own story better, is not as obvious and might need some explanation.

IT has, for the most part, stood silent as critics have berated it for poor service, missed deadlines, and bloated budgets. In other cases, IT's response has been seen as inadequate, or worse, defensive. Both business and IT senior management tend to agree that IT has not been very effective in justifying its actions and its costs. Making matters worse, the negative attitude coming from users, real or imagined, dissuades IT from asking for help when a problem arises that is not obvious to the business. Instead, *fortress IT* hides problems, never to be shared with outsiders if at all possible.

The for-profits have considerable skill and success at building positive brand images and in marketing their products and services. Their knowledge can certainly help IT management build a positive image of IT that encourages constructive user communication and involvement.

Which brings us to the awkward reality of IT's situation. While there are a plethora of books published by business gurus for managing a for-profit organization, there are very few books published for managing a cost center. The revenue generators have their business heroes, such as Porter, Deming, and Drucker, but where are the overhead heroes? It appears there are none. If cost center managers want business guru help, then they will have to adapt the advice written for the revenue generators. This is the strategy behind market-driven management—taking the best advice from the for-profit business gurus and adapting it for the overhead manager.

Market-Driven Management

If any leader of a support organization is to acquire expert help in running his or her cost center, then that leader will have to settle for the advice given to the revenue generators. Some ideas can be directly applied to an overhead organization. Others must be modified or adapted to furnish the best value. Applying the best thinking on how to run a for-profit business to IT is called market-driven management (MDM). The name was chosen to suggest the impact that free-market processes can have on the captive markets found *inside* most enterprises. MDM is a program of using proven business techniques to help IT provide the technology-based services and support required by both senior business management clients and technology consumers.

MDM consists of seven components: (1) IT governance, (2) IT strategy and planning, (3) portfolio management, (4) customer management, (5) market intelligence, (6) service-offering management, and (7) performance management. Most of these components will be familiar to IT. None of the most recognized components, such as IT governance or portfolio management, have been radically changed from the familiar. MDM does not change them, but rather supplements them with methods, tactics, and techniques that can significantly expand their effectiveness. Similar to an engine additive for your car, MDM can improve the performance of IT governance.

Other MDM components will be new to most IT organizations. Service-offering management, for example, builds on the experience of successful technology vendors. It incorporates into IT what technology vendors do to design and deliver IT services customers want and are willing to pay for.

Who Can Benefit from Market-Driven Management?

Will the for-profit-based MDM help every IT organization? No, at least not to the same extent. The benefits derived from MDM depend on the level of sophistication of the IT organization. Some IT departments have fundamental problems providing basic services. For them, keeping the systems up and running takes all of their energies. Looking at for-profit business techniques might not be the most effective use of their time. Other IT organizations are already doing what the for-profits are doing, so the MDM benefits for them might be limited. However, most IT shops could gain from one or more of the for-profits' techniques.

As Exhibit 1.2 shows, approximately 10 to 20 percent of the IT organizations are in the *barely useful* band on the chart. They provide basic services, mostly to the support areas such as finance and human resources. IT support for direct revenue generation (e.g., e-commerce, real-time inventory, just-in-time manufacturing, etc.) is minimal to nonexistent. IT staff spend most of their time responding to problems and putting out fires. IT's goal is to get through the day without a major disaster. One day

Exhibit 1.2   IT Value Matrix

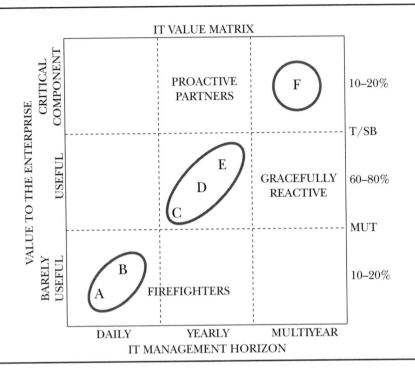

at a time also happens to be their planning horizon. They are an almost totally reactive organization. IT departments A and B in Exhibit 1.2 would be in this category. A good name for this group is *Firefighters*.

Most IT organizations are in the *useful* band of the chart. They get by, and would be viewed by their internal customers, as just okay. They provide the basic services the enterprise needs. They do a fine job supporting other core services, such as finance and HR, and are starting to help in the direct revenue-generating areas. The company revenue generators feel that IT is a useful although not critical function. They would never think of IT as their business partner. IT still puts out fires and spends too much time on remediation, but its staff have developed skills and internal processes to the point that their firefighting is smooth and coordinated.

Compared with the chaos of the *Firefighters*, this group's work looks like a ballet. They are still reactive, but they are *Gracefully Reactive*—a good description of this group. Their experience and skills disguise just how reactive they really are. They are like "the man behind the curtain" in the *Wizard of Oz*. As long as their internal clients keep looking at the stage, and not behind the curtain, IT appears to have its act together. They are good at annual planning and budgeting, even if the plans are little more than annotated budgets. Thinking beyond the next 12 months or trying to anticipate business needs is rare. They are IT departments C, D, and E on Exhibit 1.2.

IT department F is in a class by itself. It does a good job providing the needed support services, but it also works with the business units to extend technology into the business itself. Rather than waiting for its internal customers to come to IT with new ideas, these IT departments seek out opportunities to work with the business to jointly develop fresh ways for embedding IT in the business. Their internal customers see them as a *critical component* of the business. Because they are so in step with the business, their IT strategy and multiyear plans are in tune with the business's strategy and multiyear plans. At the very most, 10 to 20 percent of the IT organizations have achieved this status. A good name for this group is *Proactive Partners*.

Firefighter organizations face some critical decisions. At the very least, IT needs to provide basic services without interruption. If they cannot do this, then they might want to consider learning a third-world language, because outsourcing might be just weeks away. Their salvation is technology. They need better technology, or, more likely, need to better manage existing technology. The solution to their problems lies in the organizational, skill, and process changes that many of the vendors, consultants, and nonprofit support organizations can help provide.

The best of the *Firefighters* has run into the minimal utility threshold (MUT), a wall that stops them from progressing beyond *barely useful*. To cross the MUT, they need to learn not just how to manage technology, but how to manage a technology organization.

Most IT organizations, between 60 and 80 percent, exist in the band just above the MUT. They provide the basic services internal customers expect. They might do it elegantly, or they just might get by while hiding their reactive activities. They have successfully learned how to manage technology. Those near the top of the *useful* band have also learned to manage the people who oversee the technology and provide the structure and processes needed to keep the IT shop humming. The downside of this group is that they still provide technology to users. Their management skills are limited to managing technology, the IT organization, the staff that supports it, and IT's internal processes.

Those at the top of the *useful* band have gone as far as they can go as they come up against the Technology/Service Boundary (T/SB). To go beyond the T/SB, they need skills beyond those required to manage a technology organization. They will need to acquire the skills necessary to run a business.

The *Proactive Partners* do not necessarily do a better job than the *Gracefully Reactive* organizations in providing basic support services and maybe even revenue-generating services. The main difference between the *Proactive Partners* and the *Gracefully Reactives* is that the *Proactive Partners* do not sit in the IT organization waiting for the phone to ring. They meet with their business users; or even better, they create opportunities to meet with business users and discuss how they can provide additional services. They function much like a technology vendor seeking out opportunities to sell IT services to the business. They recognize that their customers do not want technology, but technology-based services. They understand that IT is not a technology organization, but a business organization whose mission is providing technology services.

Many resources are available for helping the *Firefighters*, but their redemption will not be found by studying the for-profits. Their role models should be other IT organizations. The *Proactive Partners* might learn a few things from the for-profits, or they could just confirm what they are doing. There might be some areas where they could sharpen skills or provide some new service, but overall, they are probably already doing what they should be doing.

The group with the most to gain from studying the for-profits is the *Gracefully Reactives*. They are the two-thirds to three-quarters of all IT organizations that are doing an acceptable-to-good job but want to do a great job. They are the people who have taken technology as far as it will go in supporting the business. However, they realize that to go further, they will have to shift from leading a technology organization to leading a business organization whose business just happens to be technology. For this group, the for-profits can provide the techniques, processes, and organizational changes that can fundamentally alter their relationship with their internal customers for the better.

Starting an IT Business

Anyone planning on starting a new business needs to ask themselves the five critical questions presented in Exhibit 1.3.

These are good questions for any business, and, with just slight modification, for any IT organization as well. Does IT have an articulated and agreed-upon purpose or mission? Who are IT's customers? Are there different types of customers (clerks, salespeople, managers) performing different business functions? What do these different customers want? What services should IT provide to its customers? How should these needed services be sourced? Finally, how do you measure IT's success?[6]

Luckily for IT, the for-profits not only know the questions to ask, but they know how to obtain the answers as well. From the for-profit perspective, what IT lacks is not technical know-how, but an understanding of its market (customers, suppliers, competitors, and partners). What the for-profits can teach IT is how to better understand its customers, manage its suppliers, beat out its competitors, and leverage its partners—all for what the business believes is an acceptable cost. This approach is the essence of MDM, which is taken right out of the for-profit's playbook and will be discussed in greater detail in the following chapters.

Exhibit 1.3   Critical Business Questions

- *What is the purpose of the business?* Does the business have a clear mission and a set of goals and objectives?

- *Who are the customers?* Is there just one type of customer, or are there various customer segments or groups?

- *What do the customers need and want from the business?* How can the business best anticipate customer needs? How will those needs be communicated?

- *What products or services should the business provide?* Should the products or serviced be developed in-house? Should parts of the products or services be subcontracted? Should the creation of the entire product or service be outsourced? Should the business be involved in this product or service at all?

- *How will success be measured?* Revenue? Net income? Customer satisfaction?

Source: George Tillmann, "In Search of Overhead Heroes,"
Strategy + Business, Issue 39, Summer 2005, pp. 14–17.

SOME ADDITIONAL THOUGHTS

> **MDM.**   The application of proven for-profit business techniques, targeted IT's customers (both senior business management clients and end-user technology consumers), in order to improve IT's transparency and perception as safe hands. MDM focuses on IT's market (customers, suppliers, competitors, and partners) in order to better support the business through the development and delivery of more valuable technology-based services.

Most IT shops are committed to providing the best service they can, and most do a decent job. Yet, despite an acceptable performance record, IT suffers dissatisfaction and second-guessing from its customers. Part of the problem is the services IT offers might be slow, unavailable, functionally weak, or simply the wrong service. However, just as likely, the reason for dissatisfaction with IT is the users' perception that IT does not listen to them, does what it wants regardless of user needs, and is too expensive. The phrase "fat, dumb, and happy" comes to mind. In the midst of the gloom, there is hope.

MDM has two distinct advantages for IT. First, it targets all of IT's customers, not just the senior business management clients. The end-user technology consumers also gain from MDM. Second, MDM applies the best for-profit thinking to the cost center situation. It looks at successful technology vendors and adopts and adapts the techniques and practices that have made them successful. The expense side of the business now has just as much to gain from the great business management writers as the revenue side.

Whatever IT, or any overhead organization, is going through, the for-profits have already been there and, in most cases, resolved the problem. MDM brings to IT some of the best thinking of the for-profit world that can be applied to common IT problems. Using MDM can help IT move from being a mediocre organization to one of the best.

NOTES

1. Jack Hope, "A Better Mousetrap," *American Heritage Magazine*, Vol. 47, Issue 6, October 1996.
2. *Ibid.*
3. "IT Budget-to-Revenue Ratio Improves IT Management," *McLean Report*, Info-Tech Research Group, July 26, 2005, http://www.infotech. com/MR/Issues/20050726/Articles/IT%20Budget-to-Revenue%20Ratio %20Improves%20IT%20Management.aspx#issue.
4. "The Chaos Report," The Standish Group, 1995.
5. Paul Strassmann and Danek Bienkowski, "IT in the 21st Century: Speaking the Language of Business," ABTCorporation, www.strassmann. com/pubs/abtcorp/.
6. George Tillmann, "In Search of Overhead Heroes," *Strategy + Business*, Issue 39, Summer 2005, pp. 14–17.

2

IT Governance

When men exercise their reason coolly and freely on a variety of distinct questions, they inevitably fall into different opinions on some of them. When they are governed by a common passion, their opinions, if they are to be called, will be the same.

—*Alexander Hamilton*

If Columbus had an advisory committee he would probably still be at the dock.

—*Arthur Goldberg*

Edwin A. Abbott wrote a short novel in 1884 called *Flatland*, the story of beings who live in a two-dimensional world.[1] The protagonist in the story is a square, who interacts with triangles, pentagons, and so forth and cannot imagine a world of three dimensions. If you draw a line between two flatlanders, they can no longer see each other because they have length and depth, but not height. The line works for them like a wall does for us. Looking at a flatlander's house is like taking the roof off one of our three-dimensional houses. Peering down, we can see multiple inhabited rooms separated by walls. We can observe the three people in the living room, two more in the kitchen, and one in the bedroom. However, they cannot see each other because of the walls separating the rooms. Although our view of the house is simpler than theirs, it provides us with more information about its structure and its inhabitants than that experienced by those inside it.

Corporate governance should work in a similar way, providing a simpler yet more informative view into the structure and inhabitants of an enterprise. Governance, done right, can create a picture of the enterprise and its people. It can also show their work, their strengths, their weaknesses, their needs, and their contributions in a way that no one person in any of the rooms of the enterprise can clearly see. Unfortunately, many organizations get governance wrong. They see its purpose as rules and not as clarity. For them, governance is used to reinforce walls and ensure that what goes on behind them is secure and unobservable. They are true flatlanders.

Information technology (IT) is expensive. Depending on the size of the company and the industry it is in, IT can cost from one-quarter to one-half of an organization's total capital expenditures.[2] IT departments' spend, as a percentage of revenue, averages between two and four percent for most companies, but can be as high as eight percent for the financial industry.[3]

J. Georges Clemenceau once said, "War is too important a matter to be left to the military." Many executives believe that IT is too important a matter to be left to the technicians. The result of this mistrust can be many strange reporting lines, numerous committees, or outsourced technology functions.

IT governance can be a contentious issue. The IT Governance Institute–PricewaterhouseCoopers report found that 76 percent of the surveyed chief executive officers (CEOs) and chief information officers (CIOs) knew of situations that IT governance could resolve. Surprisingly, only 42 percent of them planned to implement an IT governance function.[4]

THE PROBLEM

There was a time when IT was little more than a reporting arm of finance. It gathered data from the operating units, did some simple number crunching, and produced reports. It was, for the most part, inconsequential to the revenue generation of the business. It did, however, have two distinct qualities: (1) it was mysterious, and (2) respectable businesspeople wanted little to do with it. Auditors once debated whether to audit "through" the computer or "around" it, referring to the question of whether auditors had to look inside at what the machine was doing. Because it was cast as a rather large calculator that never made a mistake, spending time knowing what was happening within the box was viewed as a waste of valuable resources.

Some things have changed. IT is now a significant part of an organization's asset portfolio, and many businesses could not exist without it. In the financial industry, often the only product that is bought, sold, or serviced is electronically stored information. As bankbooks disappear, stock certificates become collector's items, and paper checks give way to statement line items, the industry would collapse without IT. With IT's move from nice-to-have to vital, it has gained the attention of senior management, which feels uncomfortable leaving such an important area to technical staff.

Some things have not changed. The mystery and antipathy surrounding IT are, in many cases, still there. Most business managers have little knowledge of, and less interest in, IT, which adds to their discomfort. They question the cost of IT and whether they are getting the services they are paying for. Worse, their fear of and disinterest in IT reinforces their feelings that IT does not sufficiently justify its actions or adequately account for its expense. Forgetting for the moment the modest hypocrisy of complaining about IT's free rein while failing to provide adequate oversight, the business does have a point. Given the vacuum created by senior business management's lack of involvement, IT has taken up the slack and made some critical business decisions. The result is a Hobson's choice, where none of the alternatives is acceptable. IT loses if it cannot get senior business management involved in critical IT decisions. Yet, it also loses if it makes those decisions without the backing of the business.

THE IT SOLUTION

The business–IT relationship should be win-win for both parties. IT wants to serve the business and the business wants IT's help. Instead, too often it turns out to be lose-lose. The business is unhappy with what it is getting from IT, and IT feels it is undervalued and unappreciated.

What do customers want from IT management? When asked, they will tell you that they do not want to run IT, but they do want to know that it is being run properly, that their needs count, and that they are getting what they pay for. More than anything, what they want from IT is management transparency and safe hands.

People want to know about what might affect them. They want to be aware of problems they might be facing, what is being done about them and by whom, and when and where they should see results. They want to make sure that they are not being taken advantage of, and that they are not, without a good reason, paying for benefits going to others. They want to be told who to talk to about things affecting them, and who can make things happen. They want to hear about it when things go wrong as well as when things go right. In short, they want the opportunity to know everything that might affect them or their business.

Customers want transparent IT processes that afford them the opportunity to know and understand the decisions IT makes, who is making the decisions, the decision processes IT uses, the reasons for those decisions, and the appeal process.

Not everyone can do everything. You must rely on your dentist to take care of your teeth, your tax accountant to file your taxes, and your surgeon to take out your appendix. You also want to feel sufficiently secure about the skills of your dentist, accountant, and surgeon, so that you do not have to constantly oversee their work, second-guess their conclusions, or get second opinions for all of their recommendations. You want to feel that when you go to the dentist, accountant, or surgeon, you are in safe hands. Safe hands refers to the trust you place in people to look out for your interests.

They are the ones who can be counted on to do the right thing without being constantly monitored. Customers want to feel that the assets in IT's charge, as well as the support IT delivers, are in safe hands.

Transparency and safe hands are more important to customers than are efficiency and effectiveness. The reason is that most customers feel that if they have transparency and safe hands, then efficiency and effectiveness will either follow directly or can be achieved with business management help. However, without transparency and safe hands, there is little hope of achieving either efficiency or effectiveness. Therefore, transparency and safe hands are the keys to meeting, and perhaps exceeding, customer expectations.

How does IT demonstrate transparency and safe hands? Experience has shown that one of the most successful ways to demonstrate both transparency and safe hands is through the effective use of IT governance. The most common IT governance mechanism is the IT Steering Committee (ITSC), although it could be called by many other names. The next section looks at a useful steering committee model that has worked for some organizations. It might not be exactly right for everyone, but its philosophy, approach to the problem, and means of involving IT's customers should be directionally correct for all organizations.

IT Steering Committee Objectives

The enterprise needs a forum for the business (corporate as well as the business units) and IT to discuss and agree on IT's operating programs and investments.

The IT Steering Committee has six objectives:

1. *Create an IT strategy.* The enterprise needs an IT strategy that is aligned with the organization's business strategy, outlining what IT needs to do over the next few years to fulfill its corporate mission.

2. *Develop multiyear and annual IT plans.* The IT strategy remains unrealized until IT has a direction-setting, high-level, multiyear plan and an actionable and detailed annual IT plan. Both plans should include a set of annual goals and objectives that the various IT units can act on and that are consistent with the enterprise's business and IT strategies.

3. *Foster collaboration between IT and the business.* IT, corporate, and the business units need to work hand-in-hand if corporate and business unit goals are to be achieved with IT's support.

4. *Approve IT's approach.* The business needs to agree on, and feel comfortable with, IT's methods and processes for realizing corporate, business unit, and IT goals. IT's approach needs to be consistent with the corporate culture, industry best practices, and all legal and regulatory

requirements. It should also be reasonable and achievable without unacceptable risk.

5. *Reach consensus on the number and deployment of IT resources.* The steering committee should ensure that the IT organization has the resources (e.g., staff, skills, hardware, software, infrastructure, organizational structure, funds, etc.) it needs to carry out its mission, and that the resources are reasonably deployed.

6. *Monitor and communicate status and results.* The steering committee needs to confirm that IT adequately and effectively monitors its activities and communicates with corporate and business units about the status of its operations, plans, budgets, investments, and so forth.

It is important that the goals of the ITSC satisfy the needs expressed by the user base and that they meet business concerns regarding IT efficiency, effectiveness, transparency, and safe hands (see Exhibit 2.1).

IT Steering Committee Structure

For most organizations, a one-size-fits-all, single steering committee will not work. An effective steering committee needs skills in business analysis, monitoring technology innovation, cost/benefit analysis, portfolio management, executive-level business decision making, and more. The workload is too great and too diverse for any single group to do an adequate job. Good results have been achieved, however, with a multilevel steering committee. The various and different committee tasks and responsibilities are assigned to different tiers or levels based on the skills and experience of the staff on that level. The first tier consists of a senior manager Executive Committee. Under

Exhibit 2.1   Mapping Customer Concerns to IT Governance Goals

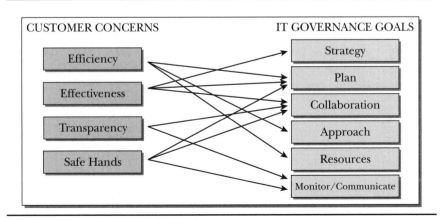

Exhibit 2.2 IT Steering Committee Structure

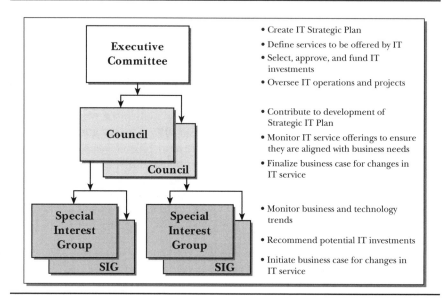

the Executive Committee are one, or more, middle-manager-staffed, senior-manager-led councils. The councils oversee third-tier, middle-manager-led, special interest groups (see Exhibit 2.1).

Executive Committee The Executive Committee is the highest level of the ITSC and the one where the critical decisions are made. It meets formally only a few times per year, usually in concert with the enterprise business cycle of planning, budgeting, monitoring, and midyear adjustments.

Executive committees work best when their membership consists of at least 6, but fewer than 18, members. Smaller groups leave too much work for each member to do and can rarely represent the entire organization. Larger groups are too unwieldy and can become bureaucratic. The members should represent most, if not all, IT constituencies, such as business units, product groups, geographies, and so forth. A rotation of members might be needed to provide all constituencies with adequate and appropriate representation. Executive Committee members should serve for multiple years. A good rule of thumb for the term of membership is to mimic the life of the strategic plan. If the business or IT has a three-year strategic plan, then a term of three years for Executive Committee membership is good. Terms should overlap so there is never a 100 percent turnover in membership in a single year.

Councils Under the Executive Committee are one or more councils, which form the deliberative and analytical bodies of the ITSC. Each council is chaired by a member of the Executive Committee and staffed with middle managers. Membership can also include a few very experienced functional and technical experts. Councils differ from each other by either the functions or constituencies they represent. For example, there could be one council for manufacturing and another for European operations. Likewise, there could be a council focusing on administrative matters while a second focuses on customer issues.

Council size varies considerably based on its focus; however, a size similar to that of the Executive Committee seems to work well. Council member terms are more volatile than Executive Committee membership, due to the subject matter of the council and forces within the business. Many organizations cannot afford to have their most experienced staff spending time outside of the business for too long. However, the Executive Committee should insist that council members prepare for a term of at least two years.

Special Interest Groups   Councils can be further divided into Special Interest Groups (SIGs), which are more transient than the permanent councils. They are the fact-finding bodies of the ITSC and can have a technology or functional focus. For example, there could be a SIG studying wireless communications to investigate how wireless technology might help the business. There could be another SIG focusing on supply-chain management application packages. SIGs can go into and out of existence as the need for them waxes and wanes. Last year's SIG on customer care could be replaced by this year's SIG dealing with securing customer information.

SIGs are led by council members. Membership can be limited to council members or open to others within the organization. Titles are less important on a SIG, and effective SIG members often come from the non-management ranks. SIG terms of membership can be the most volatile, running from a few weeks to many years. The determinant is how long a special interest or knowledge is needed. Some skills might be needed for just a few months, whereas others will have an ongoing function in the SIG.

IT Steering Committee Members

Finding the right members is perhaps the most critical task in setting up a successful governance function. The right SIG members provide the needed input to the ITSC process with their hands-on knowledge of what the business needs or what technology has to offer. The councils are the workhorse of the committee, building the business cases that are presented to the Executive Committee for approval. The Executive Committee is where the critical decisions are made that ultimately determine the success or failure of the ITSC. Pick the wrong people for the Executive Committee, and it does not matter what else is done right; the governance function will fail. Pick the right people, and they can make the needed corrections if the other steering committee components are flawed.

Executive Committee   Having the right people on the Executive Committee can make or break the entire ITSC. There are two criteria for selecting Executive Committee members. First, the Executive Committee needs to be staffed with senior leaders who (1) have significant clout within the organization; (2) have the vision to represent the entire organization and not just their constituency; (3) can spare the time to actively participate; and (4) are not afraid to make decisions that will commit the resources of the entire organization. Second, the Executive Committee needs adequate representation from across the entire organization so that all constituencies feel that they are a part of the decision process.

If the Executive Committee members are too junior, then they will have little or no influence within the organization. Either their decisions will be ignored or they will need to have them cleared by others. If Executive Committee decisions require approval from elsewhere within the organization, then the wrong people are on the committee. Executive Committee members must have the authority to commit the resources of the firm without being second-guessed or overridden. Having no IT governance function is better than having one that is powerless. It would be better to have the CIO make all necessary decisions alone than to saddle him or her with a powerless overseer.

Good Executive Committee candidates are business unit leaders or their direct reports; geographic leaders, such as the head of Europe or the Far East; and corporate officers, such as the chief financial officer (CFO), chief operating officer (COO), or head of human resources. The CIO, as well as one or more of the direct reports, should be members. In some organizations, it might not be possible for all constituencies (i.e., lines of business, customer bases, geographies, etc.) to be represented simultaneously. In this case, a rotation process might be needed to ensure that all constituencies are either directly represented or will get their turn.

Most critical of all is the selection of the chairperson, particularly during the first years of the ITSC. How the committee will be viewed, and in a large part its future success or failure, will depend on the first chairperson. If he or she is a strong leader, who keeps the committee on point and making progress, and if the recommendations and decisions of the committee are respected throughout the organization, then the ITSC will be successful. However, if the first leader is weak, if meetings are unattended and rambling, and if recommendations and decisions are ignored, then it would be better that the ITSC was never created.

Councils   Council members are usually middle managers, but they can also be functional, technical, or business experts, who have the time and inclination to do the heavy lifting of the committee. They should be the knowledge leaders in their area, willing to work as part of a team to better the organization. Staff should be limited to membership in one council at a time.

Senior managers should consider council membership as a rare opportunity for their best and brightest middle managers and functional, technical, or business experts. The benefits of membership include an opportunity to work with the best and the brightest staff from other parts of the organization, a chance to gain a broader knowledge of the enterprise, and an opportunity to acquire valuable business governance skills.

Special Interest Groups SIG members can come exclusively from the ranks of the councils or from other interested parties in the organization. Normally, SIG members should either be knowledgeable in the subject area of the SIG or have an interest in introducing the subject into the business. For example, a SIG on handheld wireless devices for warehouse management could be staffed with wireless device experts, as well as business staff interested in introducing the technology into company warehouses. Length of membership could be as short as the length of time needed to support one part of one SIG, or could extend to memberships in multiple SIGs over long periods.

IT Steering Committee Roles and Responsibilities

One of the most important decisions that needs to be made about the ITSC is its role and the scope of its responsibility. Should the ITSC limit its responsibility to the corporate IT organization, or should it include all IT throughout the enterprise? In most companies, the IT organization is only responsible for a portion of total IT in use throughout the enterprise. The CIO might own the shared functions, such as infrastructure, corporate servers, and the network, while the business units, or individual offices, own the personal computers (PCs), their local area networks, and even the servers located in their offices.

There are legal and regulatory reasons for having some local offices own local IT equipment. For example, tax laws can make local ownership of PCs, printers, local servers, and so forth, more financially attractive than nonlocal ownership. In some counties, only locally produced hardware and software can be acquired without paying punishing taxes. This factor makes a case not only for local ownership, but also for local support, because only local staff will have the knowledge and experience to support the locally manufactured devices.

It is not uncommon for half of an enterprise's total IT expenditures, sometimes called "shadow spend," to be outside of the IT department. Senior management must agree on how much autonomy business units and offices have in purchasing and owning technology and under what circumstances they must submit to a centralized corporate authority.

The authority issue is not always a clean split between central and local control. There can be different central versus local decisions for standards development, asset selection, purchasing, and support. For example, although an enterprise might charter the centralized IT organization to issue hardware and software standards, and to select the products that meet the standards, the enterprise might give authority to local offices to purchase and support those products.

The determination of ITSC's scope and responsibility is fundamental to the governance organization, and perhaps the first test of its effectiveness. If the issue was not satisfactorily resolved when the ITSC was formed, then its resolution is an early, if not the first, task for the new committee. The committee members should work with business leaders to define ITSC's responsibility, while confirming that it is both explicit and consistent with the enterprise's strategy and goals. Then the ITSC needs to ensure that its role and responsibilities are well established in its charter, processes, decisions, and communications.

The centralization/decentralization issue, always a hot topic in any organization, is a good early test for the ITSC. If it can articulate and enforce the enterprise's position on IT authority, it stands a greater chance of success.

Special Interest Groups   Each SIG is assigned an area of responsibility. Its focus could be functional, as in finance or payroll; it could be business-oriented, as in product development; or it could be technical, as in wireless communications. The SIG members need to keep abreast of their area of responsibility. They should identify opportunities in which the business could benefit from their subject. Finally, they should present to the council suggestions on new or different possible uses of technology. Opportunities could be suited for the entire company, or for smaller constituencies, such as finance in Asia. If the council believes the SIG is nearing a consensus, it can request that the SIG create a business case.

SIGs can function as one large team, or they can be further divided into numerous smaller teams, depending on the work at hand. SIGs should be designed to require few, if any, formal meetings. Conference calls, e-mail, and collaboration tools might be all that is needed to keep the SIG on track.

Councils   The councils recommend technology-related actions to the Executive Committee. The recommendations could be to expand existing technology into new areas, such as knowledge management specific to Latin America, institute new uses of technology already in use within the enterprise (e.g., integrate supply-chain management), or introduce emerging technology, such as handheld devices for inventory clerks. The recommendations should come in the form of a business case that lays out the benefits to the firm, all costs, and the time required for implementing the program.

Council members should spend less than 25 percent of their total steering committee time commitment on council meetings. Seventy-five percent of their effort should be spent in researching and producing business cases for potential IT investments. Avoid including council members whose only steering committee involvement is showing up for council meetings. They produce little, ask obvious questions at meetings, waste more productive members' time, and set a bad example. The success of the councils will depend on recruiting council members who will put in the time outside of the meeting room.

Executive Committee   The Executive Committee is the decision-making body for the ITSC. Its function is similar to a judicial panel in that the committee hears the arguments made by the councils regarding recommended IT actions. Unlike a judge, the committee can also obtain input into the decision-making process from sources outside the committee or the councils, such as the CEO, business unit heads, general staff, and even customers or potential customers. Meetings and the preparations for meetings will consume more than 90 percent of the total time Executive Committee members need to commit to the steering committee. The various ITSC operational functions can be seen in Exhibit 2.3.

IT Steering Committee Processes

Three ITSC processes dominate all others. The first process is the approval and oversight of the IT strategy, from the multiyear plan down to the annual operating budget. The steering committee, particularly the Executive Committee, needs to feel comfortable with the way IT plans to use corporate assets and deliver customer services. Particular attention

Exhibit 2.3   IT Steering Committee Operations

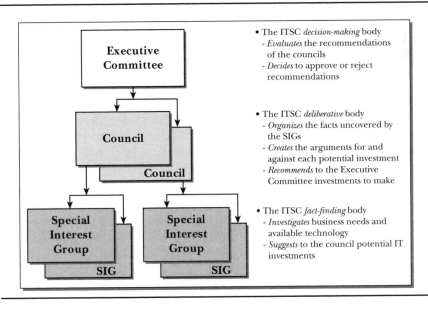

- The ITSC *decision-making* body
  - *Evaluates* the recommendations of the councils
  - *Decides* to approve or reject recommendations

- The ITSC *deliberative* body
  - *Organizes* the facts uncovered by the SIGs
  - *Creates* the arguments for and against each potential investment
  - *Recommends* to the Executive Committee investments to make

- The ITSC *fact-finding* body
  - *Investigates* business needs and available technology
  - *Suggests* to the council potential IT investments

Executive Committee

Council

Council

Special Interest Group

Special Interest Group

SIG

SIG

should be paid to IT's approach to performance monitoring (Does IT have the capability to know the status of the services it provides?) and risk management (Does IT understand the organization's tolerance for risk, and to what extent does the risk need to be mitigated?). The IT strategy and planning processes will be looked at in greater detail in Chapter 3.

Second, the steering committee needs to oversee the IT project portfolio by reviewing and approving appropriate investments. The process starts with the SIGs and councils preparing business cases. A series of reviews and screens help members select the cases that are most important. These most important business cases are then submitted to the Executive Committee for approval. Before deciding which projects to approve, the Executive Committee needs to understand the organization's appetite for investment and the availability of resources, including funds. Once projects are approved, the Executive Committee needs to charge IT with their execution and ensure that funding remains available. The project approval process will be looked at in greater detail in Chapter 4.

Finally, the steering committee needs to provide managerial oversight for the implementation of the approved projects.

IT Steering Committee Deliverables

The ITSC plays a role, as either an author or an audience, for several critical IT deliverables, including:

- *IT strategy.* An IT strategy is a clear articulation of the direction IT will be taking. It is driven by an understanding of where the business, the market, and the technology are going. Written more in business than technical language, the IT strategy will become a principal vehicle for communicating with IT's customers. Information for the IT strategy comes from documents and interviews with corporate and senior business-unit managers, ITSC members, and IT managers.

   The creation of the IT strategy should be a collaborative effort between IT and the ITSC. The audience for the IT strategy document is all senior managers, including corporate, business unit, ITSC members, and IT staff.

- *Multiyear IT plan.* The multiyear plan is a high-level document, including schedules, resource requirements, dependencies, and costs for executing the IT strategy. It should have the same life as the IT strategy. If the IT strategy is for three years, then the multiyear plan should also be for three years. The plan is created by IT from the IT strategy and from interviews with IT staff. The audience for the plan is ITSC members and IT staff.

- *Annual IT operating plan.* The operating plan consists of the detailed approach, schedule, and budget needed to keep IT as an ongoing service for the coming or current year. Included are the cost of maintaining all assets and services (e.g., staff, skills, hardware, software, maintenance, etc.) and any programs for changing or updating services. IT is responsible for creating the annual IT operating plan, which will be used extensively by the ITSC and IT.

- *Business case.* A business case is a document articulating the purpose, costs, and benefits of a potential IT investment. The business case should have sufficient breadth and detail to explain the investment objectives, business and technical risks, and competitive pressures, as well as the potential competitor response, schedules, timelines, and alternatives. It should also discuss the impact on the business of investing in the proposed project, as well as the implications of not investing in it. The document needs to be of a sufficiently high level in tone and length that senior executives can read it in a short period, yet sufficiently detailed that unanswered questions raised by the business case are kept to a minimum.

  The councils and SIGs are the primary authors of the business case. They use information from corporate, the business units, ITSC councils, SIGs, and outside vendors to create it. A business case created by a SIG is aimed at convincing the council to recommend the project. A business case created by a council is aimed at convincing the Executive Committee to approve it.

- *Annual IT investment plan.* IT, with help from the SIGs and councils, bundles all of the investments (projects) approved by the ITSC into a single annual IT investment plan, showing the approach, schedule, resources, and budget for every investment. The annual IT investment plan is useful information for corporate and the business units, as well as for the ITSC and IT.

IT Steering Committee Reporting Structure

To whom should the ITSC report? There are seven options: the Board of Directors, the CEO, the CIO, a C-level executive other than the CIO or CEO, a business unit head, the company's enterprise management committee, or no one at all. All of these options have worked or been recommended by one organization or another.

Board of Directors   The Board of Directors is charged with representing the owners or stockholders in the hiring, firing, and monitoring of the management of the company. Their primary hiring responsibility is to retain a company president. Once the president position is filled, the board can help in the hiring of the president's senior team. Although the board hires the management of the company, it does not manage the company itself. It might approve the company budget, but it has no direct budget responsibility. To aid in its monitoring function, the board usually maintains several committees, such as finance, compensation, and audit, which are charged with keeping the board informed about how well management is doing its job.

Some people see the ITSC as similar to the committees that report to the Board of Directors. Like the board's audit or finance committees, the ITSC oversees the use of corporate assets and monitors the organizations and processes that use those assets. Because its function is so similar to a board committee, advocates feel that having the ITSC report to the board makes sense. Reporting to the board has the advantage of helping ensure that IT's strategy and multiyear plans are well aligned with the business. This is the position of the IT Governance Institute.[5]

On the downside, the board has very little say in the day-to-day running of the company. It will not be very helpful in making the critical IT decisions, funding those decisions, or making sure that the business and IT work together successfully.

CEO   You cannot do better than having the ITSC report to the CEO. There is no better way of guaranteeing that committee decisions will be taken seriously. The CEO's weight behind the IT strategy, the IT plan, or IT investment decisions is invaluable. However, many CEOs try to limit their direct reports, both staff and committees. They feel that either they cannot devote the time needed, or they would prefer that committee decisions be screened by an additional layer of senior management before they wind up on the CEO's desk.

CIO   The ITSC can report to the CIO. This works best if the sole purpose for the ITSC is to improve IT's understanding of what its customers want, and for IT's customers to understand what IT is doing. However, if there are issues about transparency, or if customers are uncertain about IT's ability to fulfill its mission, then having the committee report to the CIO can be ineffective. One of the virtues of the ITSC is that it can be seen as both independent of IT and as representing the business to IT. Both benefits can be lost if the committee reports to the CIO.

C-Level Executive (Other than the CEO or CIO)   There are two C-level options: (1) have the ITSC report to a C-level executive who is not the CIO's boss, or (2) have the ITSC report to a C-level executive who is the CIO's boss. Having the CIO report to one C-level executive and the ITSC to another makes little sense. This becomes the classic dilemma of answering to two bosses, which rarely works.

Therefore, the question remains, should the ITSC report to the CIO's boss? This solution is popular with many organizations and should work if three conditions are met. First, the executive to whom the CIO reports must not have any of the same difficulties working with the business as the CIO might have. Business staff must believe that the CIO's superior is one of their own and not "one of *them*." Second, IT's customers need to be sufficiently comfortable with the skills, experience, and judgment of the CIO's boss, not to question his or her decisions about IT's organization, processes, funding, or investment decisions. Third, there cannot be any unresolved issues about transparency or feelings that the business is misrepresented or underrepresented. If some of the concerns expressed about the CIO could also be attributed to the CIO's boss, then little is gained by having the ITSC report to the CIO's superior.

Business Unit Head   When a company has multiple business units in different geographies, or of unequal size or status, it is not uncommon for one business unit to own the infrastructure that other business units use. It might be that the global CIO reports to the head of the largest, oldest business unit in the company's home country (i.e., the primary business unit), rather than to a newer, smaller, or more remote business unit. If the primary business unit can function as a shared service and is adept at servicing the other business units, then the ITSC could report to the head of the primary business unit. Sometimes business unit management has concerns that it is not getting its fair share of IT. If this is the case, then having the ITSC report to a single business unit head will not be effective.

Enterprise Management Committee   Most companies have a committee of senior executives from across the organization that either reports directly to, or is chaired by, the CEO. It can go by various names, such as the executive committee, management committee, or leadership team. The management committee might have decision authority, or it might function simply as an advisory body for the CEO. The members represent not only their individual organizations, but also the entire enterprise, both profit and cost centers, corporate and business units, locally or across the globe. It routinely has other committees or subcommittees reporting to it. One of those committees could be the ITSC.

The management committee is a good choice for a successful direct report for the ITSC because it represents the broadest view of the organization. It also contains a large concentration of senior managers from across the company. Finally, it can make recommendations or decisions, including funding decisions, that bear the influence of the entire enterprise. Even better would be having one or more members of the enterprise management committee serve on the ITSC.

No One At All   What would be unworkable for most organizations might be the right answer for a few. Organizations that are primarily committee-run, such as academic institutions, loose federations, nonprofits, and some partnerships, might be best served by an ITSC with no formal ownership. The implication is that the committee reports to the entire partnership, faculty, or owners.

The advantage of such a structure is cultural—it is the way the organization does things. If the enterprise is one of the handful that have a culture in which all decisions are made in committee and then everyone abides by those decisions, then this model might work. The disadvantages are obvious, although no more so than for any other committee reporting to no one in particular. They include uncertainty of direction, a lack of authority, and indecisiveness.

Of the seven options, having the ITSC report to the company enterprise management committee, the CEO, or the CIO's boss are probably the most effective. If the CIO cannot persuade one of these parties to sponsor the ITSC, then the CIO might have to step in and take charge of it.

IT Steering Committee Communication

Weill and Ross, in their book *IT Governance,* report that the primary predictor of governance success was the number of senior managers who could accurately describe the company's IT governance.[6] The more senior managers who could correctly depict how their IT governance process worked, the more successful the IT governance organization would be.

Why Is There No Finance or HR Governance Organization?

If having a governance organization for information technology (IT) is such a good idea, why do you not see one for finance, human resources (HR), and the other cost centers? Good question, and although maybe they should have them, they don't for five reasons:

1. Finance and the other cost centers are well-established, business-like organizations. Accounting started thousands of years ago, and modern accounting traces its history back to Luca Pacioli's 1494 *Summa de Arithmetica.* HR may not be able to trace its origin to an exact date, but acquiring and managing the 20,000 workers needed to build the great pyramids of Egypt probably gave HR a good start. In addition, most senior business managers feel more comfortable with finance, HR, and the like. Many of them spent some time there during their climb to the top.

2. IT budgets are bigger and more complex, and involve strange things like routers and sniffers. Ninety percent of the finance budget is either headcount or headcount-related costs, such as benefits, occupancy, and training. The same would be true for the other overhead areas, except IT. IT routinely spends only about half of its budget on staff and staff-related costs. The other half takes up many pages of incomprehensible items that many non-IT managers find, well, incomprehensible.

3. Each year, the IT budget includes a considerable number of large, one-time investments. These investments are usually not IT initiatives, but rather the firm deciding to invest in itself. IT is just the enabler or manager of these corporate projects. Therefore, it is only logical that the business should decide on, fund, and oversee its investments.

   Finance and HR rarely have large one-time investments, so similar oversight is not needed. When an occasion for making a large non-IT investment does arise, the business often sets up a special committee or task force to oversee it. For example, the question of where the company should build its new manufacturing plant is often not left to the manufacturing division but to a corporate-wide team. Its job is to decide whether the new plant should be built in India, Mexico, or Detroit. A different committee might be charged with overseeing the construction of the facility. Because these investments occur only occasionally, the committees that oversee them need not be permanent bodies.

4. IT operations are often more critical to the revenue-generating capability of the company than are functions in the other cost centers. Most HR departments could cease operations for a day or two with little impact on the bottom line, but the same is not true for IT. Because of its operational criticality, senior business management wants to be confident that proper precautions are in place to ensure continued operations.

5. Over the years, IT has acquired a reputation for spending large sums of money unwisely. Until senior managers are comfortable that IT has its act together, they are going to want to monitor IT spending.

The newness, distinctness, and unfamiliarity of IT make it a prime candidate for special treatment, and a special group, the IT Steering Committee, to monitor its actions.

The better information is shared about the ITSC, its purpose, members, processes, and decisions, the better it is for the entire organization. Customers might not want to get involved in IT oversight, but they do want to know that someone is looking out for them and making sure that their interests are represented. Communicating ITSC makeup and activities contributes to three of the success criteria for IT: effectiveness, transparency, and safe hands.

IT's Role in IT Governance

IT should play an active role in the ITSC without being seen as running or unduly influencing it. Someone is needed to set up meetings, prepare documents, contact vendors, perform research, and function as technical experts and resources for the committee members. IT is the best qualified to fill this role. The challenge for IT is to be the arms and legs of the steering committee, without being seen as its head or soul.

As mentioned earlier, the chairperson of the ITSC needs to be a very senior and well-respected executive in the enterprise. However, someone so senior will not have the time to lead the necessary administrative tasks associated with running the Executive Committee, much less the entire ITSC. The ITSC needs an executive director or some similar position to run the day-to-day housekeeping responsibilities of the committee. Scheduling meetings, managing the agenda, supervising membership, and other similar tasks need to be overseen by a manager who can combine administrative and diplomatic skills. A senior IT manager could fill this role. Having an IT person perform this function helps to keep IT in the loop on current events and is a good learning assignment for an up-and-coming manager.

A second role IT can play is to provide the necessary support to the steering committee, particularly the councils and SIGs. Although the councils and SIGs are charged with developing the business cases for potential projects, it is doubtful that they will have all of the skills or the time necessary to do a good job. IT should be available to help the councils and SIGs do the functional analysis, high-level design, vendor interaction, and cost/benefit analysis needed to produce an acceptable business case.

This relationship will require some diplomatic skills, because simply having the councils turn the work over to IT is unfair, undesirable, and unworkable. The main purpose of the steering committee is to provide a vehicle for the business to let IT know what it needs. Having IT create the business cases defeats this purpose, because it is IT telling the business what IT thinks the business needs. IT needs to support the councils without taking on, or overly influencing, their work. It needs to help in producing the work, but the councils still need to own the work.

There is one area where the user-led councils are not very effective. Non-IT people have a very difficult time understanding IT infrastructure. They struggle to know when it is working well and what has to be done when it is not. Customers might have the inside track about customer service improvements, but they are uninformed when it comes to dealing with router or PBX replacement needs. They might know what their own business unit needs are, but they wrestle with the requirements of a shared service.

Whatever number of councils the ITSC creates, an additional council is needed to deal strictly with IT infrastructure. The Infrastructure Council should function the same way as any of the other councils, from needs analysis to business case development. The scope of its work will be limited to shared infrastructure and standards issues. The Infrastructure Council should be run and staffed by IT, but report to the Executive Committee, as do the other councils. IT personnel, customers, or anyone else in the organizations with the interest and necessary skills can join the Infrastructure Council SIGs. This council is responsible for presenting recommendations to the ITSC for infrastructure upgrades, standards changes, security policies, and so forth.

Does every organization need IT governance? If IT gets along well with its user base, then it might not be needed. IT governance might be superfluous if there are no questions about IT costs, what investments should be made, or whether IT is fair in doing its job. For the remainder, IT governance is a way to increase customer knowledge of how IT works, improve their participation in IT decisions, and increase their trust in IT to successfully carry out its mission.

IT's solution of applying a steering committee to the problem of a disenfranchised customer base is a good one and should go a long way in resolving customer concerns about IT. However, IT can learn some techniques, tips, and tricks from the business world. The for-profits have been effectively using steering committees for many years, from the lofty board of directors right down to the holiday party decoration committee. Their experiences can help IT squeeze the most benefit out of IT governance.

WHAT THE FOR-PROFITS CAN TEACH IT

IT governance is not the only type of business governance. Almost every public corporation anywhere in the world has a board of directors, or some similarly named body, to oversee the management of the company. Directors are usually experienced and competent executives, often senior managers in other companies, who are elected by the shareholders to represent them and their interests. They are busy people who do not have a lot of extra time on their hands. Yet, most board directors manage to successfully oversee very large and complex organizations. How do they do it, and can any lessons be applied to handling the ITSC's Executive Committee?

Keep Senior Manager Discussions at a High Level and to the Point

Successful board meetings have tight but complete agendas, culled to the relevant points so that members can make many of the decisions needed without much debate. Executive Committee members, like board members, are senior executives. They have neither the time nor the inclination to get involved in detailed and drawn-out discussions about technology, standards, or most any topic IT can raise. Because IT controls the agenda through the Executive Director role, it can assure the Executive Committee members that meeting agendas will be on-point, at a sufficiently high level, and focused on the actions the committee needs to take.

Senior managers expect high-level summaries, sparse on technical jargon and long on business concepts, that can be presented in just a few pages, and read in just a few minutes. They expect that the detail work has been done by subordinate organizations and that both the presented and supporting numbers and facts are correct and have been checked and rechecked.

Except in a few cases, they do not want a long discussion on a topic. All necessary and relevant debate should have gone on before the subject was handed to the Executive Committee. They want facts, presented at a high level, but backed up with detail. Most important, they want to understand their role. Are they there to hear a status report, make a decision, or take some particular action?

When debate is called for, it should be on a subject that no other organization could handle in the place of the Executive Committee. Even then, the councils and IT need to ensure that the undisputed facts are laid out in a clear and concise way and that any disputed data is so labeled.

Delegate

Boards of directors have several committees that perform the necessary preliminary work and prepare the questions, issues, and recommendations that need to be addressed by the full board. These committees will not put something before the board until it is complete, concise, and actionable. Nothing should go to the Executive Committee that could be handled by a subcommittee or one of the councils. However, no decisions should be made by a council that should go to the Executive Committee.

How does one decide? If the issue involves the entire organization, it should go to the Executive Committee. The Executive Committee is primarily in place for making decisions and not for fact-finding or lengthy debate. Issues should not go to the Executive Committee until all of the facts are known, and any disagreements laid out, both pro and con. The Executive Committee's role is to review the information presented by the councils and SIGs, and vote on the action to be taken. Nothing will turn senior managers off quicker than wasting their time with incomplete analysis or seeing that decision-making groundwork has not been laid.

Premeeting Reading Materials

Board members do not go into a board meeting to learn the facts. They want to know the facts ahead of time and use meeting time for any needed discussion or debate before making any decisions. Learning the facts is something that can be done much more quickly, and with greater understanding and retention, outside a meeting room.

The U.S. Supreme Court is a good example. Each side in a case has only half an hour to present its verbal arguments before the court. The short time works because the Justices have read the written arguments, prepared by each side, beforehand. These written arguments can go on for many pages and take considerably more than 30 minutes to read and understand.

Corporations routinely ensure that board members have reading materials on the agenda items in sufficient time before a meeting so that they can be read and understood. This also gives board members an opportunity to discuss items with others before the meeting.

The same should be done for the Executive Committee and for the councils. Sending agenda materials to all members a few days before the meeting gives them time to read and understand the facts and issues before they step into the meeting room.

Keep Documents and Presentations Short and Simple

There once was an order-of-magnitude rule—whatever you present to middle managers should be an order of magnitude (power of 10) shorter than what you present to staff and junior managers. In addition, whatever you present to senior managers should be an order of magnitude shorter than what you present to middle managers. The rule is a bit of an exaggeration, but it is not uncommon to see the 150-page report to junior managers become a 25-page report to middle managers and a 5- to 10-page report to senior managers.

Do not expect to walk a committee of senior managers through a 100-page document at a meeting, even if they had a chance to see it ahead of time. Presentations should be crisp and to the point. Longer material, background information, spreadsheets, and the like should be contained in an appendix. Appendix material can be referenced by the presenter, or by a committee member, as needed. It is not uncommon for a board of directors' presentation of only 10 or 15 slides to be accompanied by a 150-page appendix.

Communicate the Purpose of the Meeting or Agenda Item

Every document, as well as every presentation, should include a statement of what the presenter wants from the committee. Is the presentation a status report, or is a decision expected?

The executive management team for a manufacturer was given a presentation by a business unit manager. The subject was the viability of marketing one of the business unit's products in a foreign country where the company currently had no presence. The business unit manager laid out the potential benefits, the issues, and the risks of such a strategy. The management team had no idea why the presentation was made and simply thanked the manager when he was done. They thought he was simply keeping them abreast of potential markets. The perplexed manager was looking for a decision giving him permission to market in that country. He left the room without hearing a yes or a no answer. If one wants something from the committee, it is important to ask for exactly what is wanted and give a deadline for when the answer is needed.

Committee members, particularly Executive Committee members, should know exactly what is expected of them. All agenda items should have an *agenda item objective.* There are three types of agenda item objectives. The first is to *inform.* The material presented to the committee is simply intended to keep the committee members abreast of a situation.

Examples could be program status, such as the current state of the new data center building program, or a situation status, such as the current circumstances regarding a telecommunications strike or a political incident in Indonesia.

The second type of objective is to *gain a sense of the committee.* The material presented is used to ask the committee's advice on a situation, a potential course of action, or a resolution. For example, the committee could be asked for its opinion of outsourcing a function or the acceptability of a particular company as a new vendor.

The third agenda item objective is to *make a decision.* Here, the presentation is requesting that the committee commit the enterprise to a course of action. It might be approving a budget, deciding to outsource telecommunications, or increasing the IT workforce.

Presell Positions

The meeting is neither the time nor the place to go into a long sales pitch on why the board or the committee should approve or reject a proposal. In the most effective boards, all-important sales pitches are made long before the meeting, in one-on-one sessions with individual board members.

The U.S. Congress is a good example. Most congressional leaders will not bring a bill to a vote until they know they have enough votes to pass it. To learn how many votes they have, the leaders need to spend time with individual representatives or senators. If they learn that too many legislators are opposed to the bill, they still have time to either try to convince the legislators to vote for it or change the bill so that it is more attractive to a wider audience. Only when they are sure they have the necessary support will they bring the legislation up for a vote.

If IT is putting an important proposal before the ITSC, then IT management should meet with the members of the committee, one-on-one, and find out if they agree. If they do not agree, then IT can either try to change the committee member's mind or change the proposal to give it greater appeal. The real work of getting a proposal through the committee does not take place in the meeting room, but in private offices days before.

No Surprises

Businesspeople usually see surprises as negative—the consequences of analysis that was not done, eventualities that were not anticipated, or outcomes that were not wanted. Lawyers have a rule about questioning a witness in court: Don't ask a question to which you don't already know the answer. For IT, that means do not raise issues at an ITSC meeting unless IT management already knows what it is going to hear.

It is important that IT be seen by the steering committee members as a competent resource. As stated earlier, one of the reasons to have the committee is to demonstrate to customers that they are in safe hands with IT.

If IT is continually losing arguments at committee meetings, if it is seen as always being on the side opposite the business, then customers might start to believe that IT is somehow out of step with the business and an organization that needs to be watched more closely. Surprises at ITSC meetings can send the negative message: "The IT people can't even manage the committee meetings; how are they going to manage IT for the enterprise?"

One way to be seen as in-step with customers is to appear to be on the same page with them at meetings. Because IT is in control of the agenda and the preselling of ideas, it should not be too difficult to minimize committee vote losses or avoid appearing oppositional.

Be Wary of Unscheduled Meetings

Ever try setting up a meeting for a group of senior managers? It can take months to get a half-dozen senior executives in one place at one time for one meeting. Even then, half might have to cancel on short notice or will simply not show up. For this reason, it is important to have only a few Executive Committee meetings, no more than four a year, and to schedule them long in advance. Publishing next year's calendar this year makes a lot of sense.

However, crises are not scheduled. Things come up, such as acquisitions, regulatory requirements, legal issues, vendor problems, and so forth, that sometimes, make it necessary to call an unscheduled meeting. Figuring out what to do when your telecommunications vendor goes out of business cannot wait three months until the entire committee can get together. A better answer is a conference call. A one-issue conference call, lasting no more than half an hour, perhaps scheduled for the early morning or late evening, can often be set up in a day or two.

To get the right people to join the Executive Committee, prospective members will need to know in advance what their time commitment will be. To keep the promise of, say, four three-hour meetings per year, it will be necessary to have members agree to the occasional committee conference call.

The burden of making the conference call work is on IT. The IT department has to schedule the event, make sure sufficient members can be on the call, and have the relevant prereads in committee members' hands before the call. Prereads might sound unnecessary or excessive for conference calls because they could hold up scheduling the call. However, committee members might be taking the conference call in a car, or in a noisy airport, or in some other inconvenient spot. Having the preread minimizes the inconvenience. The document does not have to be anything special, perhaps just a few talking points in an e-mail, to keep the committee members on track.

Know Who the Real Players Are

On every committee, just as in every department in every company, there are the players and the observers. The players are the ones who make things happen, who take charge of the proceedings, and whose opinion moves the organization. Observers are there to support the players. They might agree or disagree with a position, but will likely do little to either foster or oppose it. Oddly, a player in one context might be an observer in another. Because being a player consumes more time and energy than being an observer, and because most senior managers cannot be players in every situation, they choose where they do and do not want to play.

On the ITSC, there are also players and observers. Perhaps one-fourth to one-third of the committee consists of players. The remainder are observers who will defer to the players. The role of IT management is to figure out who is who. Knowing who the players are has two benefits. First, the players are the ones you need to get on your side. Preselling is important for all committee members, but it is far more important to presell the players than the observers. This not only makes the preselling task easier, but also gives IT an opportunity to spend more time preselling players. Second, there are times when decisions or approvals are needed right away. When it is not possible to have a conference call of the entire committee, IT can often get the go-ahead they need from the players.

The player/observer distinction is also important in choosing the chairpersons of the Executive Committee and of the councils. Obviously, players are desirable for all of these positions.

Beyond the Executive Committee

The lessons learned from the for-profit boardrooms are applicable to more than just the ITSC Executive Committee. While the Executive Committee might be the primary beneficiary of these techniques and tips, at least some of them can also be used for the councils and even the SIGs. The advantages derived from premeeting reading materials, agenda item objectives, preselling, and knowing the players, can also be useful for the councils and the SIGs. In addition, the councils can gain from knowing what to delegate to the SIGs. In fact, the boardroom techniques presented in this chapter can be useful for almost any committee at any level.

SOME ADDITIONAL THOUGHTS

IT governance. The organization, processes, and deliverables by which the enterprise recognizes the roles that both the business and IT need to play in order to successfully execute the enterprise's strategy. This involves (1) the business informing IT of its business direction and technology needs; (2) IT responding to the business with the resources needed to satisfy those needs; and (3) the trade-offs and compromises worked out between them to arrive at an agreed-upon and funded IT agenda.

IT governance serves many purposes. Certainly one is offering the opportunity for the business to tell IT what it wants. Another is having the business make the tough trade-offs concerning which projects to fund and which to hold for another year. Few CIOs would object to turning over to a business-run committee the unpleasant task of telling a business unit head or the CFO that the pet project they want is not going to happen.

IT STEERING COMMITTEE

DOs	DON'Ts
• Do get the right people on the Executive Committee. It is more important than any other committee component. • Do learn who the real players are. Work closely with them. • Do have all agendas well thought out and at the proper level for the audience. • Do take every opportunity to showboat IT (transparency and safe hands).	• Don't get bogged down in low-level matters, small investments, or any subject that is not worthy of senior-manager-level attention. • Don't let nonworkers on councils or SIGs, and don't let council or SIG work quality slip, even if you have to buttress the council or SIG with IT staff.

Good IT governance involves psychology as much as it does the traditional governance components of structure and process. Many CIOs find that the most significant benefit of an effective IT governance function is the opportunity to sell IT to its customers. Showing that IT's processes are transparent, and that it is a set of safe hands that can be trusted with running the organization's technology function, can be invaluable for IT.

The Higher Priority

Most consultants and information technology (IT) senior managers will agree that a good IT strategy involves senior IT managers and senior business managers working together. For most, the whole purpose of the collaboration is to have a good IT strategy.

Market-driven management (MDM) reverses that notion. One of the objectives of MDM is fostering collaboration between IT and the business. The IT strategy is a *means* to that end. Expressed differently, for most experts, the goal is an IT strategy, while business–IT collaboration is a means to that end. This is true for MDM, but only secondarily. The primary reason for an IT strategy in MDM is to get the business and IT working closely together.

IT governance is a benefit for IT staff as well. There is nothing more frustrating than working hard, nights and weekends, to complete a project, only to find that the customer is underwhelmed with the results. IT governance helps ensure that the purpose, expectations, and realities of IT's efforts are well understood by both IT and customers. Properly managed expectations can help demonstrate both the transparency of processes and the competence of IT as a set of safe hands.

REFERENCES

The following are some literature, Web sites, and organizations that might be useful.

Some Representative Literature

Anson, Mark, Ted White, and Ho Ho. "Good Corporate Governance Works: More Evidence from CalPERS," *Journal of Asset Management* (February 2004), pp. 149–156.

Board Briefing on IT Governance, 2nd Edition. IT Governance Institute, 2003.

Brand, Koen, and Harry Boonen. *IT Governance: A Pocket Guide Based on COBIT*. Van Haren Publishing, 2005.

Cameron, Bobby. *Transforming IT Governance, November 2002*. Forrester Research, 2002.

IT Governance Global Status Report. IT Governance Institute and PricewaterhouseCoopers, 2004.

Lorsch, Jay, and Martin Lipton. "A Modest Proposal for Improved Corporate Governance," *The Business Lawyer*, Vol. 48, No. 1 (November 1992).

Shultz, Susan. *The Board Book: Making Your Corporate Board a Strategic Force in Your Company's Success*. AMACOM, 2002.

Symons, Craig. *IT Governance: Steering Committee Do's and Don'ts*. Giga Research, 2003.

Van Grembergen, Wim. *Strategies for Information Technology Governance*. Idea Group Publishing, 2003.

Ward, Ralph. *Improving Corporate Boards: The Boardroom Insider Guidebook*. John Wiley & Sons, 2000.

Weill, Peter, and Jeanne W. Ross. *IT Governance*. Harvard Business School Press, 2004.

Some Helpful Organizations and Web Sites

> *IT Governance Institute.* The ITGI publishes materials on IT governance and oversight, and is the publisher of the Control Objectives for Information and Related Technology (COBIT), a toolkit of IT governance. www.itgi.org

> *BoardSource.* Publishes materials about how boards of directors function in the United States (formerly The National Center for Nonprofit Boards). http://www.ncnb.org/

> *ISACA.* An organization dedicated to corporate governance, particularly control issues, security, and auditing. http://www.isaca.org/

> *Institute on Governance.* A Canadian organization dealing with nonprofit board structures, performance measurement, policy creation, and the like. Although the subject is not-for-profit boards, much is applicable to IT governance. http://www.iog.ca/

> *Voluntary Sector Roundtable's Board Development Materials.* A Canadian organization providing not-for-profit board information. http://www.boarddevelopment.org/

> *Authenticity Consulting, LLC.* A consulting company to help nonprofits, but its Web site sometimes has information that would be useful to running an IT Steering Committee, such as how to set up advisory (council) groups. http://www.authenticityconsulting.com/pubs/BD_gdes/BD_pubs.htm

Some of the best information on how boards operate does not come from books, but from the materials posted on the Web by large corporations. Look for Web pages with names like "Corporate Governance Guidelines." They can lay out the board's mission, strategy, membership requirements, how often they meet, availability of preread materials, and many other interesting facts. Not all of this information is available at each site, but by visiting several sites, one will get a good picture of how these organizations function.

NOTES

1. Edwin A. Abbott, *Flatland,* New American Library, 1984.
2. Department of Commerce, *The Emerging Digital Economy,* April 1998, p. 6.
3. *The Economics of IT,* Forrester Research, May 2005.
4. *IT Governance Global Status Report,* IT Governance Institute and PricewaterhouseCoopers, 2004.
5. *Board Briefing on IT Governance,* 2nd Edition, The IT Governance Institute, 2003.
6. Peter Weill and Jeanne W. Ross, *IT Governance,* Harvard Business School Press, 2004, p. 124.

3

IT Strategy and Planning

> All men can see these tactics whereby
> I conquer, but what none can see is the strategy
> out of which victory is evolved.
>
> —*Sun Tzu*

> Always plan ahead. It wasn't raining
> when Noah built the ark.
>
> —*Richard C. Cushing*

In 1830, Charles Lyell published his *Principles of Geology* and changed forever the way science looked at the world. Before Lyell, the prevailing view held by geologists was known as catastrophism—everything in the world (rocks, mountains, rivers, seas, and living creatures) was created as the result of one single catastrophic event. All change stopped after the catastrophe was over, with the earth remaining unchanged ever since. No new mountains, no new rivers, no new creatures.

Lyell was a uniformitarian. He believed that geologic forces, working over very long periods of time, had radically altered the surface of the earth. Moreover, these powerful, slow-moving, yet constant forces continue to change the world to this day. Twenty-nine years later, Charles Darwin, in his *On the Origin of Species*, would use Lyell's theory to say that if the earth changes, then, to survive, the life the earth supports must also change. Science learned in the first half of the nineteenth century that change is everywhere and inevitable. The business world did not learn it for another 120 years.

THE PROBLEM

Throughout the early post–World War II period, business in the United States boomed. The demand for goods was so high that businesses had to do little to sell their products. However, by the mid-1950s, demand started to slow. Returning veterans had purchased the houses they were going to live in, the cars they would need to commute from the suburbs, and the washing machines and other labor-saving devices that would transform housework. Businesses became aware that they could no longer just wait passively for the orders to flow in. They would now have to work harder to make their products more attractive to consumers.

Michael Porter, in his landmark book, *Competitive Strategy*, starts the first sentence of the first chapter with, "The essence of formulating competitive strategy is relating a company to its environment."[1] The problem is change. Business strategy is needed because the environment changes—in this case, the business environment. Each time it changes, a new strategy to cope with it must be formulated.

Business strategy is based on the recognition that change is an inevitable part of the business environment. To survive, companies must formulate a response to the change and then see that the response permeates their organizational structure, processes, products, and culture. For example, in the 1950s, it became apparent to all that the boom was over and that companies would have to compete more vigorously with their competitors for consumer dollars. Some adopted a strategy of competing on price. They would offer their products at a lower price than their competitors would. Others decided to compete on quality, striving to make their products the best on the market. A third group decided to compete on the concept of brand. They would persuade consumers to buy their products, based not on price, not on quality, but on name recognition.

Strategies are very stable during periods of business environment constancy, but change rapidly during times of business environment fluctuation. IT's challenge is keeping up with the business strategy changes. If the business strategy goes in a new direction, then the technology needed to support the business must also take a new direction. What technology changes are needed, and when they are required, is the focus of IT strategy.

THE IT SOLUTION

IT strategy is a response to the business strategy. It tells the organization's senior executives that IT (1) has heard their concerns about the business; (2) understands the technology implications of the business strategy, including what IT can do, when it must do it, and what it will cost; and (3) is ready and willing to make the necessary technology changes to adapt to the business strategy.

An IT strategy is a way of aligning the efforts of IT with the efforts of the business. It is also a way of marshalling staff behind a single flag or call to action. It becomes IT's *raison d'etre*—what it must do to fulfill its mission and purpose in the enterprise. Unfortunately, the simple has become complex. Inexact language, overselling, and poor strategy development have

Exhibit 3.1   Strategy Components

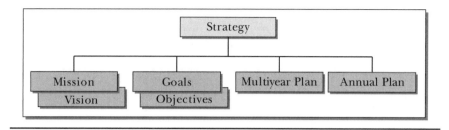

made strategy confusing, overhyped, and underleveraged. This chapter tries to untangle a surprisingly simple and very useful tool.

The word *strategy* can be confusing because it represents a whole class of processes and deliverables, as well as one process and one specific deliverable. In its broadest sense, a strategy includes a mission statement, a vision statement, goals, objectives, a multiyear plan, and an annual plan (see Exhibit 3.1). Unfortunately, these terms are neither hard and fast nor universally used. For example, one organization's mission might be another's goal. Some use very different language. For example, Johnson & Johnson, the giant healthcare products company, does not have a mission statement; instead, it has what it calls its "credo." Some use the word *strategy* to mean simply the multiyear plan. This chapter focuses on the broader interpretation of strategy and the components that make it up.

Strategy Components: Mission Statement, Vision Statement, Goals, and Objectives

A *mission statement* is a very short, usually one- to three-sentence, statement of the organization's purpose. It is the highest-level articulation of why the organization exists. Because it is written at such a high level, it usually has a rather long life. Companies can go decades without feeling the need to modify their mission statements. Conversely, if an organization changes its mission every few years, it might be an indicator that something is wrong with either the organization or the environment in which it exists. Exhibit 3.2 contains the mission statement for a pharmaceutical company.

Exhibit 3.2   Merck & Co. Mission Statement

The mission of Merck is to provide society with superior products and services by developing innovations and solutions that improve the quality of life and satisfy customer needs, and to provide employees with meaningful work and advancement opportunities, and investors with a superior rate of return.

Source: Merck & Co., Inc. Web site www.merck.com.

Exhibit 3.3   State Farm Mutual Automobile Insurance Company Vision
Statement

Our vision for the future is to be the customer's first and best choice in
the products and services we provide. We will continue to be the leader
in the insurance industry and we will become a leader in the financial
services arena. Our customers' needs will determine our path. Our values
will guide us.

Source: Copyright, State Farm Mutual Automobile Insurance Company 1998.
Used by permission. www.statefarm.com/about/mission.asp.

A *vision statement* is a broad picture of where the organization will be
sometime in the future. The statement might say that by the end of the
decade, the company will be the largest thumbscrew supplier on the west
coast. Exhibit 3.3 contains an insurance company's vision of becoming its
clients' preferred partner.

For many companies, the vision and mission statements are mutually
exclusive. They have one or the other. Some organizations have both, as in
the case of a global packaged goods company in Exhibit 3.4.

A *goal* is an articulation of the intended results, outcome, or benefits
of the mission.

An *objective* is a more detailed or specific description of what is to be
achieved. Objectives sometimes include time frames, responsibilities, and an
approach for achieving the goals. An objective is often sufficiently concrete
that its success can be measured. Exhibit 3.5 lists the goal and objectives for
a financial company.

It is easy to be confused by the subtle differences between some goals
and objectives. This is perhaps why they are sometimes lumped together.
Joining goals and objectives into one title is one way of getting around a
somewhat elusive distinction.

Exhibit 3.4   Sara Lee Corporation Mission and Vision Statements

---

Our Mission
To simply delight you . . . every day.

Our Vision
To be the first choice of consumers and customers around the world by
bringing together innovative ideas, continuous improvement and people
who make things happen.

Source: Sara Lee Corporation, www.saralee.com/AboutSaraLee/OurMission.aspx.

Exhibit 3.5   Principal Financial Group Goals and Objectives

Our goal is to be a domestic leader in providing innovative and leading-edge banking solutions that deliver exceptional value to our customers . . .
   Our primary objectives:

- Reliably deliver quality banking products and services to our customers at a fair value for them and a fair return for Principal Bank.

- Provide the financial "glue" that ties together the separate products and services purchased by customers of the Principal Financial Group.

- Ensure our systems and processes are operationally efficient and can meet the needs of our growing bank.

Source: Principal Bank, a member of The Principal Financial Group, Web site www.principal.com.

Should IT follow the business world, and have a mission statement, a vision statement, goals, and objectives? It depends on the size and breadth of the IT organization. Large IT organizations, those that must support several very different types of customers, or those that provide very critical, revenue-generating services to the business, should probably have a mission statement, a vision statement, goals, and objectives. However, smaller IT shops, or those less involved with the revenue-generating side of the business, might find that having them all is overkill. However, regardless of size or purpose, all IT organizations should have at least a mission or vision statement and a set of goals or objectives.

Exhibit 3.6 contains an example of a simple mission statement for an IT organization that supports professional staff who travel extensively.

IT mission and vision statements should be short. A good rule of thumb is that they should be "T-shirtable" (able, or almost able, to fit on T-shirts, coffee cups, posters, and the like). Anything longer, and they will lose their punch.

IT goals also need to be short and to the point. The samples in Exhibit 3.7 would be appropriate.

If there are goals, then objectives might not be needed; however, they would never be inappropriate. For example, the first goal, *Provide the absolute best operational service*, could have the objectives in Exhibit 3.8.

Exhibit 3.6   Sample IT Mission Statement

Corporate IT provides high-quality, cost-effective technology services to support the firm's staff, whether in the office or in the field.

Exhibit 3.7   Sample IT Goals
• Provide the absolute best operational service.
• Develop a service culture.
• Focus on our internal customers.
• Become an information-driven organization.
• Develop exceptional professionals.

IT mission, vision, goals, and objectives are very effective ways of communicating to senior management, to IT consumers, and to IT personnel what the IT organization is about, and also, at the most fundamental level, why it exists.

Strategy Components: IT Multiyear Plan

A *multiyear plan*, also called a long-term plan, is a high-level document consisting of the schedules, benefits, resource requirements, dependencies, and costs of executing the organization's mission for the next three, five, or more years. The multiyear plan is sufficiently important that some organizations reserve the word *strategy* for it alone. They do not consider the mission statement or objectives part of the strategy.

For IT, the multiyear plan is where the rubber meets the road: It is the primary deliverable for determining and communicating the IT organization's direction and planned course of action for the coming years.

The typical plan consists of five parts. The first is an analysis of the current business environment. The second is a look at the current technology environment. The third is the business's best educated guess of what the future business environment will look like. The fourth part is IT's analysis of the future technology environment needed to support the projected future business environment. The last part identifies the gaps between the current and future technology environments and the initiatives needed to fill those gaps. These five parts not only form the high-level work steps for

Exhibit 3.8   Sample IT Objectives for the Goal: *Provide the Absolute Best Operational Service*
• Provide consistent services with the highest availability, reliability, security, and cost-effectiveness.
• Achieve a high degree of measurable customer satisfaction.
• Ensure seamless service integration—the same service, working the same way, anywhere in the world.

the multiyear plan, but they can also become the organization and major chapters of the plan document.

Current Environment   The *Current Environment* section is an analysis of how the business and IT currently function. It forms the baseline for an understanding of what, if any, IT changes are needed for the future. It is usually not a difficult section to produce, because it is a re-articulation of what the business and IT should already know. However, it is a cornerstone for what is to come.

Current Business Environment
The purpose of looking at the current business environment is to establish the starting point for any future vision. In addition, it defines what is, or should be, the purpose and goals of the current technology environment. Finally, it gives IT an opportunity to show senior business management that it understands the concerns of the business. A good understanding of the current business environment should include an articulation of the business's purposes, direction, and the challenges it faces.

Mission, Vision, Goals, and Objectives
This section starts with a statement of what the business is trying to achieve. A simple reaffirmation of mission, goals, and objectives is sufficient. Is the business strategy to be a low-cost provider or a premium merchant? Does the business want to generate a significant amount of its sales internationally in new markets or domestically in the tried-and-true markets? Is the emphasis to gain market share or to maximize profits?

While some companies publish their goals and objectives, others are more taciturn. A few short interviews with senior management can confirm whether IT has collected the right information.

Current Strategy and Execution
This section is to confirm that IT understands the current business strategy (business multiyear plan). How does the business plan to achieve its goals and objectives? Being a low-cost provider means that the production costs must be low. What is the strategy to get and keep costs down? If the intention is to enter new markets in Latin America, how does the company plan to do this? Partner with local firms? Buy a local company? Set up a brand-new operation in Latin America?

Obtaining and understanding the business strategy is not always easy. As Exhibit 3.9 shows, there are explicit and implicit business strategies. Explicit strategies are those published in a business strategy document. It states, in one logical place, the company's mission, goals, multiyear plan, and so forth. An implicit business strategy means that a business strategy exists, but it is not something one will find in a single document. It might be spread over various reports, memos, e-mails, meeting minutes, and sometimes just in people's heads.

Exhibit 3.9 IT Access to the Business Strategy

	SHARED	NOT SHARED
IMPLICIT	**Somewhat Difficult** - Source: Multiple documents - Interviews to confirm	**Most Difficult** - Source: Permission to *look* for documents - Detailed interviews
EXPLICIT	**Easiest** - Source: One document - Short interviews to confirm (if needed)	**Somewhat Difficult** - Source: Permission to *see* document - Interviews to confirm

A strategy can be shared or not shared. A shared strategy is one that is accessible by a large number of managers, if not all corporate staff. Some firms even publish part or all of their business strategy in shareholder reports or on their Web sites. Other enterprises do not share their strategy and restrict part or all of its distribution to just a few executives.

IT should work to obtain as much of the business strategy as it can. If strategy documents do not exist, or if they are not accessible, IT will need to compensate for their absence by interviewing senior business managers. As Exhibit 3.9 points out, the level of effort IT will have to apply to obtain and understand the business strategy depends on whether it is explicit, implicit, shared, or not shared.

Assessment of How Well the Strategy Is Working

There are multiple sources for uncovering a business strategy and understanding how well it is being executed (see Exhibit 3.10). Strangely enough, while the business strategy might involve some level of secrecy, how well the company is doing is often water cooler scuttlebutt.

As long as it does not create an internal crisis or get the CIO fired, documenting a synopsis of how well the strategy is working, and the reasons why it is (or is not) working, can be quite useful. The goal is not to be the most knowledgeable person on the unemployment line, but to understand where things are going right and where things could be done better. The focus should be on improvement, not blame. The key question is: What should be learned from this assessment?

Exhibit 3.10 Understanding the Business Strategy

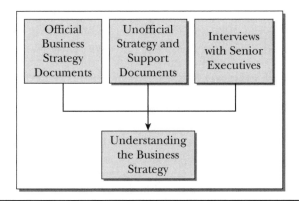

Evolving Threats and Opportunities

As stated earlier, a strategy involves responding to change. The change can come from within the company, but more often, it is change coming from outside the enterprise. A common reason for changing a business strategy is a perception of internal or external threats and opportunities. Understanding threats and opportunities involves asking some telling questions: Is the customer base changing? Is it aging or becoming younger? Are customers developing tastes that are more or less sophisticated? Are the suppliers consolidating, becoming competitors, or lowering prices? Are competitors merging, going out of business, or moving overseas?

IT should document all known threats and opportunities. Detail is not necessary and can even be detrimental. The goal is to show that IT understands the current market forces affecting the business.

Current Technology Environment

IT should document the current technology environment to form a baseline for understanding technology changes that will be needed in the future. This information will be useful for the plans and funding requests IT might eventually have to make to accommodate new business initiatives. It will also help business managers understand what IT will need to do to meet its future market demands.

Mission, Vision, Goals, and Objectives

It might seem to be an error placing IT's mission, vision, goals, and objectives in the multiyear plan when they are strategy components in their own right. The reason is simple. Placing them in the multiyear plan is an opportunity to, once again, remind the enterprise that IT is dedicated to the business's success. These components are short and take up little space, but their reiteration is a mantra that IT should emphasize whenever possible.

Current IT Strategy and Execution

Unless IT is in total chaos, it has been working under a set of assumptions and guidelines that can be called the current IT strategy. It might not be published or even on paper, and it might not be for multiple years, but there is probably a set of shared goals, expectations, and approaches across the IT department. Pull them together into a single document, and *voilà!*, there is at least a *de facto* IT strategy.

Assessment of How Well the IT Strategy Is Working

This is the time to come clean. How well is the IT strategy actually doing? Is it consistent with the business strategy or business direction? Is it consistent across IT? Is it complete? Does it do the job that needs to be done? Be brief and be honest. No Uriah Heep whining, but beware: Get caught stretching the truth too far, and credibility will suffer, a potentially fatal senior manager error.

Evolving IT Threats and Opportunities

The first question to answer is what impact do the current *business* threats and opportunities have on IT? For example, a threat (and opportunity) would be customers wanting to submit orders using the Web, a service IT does not currently support. Another example would be customers wanting 24-hour online shopping, when IT is currently unable to comply because the system has a traditional online/batch-window architecture.

Second, what current *technology* threats and opportunities are there? Will changing economics for outsourcing or offshoring affect IT? Will cell phone or personal digital assistant (PDA) use change the way IT currently supports e-commerce?

Future Environment   IT needs to understand how the world is changing. It should start by documenting the pressures and opportunities the business feels it will be facing in the near future. For example, the *Evolving Threats and Opportunities* section of the *Current Environment* deals with threats and opportunities currently emerging, while this section deals with what is likely to occur in the coming years. This section should put together a projected picture of the business and technology environments for two, three, or more years into the future. The goal is to understand what IT will need to do and what it will need to look like (e.g., organizational structure, processes, resources, etc.) to accommodate the anticipated business environment.

Future Business Environment
There are at least six sources of future business change:

1. *Customers.* How will the customer base be different three, five, or more years from now? Will their needs or wants be the same? Will change center on quality or cost? For example, will consumers demand better

products, as happened in the automotive industry, or exert pricing pressure, as the airlines experienced? Are customers getting older and thus more set in their buying patterns, or younger and more susceptible to lifestyle advertising? Will the average household income rise or fall, thus affecting what customers can afford to purchase? Customers might not change, but their numbers might, either growing or diminishing, or they might move from the cities to the suburbs, or from the United States to overseas.

2. *Suppliers.* How will suppliers be different three to five years from now? Will their products change in quality, price, or service? If supplier costs increase, will our prices need to be higher? How will that affect customers? Will they be willing to pay more or will they buy less? Will customers substitute some other (cheaper, superior) product in place of ours? Will our suppliers try to market directly to our customers (a process called disintermediation), thus cutting us out of the transaction? Will we be able to substitute one supplier for another?

3. *Distribution Channels.* Distribution channels are the means by which a company delivers its products and provides its services. Changes in distribution channels can affect costs as well as the time it takes to deliver products and services. They can contribute to, or detract from, the customer experience. For example, a small private branch exchange (PBX) provider, that delivers products through an in-house sales-and-service force might discover that its competitors are using computer stores for sales and the Internet for service, significantly lowering costs. How will the organization respond?

4. *Resources.* Resources consist of the people, equipment, materials, and infrastructure needed to provision, build, sell, and service products. Changes in availability, productivity, and cost can significantly change a company's products or services. Changes can include the way the products are produced, delivered, and serviced, as well as the prices that must be charged for them.

5. *Regulations.* Government laws and regulatory agency rules can significantly change the business landscape. In 1920, the manufacture, sale, and transport of alcoholic beverages was made illegal in the United States. About the same time, the selling of alcoholic beverages was made illegal in most provinces in Canada, but not their production. The business landscape in both countries changed dramatically. In the United States, no one could legally produce or sell alcohol. In Canada, they could produce alcohol but could not sell it to consumers. Where did all the Canadian-produced alcohol go? Across the Detroit River and Great Lakes, into the United States.

Smoking bans have greatly affected U.S. businesses, providing advantages to health insurers and most employers (people are healthier), and disadvantages to tobacco, cigarette lighter, and ashtray companies. In 1970, U.S. airline ticket prices were regulated, forcing airlines to compete on service. Today, ticket prices are unregulated, and airlines compete on price. Regulations can have a very profound effect on businesses.

6. *Competitors.* Twenty years ago, most people bought eyeglasses from solo practitioner optometrists, books from mom-and-pop bookstores, and drugs from family-owned pharmacies. Today, eyeglasses, books, and drugs are often purchased from large chain stores. Small retail stores cannot compete with the large chains on price, so if they are to survive, they need to find another way to compete with the big guys. Some have found a new niche by providing better, more personalized service than the big chains. Being able to anticipate and mitigate competitive pressures might be necessary for their survival.

Assumptions About the Business Future
Sometimes the business strategy is in a condition and format that makes it easy for IT to use. Other times the strategy might be a bit arcane, or at too high a level, or even at too detailed a level for easy IT use. Finally, sometimes there might not be a single explicit business strategy. Rather, it might implicitly exist in dozens of memos written over many months.

In all of these cases, it is wise for IT to take the business strategy, implicit or explicit, shared or not shared, and break it down into a list of future business assumptions. Each assumption in the list should be no longer than one or two sentences. A Future Business Assumptions List, which is illustrated in Exhibit 3.11, is a very simply stated summary of every statement made by senior business managers regarding how the market or the business unit will, might, or must change. Some statements might contradict others, some might not make any sense, but at least some will be on target. IT should document them all. Sorting them out will take place after they are all collected.

After the Future Business Assumptions List is complete, it should be taken to several senior business mangers for review and comment. Business managers can then correct errors, fill in gaps, resolve inconsistencies, or confirm that IT has it right. In some cases, what is written will stimulate useful memories or spark discussions in new areas.

Creating a Future Business Assumptions List gives IT an opportunity to test its understanding of what the business strategy is saying and even expand it where the business strategy is incomplete. For example, take the business strategy statement, "Growth in Asia will double over the next five years." Is the growth in revenue, net income, orders, staff, or number of customers? IT's response could be different for each of these scenarios. Will the doubling over the five years take place all at once or be spread out over the five years? If it is not evenly spread over the five years, will most of the growth occur

Exhibit 3.11   Sample Future Business Assumptions List

- The customer base will grow at 8 percent per year, sales at 10 percent, and revenue at 7 percent.
- The most significant customer growth will be in the U.S. Southwest, while the least growth will occur in the Southeast.
- Growth in Asia will double over the next 5 years.
- The current product portfolio of 12 products will probably change over the next 5 years, with a net increase of between 6 and 12 new products, and a discontinuation of 4 to 6 older and less popular products.
- Competitors will continue to shift from in-house support through walk-in facilities to overseas call centers and Internet support.
- We will probably have to do the same for our basic products.
- However, the customers of our high-end products are likely to require even more hands-on service.
- Growth in Europe will probably mean we have to modify our high-end product line for that market and provide local support.

in the first two years or in the last two? If IT is unsure of the meaning of an assumption or if an assumption raises questions, then the questions should be placed at the end of the assumptions list and the appropriate business staff interviewed to resolve them.

Some parts of the business strategy will not affect IT. For example, IT might not be affected by expanding the pool of customers who are offered discounts. There is a natural tendency to exclude from the Future Business Assumptions List strategy activities that will not affect IT. This is a mistake. There are two reasons the Future Business Assumptions List should include all parts of the business strategy, whether IT considers them IT-relevant or not. First, one never knows. When reviewing the future business assumptions with a business manager, he or she might suddenly say or remember a piece of information that changes IT's own strategy. Second, business managers might not recognize that IT left a piece of its strategy out of the Future Business Assumptions List because IT thought it was irrelevant. Rather, they might conclude that IT left it out because IT staff were remiss or inattentive—not an image IT should want to convey.

So far, this chapter assumes that the business has a business strategy, although it might be implicit rather than explicit, or not shared rather than shared. What should IT do if the business does not appear to have a business strategy at all? Every company has a business strategy, but surprisingly, some businesses do not document it. This is particularly true if the business is very stable or has been quite profitable for a long period of time. Successful companies often do not see a need to follow business best practices and document, discuss, and reaffirm their long-running strategy. This is unfortunate because, when there is a downturn, companies that have been successful for very long periods often have a much harder time recognizing the severity of the situation and taking corrective action.

If there is no explicit or implicit business strategy, or if it is not shared, then IT will need to create a substitute. It does not have to be a fancy document; in fact, this is one of the advantages of a Future Business Assumptions List. IT will need to put together a set of business assumptions based on any sundry pieces of information about the business it can find, along with the information gathered from any personal interviews with business leaders. IT should then create a Future Business Assumptions List based on the material and information it was able to gather. The list might be short or superficial, but it is better than nothing. When completed, the assumptions should be taken back to the business leaders to verify that the information is correct. The assumptions can then function as a business strategy surrogate. To update what was stated earlier in the chapter, the list of business strategy types (explicit, implicit, shared, and not shared) should be amended to add surrogate.

Some IT organizations might want to skip creating a Future Business Assumptions List, particularly if they see it as redundant with the business strategy. This is a mistake. The Future Business Assumptions List will prove to be one of the most valuable documents IT possesses. The value of having the business strategy dissected into a series of Future Business Assumptions List bullet points, which can then be reviewed by business managers, is sufficiently valuable to IT that it should be required for all IT organizations, even those where the business has a clear, concise, and explicit business strategy. A valid and up-to-date Future Business Assumptions List is the foundation for IT's understanding of the business, and it also defines IT's strategy. Its few pages will dictate future IT staffing levels, capital expenditures, and daily operations. It is one of IT's crown jewels.

Future Technology Environment

The future business environment paints a picture of how the organization sees the business evolving over the next three, five, or more years. As goes the business, so goes the technology. The future technology environment section describes what IT determines it needs to do to accommodate the business changes.

This is where the future business assumptions earn their keep, because they become the catalyst for converting a business strategy into an IT strategy (Exhibit 3.12). It is far easier to go through the Future Business Assumptions List, one line item at a time, listing how technology will have to change to accommodate the business, than it is to wade through the

Exhibit 3.12   Sources for the IT Strategy

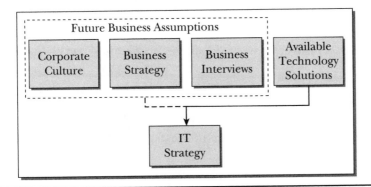

original business documents. For each bullet point on the Future Business Assumptions List, IT should determine the changes needed to the following:

- *Applications.* What new applications will be needed or what existing applications will need to be modified? Does IT have the right tools and resources to make the necessary changes? If not, can IT get them?

- *Network.* Does IT have the reliability and capacity when and where it will be needed in the future? If growth is to be in a new or remote region, does IT have a relationship with, or at least knowledge of, the vendors who do the best job in that area?

- *Data center.* Will new computer or storage devices be needed? Will the hours and days of operation change? Are there legal or regulatory impediments to storing data (customer, employee, product) or executing programs (encryption) in one location as opposed to another? Will backup or recovery need to change?

- *IT customer tools (hardware and software).* Will the user's technology toolkit have to change? Will new devices be added (e.g., laptops, cell phones, PDAs)? Are there regional or national differences (e.g., languages, laws, customs, standards) that need to be taken into account? What support documents, training classes, and so forth will need to be changed or upgraded?

- *IT customer support.* How will IT support the old and new users? How will it support the old and new tools and equipment? Will all customers, all regions, and all offices receive the same or different support? Will there be new languages spoken by new IT customers? Will there be new or changed hours of operation or customs to accommodate?

- *Security.* What new threats will IT face, and what new protection measures must it implement? What impact will national and regional laws and regulatory rules have on IT's customers or on IT's ability to do its job? How will IT protect corporate assets (i.e., hardware, software, data, and personnel) in every location where the business has a presence?

- *Planning.* Will the changes affect IT planning? Do new regions or businesses need to be added to the planning process? How will IT balance central versus distributed planning?

- *Performance measurement and management reporting.* How will IT ensure that it can account for all necessary changes, determine that they are working as expected, and convey that information to the right customers?

IT can easily understand the impact of future business changes on technology if it documents the effect the business assumption has on technology. It is a simple case of cause and effect. If growth in Asia means that the number of servers in Hong Kong must increase, then the business growth assumption caused the server technology change. If, in the future, the business assumption changes, then the technology that is the effect of that cause can easily be identified and changed.

Exhibit 3.13 illustrates how one bullet point item from the Future Business Assumptions List (see Exhibit 3.11) drives the technology changes IT needs to make.

The link between the bullet point items on the Future Business Assumptions List and the technology changes they generate will become even more important if there are future modifications to the business plan. Imagine that after the business strategy, future business assumptions, IT strategy, and IT plans are complete, the business changes a fundamental part of its business strategy. The business once assumed that it would grow 10 percent in Australia and shrink by 15 percent in Brazil. It now believes that it will grow 20 percent in Australia and 5 percent in Brazil. IT must determine whether this new information changes its IT strategy and plans. This can be a daunting task, but it is made considerably easier by using the Future Business Assumptions List. All IT needs to do is to identify the IT implications listed that are the result of the original assumptions and make the appropriate changes.

Gaps and Required Initiatives   The last step in the multiyear plan is to review the list of technology changes, combine them as needed, and create a list of the IT initiatives needed to fill the anticipated gaps in IT's services. For example, the planned growth in Asia (from the Future Business Environment) underscores that the disaster recovery data center in Asia, which is running at capacity (from the Current Technology Environment), needs to expand (from the Future Technology Environment). Ideally, this list of initiatives, from maintenance to new investments, will become the projects the organization will approve and fund to meet business expectations.

Exhibit 3.13   Sample Technology Implications Driven by the Future Business Assumptions List

Future Business Assumption: Growth in Asia will double over the next five years.

Technology Implications:

- *Applications*. Growth in Asia will probably not affect the functionality of any applications. However, doubling the number of customers, orders, and transactions will strain the batch window and the database structure. A new database management system with more indices will be needed.

- *Network*. The wide area network and a number of local area networks in Asia will have to be expanded. Hong Kong can handle the traffic, but Singapore and Tokyo will need to be re-architected.

- *Question Raised by This Analysis: Will business in all Asian offices double over the next five years or just in some?*

- *Data Center*. The Tokyo data center can handle the expanded load (including the new servers), but the Hong Kong disaster recovery site will need to add servers and storage units.

- *Question Raised by This Analysis: Does Hong Kong have the needed floor space, cooling, and power?*

- *IT Customer Tools (Hardware and Software)*. No new tools are anticipated.

- *Question Raised by This Analysis: How will the staffing in Asia change? Will it double?*

- *IT Customer Support*. If no new offices are needed, then IT only needs to hire more staff.

- *Question Raised by This Analysis: Will new offices be needed and will they require additional staff?*

- *Security*. If no new offices are added, then IT can accommodate the business increase.

- *Question Raised by This Analysis: Will new offices be created in different countries? New countries might have different laws and regulations concerning security and data protection.*

- *Planning*. No planning changes are anticipated if there are no new offices.

- *Question Raised by This Analysis: Will new offices be created? New offices will require new planning.*

- *Performance Measurement and Management Reporting*. No changes anticipated.

For each initiative IT should identify:

- *Resources needed.* Equipment (current and to-purchase), staff (existing and those who will need to be hired), and training that will be needed if IT is to have the necessary services in place for the anticipated business changes

- *Timelines.* When the resources will need to be delivered and when they will be ready for use

- *Cost.* What the resources will cost, both up front and over the life of the investment

The resources required, timelines, and costs should be high-level estimates. More detail is not needed because, before any projects are approved, the IT Steering Committee will conduct a more in-depth analysis.

While the average business strategy tries to anticipate the future for from three to ten years out, the average IT strategy is usually for about three years. The difference exists because very few IT professionals are comfortable predicting what technology will be like five or more years into the future. Three years makes the prediction possible, especially given the depreciation life of many technology assets. Technology might change tomorrow, but due to depreciation rules, if IT buys a capital item today, it is likely to be stuck with it for at least the next three or four years. However, regardless of the capital depreciation rules, trying to anticipate changes in technology more than three years out is considered by many to be science fiction.

Do not be confused by the terms *multiyear plan* or *three-year plan*. Creating a strategy for a three-year period of time is an annual event. Each year, the IT staff needs to review the plan, delete the coming year, make whatever changes are needed to the remaining years, and add a new year at the end. For example, in constructing a new three-year plan, year one is dropped (it becomes the new annual plan), year two becomes year one, year three becomes year two, and a new year three is created. Each year, IT needs to meet with business managers and reaffirm that the future business assumptions gathered during the prior year are still valid. Not every business is good at keeping the business strategy up-to-date. A few interviews with IT's customers should either confirm the business assumptions or illuminate a need to modify them to reflect current business thinking. IT can then adjust its multiyear plan to accommodate the changes.

Strategy Components: The IT Annual Plan

An *annual plan* consists of a detailed approach, schedule, and budget laying out what initiatives are needed to achieve IT's goals for the coming year. Plans usually state the work steps for each initiative, who has to perform what tasks, what they will need to do, exactly what the organization will have when the initiative is complete, when it can start, how long it will take, and what it will cost.

Even IT organizations that do not have a mission statement, published goals, or a formal multiyear plan probably have some semblance of an annual plan, even if it is just its IT budget. However, a good and robust annual plan is an opportunity for IT to reconnect with its customers, reaffirm its goals, and manage expectations for the coming year.

A good annual plan is similar to the multiyear plan, although more detailed and covering only the coming or current year. Although it need not include a restatement of IT's mission or objectives, it never hurts to remind the business of the role IT plays in the business's success. This reminder takes up little space and presents a good introduction to the technology information in the rest of the plan.

The annual plan should distinguish between operating issues and needed investments. IT should separate its operating and investment (project) plans and budgets, reserving the operating plan for maintaining the current IT services and the investment plan for the projects and activities surrounding new or greatly expanded services.

Operating Plan   Separate out all activities, resources, and costs associated with keeping the enterprise's "lights on." Data center operations, application maintenance, and end-user support are all parts of the tasks and costs associated with maintaining IT services. They are all components of IT's operating plan.

The operating plan should lay out IT's operating mission and goals, the services it provides, how performance is measured, what will be new this year, and the costs to provide these services. Central to the operating plan is understanding the cost drivers. A *cost driver* is a factor that causes a change in the consumption of a resource. Usually quantifiable, cost drivers determine how the costs of an associated item will increase or decrease based on the change in some condition or event. How much will the food cost for a birthday party? There is a very good chance that the cost to feed a dozen people is half the cost of feeding two dozen. A good cost driver for determining the cost to feed partygoers is the number of people attending. If it costs $22 to feed one person, it will probably cost $220 to feed ten.

In IT, the driver for the cost of personal computers (PCs) in a business unit is typically the number of PC users in the unit. If the unit headcount of PC users is projected to increase 10 percent next year, then the cost of PCs, PC software, and support is likely to rise about 10 percent. Drivers can be headcount, sales orders, number of customers, transactions, or any number of other factors.

Tied tightly to the cost driver is the technology conversion factor. It is important to know the relationship between the two. For example, if headcount increases 10 percent, then the cost for PCs will likely rise 10 percent.

The business cost driver (headcount) is in a one-to-one relationship with the technology cost to support it (number of PCs needed.)

Not all ratios of business cost drivers to technology cost are 1:1. Take the example of a payroll system: If the number of employees grows by 10 percent, will the payroll-related technology costs to support that growth also grow by 10 percent? Probably not. The software, if it was purchased or developed internally, will probably not cost any more. Rather than buying a new server, IT could just run the payroll application longer. No additional operators or supervisors will likely be needed. However, more electricity will be consumed, more paper reports printed, and more checks cut. Help-desk problems might increase by 10 percent, as might the number of data center incidents. Doing some arithmetic, IT might conclude that for every 1 percent increase in staff, payroll processing costs increase 0.5 percent, so the ratio of business-to-technology cost is 2:1. The technology conversion factor is, therefore, 0.5. The *technology conversion factor* is the adjustment applied to the cost driver to account for mitigating factors such as the effect of economies of scale.

Cost drivers work hand-in-hand with the future business assumptions. Take the future business assumption that business revenue will grow by 20 percent per year for the next three years in Peru, while headcount will increase by 15 percent per year. The impact of Peru's growth on the network, data center, PCs, and customer support can be calculated if the business cost drivers and the technology conversion factors for the network, data center, PCs, and customer support are known.

Exhibit 3.14 shows how future business assumptions can be used to calculate future IT growth and costs. If cost drivers are well understood,

Exhibit 3.14   Business Cost Drivers Applied to IT

IT Component	Business Driver	Business Growth	Technology Conversion Factor	IT Growth
Network	Business Transactions	20%	Network growth 10 percent greater than business growth. TCF=1.1	22%
Data Center	Business Transactions	20%	Data center grows at 85% of business transaction growth. TCF=0.85	17%
PCs	Headcount	15%	One-to-one. TCF=1.0	15%
Customer Support	Headcount	15%	Headcount to support ratio 1.0:0.8. TCF=0.8	12%

and the technology conversion factors are known, then the IT implications of the business increasing in Peru can be fairly accurately determined.

Determining and using cost drivers and technology conversion factors is an acquired skill. It will take time, years perhaps, before IT will come up with drivers and conversion factors that are sufficiently accurate to be useful. However, IT must start somewhere, and the sooner IT begins the trial-and-error process, the sooner it will gain useful information.

Investment (Project) Plan   All new investments and significant maintenance and enhancements, such as providing staff with PDAs or purchasing a customer resource-management application, should be included in a separate investment plan. The investment plan lays out all of the approved major initiatives or investments to be started, continued, or completed during the year. For each investment, IT should indicate its purpose, its benefits, when it will be started and completed, all associated costs, and when and by whom it was approved and funded.

Why separate the operating and investment plans? There are three main reasons. First, separating the operating and investment plans paints a more accurate picture of IT's ability to manage its resources. Businesses want support areas, such as IT, to track with enterprise growth, although ideally at a slower rate. For example, if the enterprise were growing annually at 7 percent over the past five years, then senior business managers would like to see the support functions growing at a similar or slightly slower rate, say 6 percent, over the past five years. However, many IT budgets "saw tooth," going up and down at different rates from year to year, often with greater swings than the enterprise has had itself (Exhibit 3.15).

Many of those swings are driven, not by the cost of providing current IT services, but by the cost of investing in new services and infrastructure. If you remove the investments from the budget, the growth line will often flatten out, showing a more consistent level of budget increase or decrease.

Exhibit 3.16 shows that if investments are removed from the IT operating budget, the budget will appear more stable and grow at a slower

Exhibit 3.15   Enterprise Growth vs. IT Budget

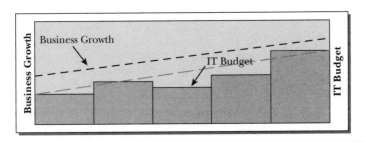

Exhibit 3.16 IT Operating Budget Compared to Business Growth

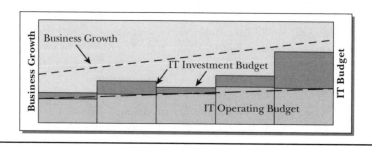

rate than the business. IT can place some operating budget increases in perspective by normalizing operating costs. Is a 10 percent operating growth in IT excessive? If the business is growing at 6 percent, maybe so. However, if the business is growing at 15 percent, then the business might be getting a bargain.

The best way to normalize cost increases and decreases is by looking at the cost per business driver unit. For example, if the major business driver for IT's end-user support cost is business headcount, and if IT's support costs are growing at a rate lower than the headcount increases in the organization, then IT is showing a per-unit cost decrease, and not an increase.

Assume that last year's end-user support budget was $500,000 for 1,000 employees. Then the unit cost is $500 per employee. If this year's customer support costs increase 10 percent to $550,000, but the number of staff has increased to 1,200 employees, then the unit cost has actually decreased to $458, or an 8.4 percent reduction in the cost to serve a single employee (see Exhibit 3.17). This is a far better number to show senior management when it questions a 10 percent increase in support costs.

Second, IT's operating costs are true IT costs. Operating costs are what IT has to pay to provide its services. IT's investments, however, are, for the most part, not IT costs at all, but decisions by the business to invest in *its* future. For example, we can imagine a company undergoing some loss of

Exhibit 3.17 IT Operating Growth Normalized

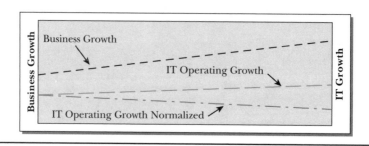

business that results in senior management requiring all support functions to cut their budgets by X percent. IT should apply the X percent cut to the operating budget. Cuts, if any, in the investment budget, should be left for the business to decide. The business might conclude that to get out of the economic downturn, it needs to invest in new products or new delivery mechanisms. It is an old business maxim that a company cannot cost-cut its way to profitability. Cost cutting simply gives the business some time and cash to make the necessary business direction changes. The business might decide that the reason the operating budget needs to be cut is to pay for needed IT investments.

Developing Staff by Developing a Strategy

Strategy development can be a difficult and time-consuming task. Some of it can be challenging, such as charting the direction for IT over the next few years. Unfortunately, much of it involves the less glamorous tasks of researching dozens of documents, perhaps hundreds of memos, down to help-desk trouble tickets. Who would want to do such work?

Because of its lack of glamour, some chief information officers (CIOs) relegate the task to the IT or corporate communications group, whose members are experts on business language, clever clip art, and document construction. These CIOs are missing an opportunity to develop some of their best staff.

An irony of life in a high-pressure department such as IT is that critical people—the ones who fix the problems, direct the staff, and make the most positive difference—are often the most professionally ill-treated. Not intentionally, of course, but they are the ones who cannot go to a seminar because they are needed back in the office.

This is an opportunity for the CIO to groom the department's best and brightest as future IT leaders without their having to leave the premises. Creating an IT strategy is an Ivy League education in a few weeks. Putting the top performers in charge of the strategy, and having them do virtually all the work, will give them an opportunity to (1) learn about the internal workings of every IT department, (2) meet and interview senior corporate and business unit staff, (3) understand the business at a level few single individuals (inside or outside of IT) will ever do, (4) work with IT's best in other IT departments, and (5) set the course of IT for the coming years.

The CIO should work them hard and demand quality from them. The result will be win-win.

Third, separating the two plans can lead to easier planning and budget approval. As stated in Chapter 2, IT governance bodies like to focus on big-ticket items, such as significant changes in services or costs. Once the steering committee has reviewed the annual operating plan two or three times, and if the operating plans are well constructed and any increases defensible and acceptable, then they are more likely to pass future operating plans with less detailed scrutiny. Instead, their focus can shift to the investment plan, where they play a more significant role in the selection, approval, and funding of company investments. A good operating plan lets the senior managers involved with IT governance focus on exceptional business issues and not on the mundane, though well-managed, operational issues.

WHAT THE FOR-PROFITS CAN TEACH IT

An IT strategy is a very effective weapon in the IT arsenal. However, there are still a few lessons in the development and use of this weapon that the business can teach the IT department. IT needs to avoid appearing to be a stranger in a strange land. If IT wants to fit in and be taken seriously, it needs to see itself, and be seen by others, as not just a technology provider, but rather as an integral part of the business. Many for-profit business organizations have learned that a well-articulated strategy can serve more purposes than just providing business direction. Used correctly, a good business strategy can be a marketing tool for customers and stockholders, as well as an apothegm or rallying cry for employees.

Know Your Target Audience

Business strategies are usually carefully written. It is not uncommon for the chief executive officer (CEO) of even a large company to spend considerable time making sure that the wording of the mission and vision statements is just right. Why? Because these documents will be read by senior managers, staff, stockholders, financial analysts, lenders, regulators, and some customers. Any document going to such an important audience needs careful *wordsmithing*.

Good businesspeople always try to see the world from the customer's perspective. They know how important it is that the audience who reads their document understand it and come away with the message the author intended. So, the wording has to be carefully selected and just right. Wording is even more critical if the document is intended for multiple audiences.

IT, however, has a tendency to write for itself and not for its customers. Technical jargon, shortcuts, abbreviations, and acronyms permeate IT documents. IT should follow the example of its business counterparts and decide who its audience is and exactly what needs to be done to effectively communicate with them. It would be far better for IT if statements such as "we are beta testing VoIP in the smaller, less critical, offices" became "we are piloting a new Internet-based telephone service in selected offices."

Use the Strategy as a Rallying Cry

Why waste a good mission statement on just senior managers? CEOs routinely use the enterprise mission statements, visions, and the recently popular values statement as a way of firing up staff morale or *esprit de corps* and getting them on board. What once existed solely in executive binders can now be found on posters, coffee cups, T-shirts, and the like. Business leaders know not to let a good marketing gimmick go to waste and that using intellectual capital for multiple purposes (strategy, stockholder reports, management presentations, team building) is more efficient than creating new material for each purpose. Moreover, there is the very true, but not well-communicated, maxim that behavior is best changed through short assertions repeated again, and again, and again. Look at political campaigns. It is often the candidate with the short, clever slogan who wins the race over the opponent who wants to debate issues. IT should use its IT strategy as a way of driving home to IT staff, as well as to IT's customers, what IT is about.

An Excuse to Have a One-on-One Meeting with Business Leaders

Nothing is worse than having an IT strategy, printing a hundred copies, and then finding out it is wrong. Imagine that, just as the reports are hitting the mailroom heralding IT's decision to finally spend millions of dollars to support the Norwegian herring snacks operation, CNN is reporting that the company is selling the division!

To avoid such unpleasant surprises, IT management should ask several senior business leaders to review the draft IT strategy for errors. The CIO or other senior IT managers should meet with the business leaders, one on one, and walk them through the document. This is the best way to

---

Should IT Contribute to the Business Strategy?

This chapter focuses on the creation of the information technology (IT) strategy. The message is that the business strategy should drive the IT strategy. This raises the question: Should the IT strategy ever drive the business strategy?

Could Amazon or eBay have a business strategy that does not rely heavily on IT? Of course not. Having the IT strategy derived from the business strategy does not preclude IT being a part—perhaps a critical part, even a driver—of the business strategy. Most company business strategies will not focus on technology to the same extent as those of Travelocity or YouTube, but that does not mean that IT should not be part of the business strategy creation process. In some cases, IT will play a critical role. In other situations, IT's involvement in the generation of the business strategy will be minimal.

A better way to look at the strategy generation process is that the creation of the business and IT strategies should be nearly simultaneous and symbiotic. For the Proactive Partners, described in Chapter 1, the development of the business and IT strategies will be a partnership of business and IT senior managers.

ensure that the business leaders actually look at the strategy document and think about each important section. Because the executives know this is a draft strategy, any errors they find need not be a cause for IT embarrassment. Then again, they just might like what they read.

IT should go further. If a salesperson gets access to a customer, especially an executive at a customer's site, few would let that opportunity go by without some soft selling. IT should do the same. Use the opportunity of sitting down with senior business leaders to ask how IT is doing, what changes those leaders would like to see, what issues (technology, business, or otherwise) they are facing, and where IT might help.

IT should not pass up any opportunity to tell the IT story (hopefully laid out in the strategy document). In addition, discussing business issues, successes, and concerns, as well as IT's role in supporting the business, can help improve the perception of IT and help build lasting relationships with senior business managers.

Joining the Club

James Whitcomb Riley is credited with saying, "If it walks like a duck and swims like a duck and quacks like a duck, I call that bird a duck." Walking like a duck, it turns out, is not a bad way of being seen as a duck. Like it or not, a common business belief is that real businesspeople have a strategy. Therefore, if the CIO wants to be seen as a real businessperson, then the CIO needs to act like one. An excellent way to start acting like a senior business manager is with an IT strategy. Creating an IT strategy shows that IT understands the business, can converse in business talk (disintermediation and supply chains, and not bits and bytes), and has a plan for how IT can be an active partner in the business.

Missions, and Visions, and Objectives, Oh My!

Does IT need a mission statement, and a vision statement, and goals and objectives, and a multiyear plan, and an annual plan? Maybe. If emphasizing the distinctions among them makes sense, then have them all. However, many companies and IT organizations have shown that they can communicate their message quite clearly without all of these different components.

For most IT organizations, an abbreviated list, as in Exhibit 3.18, is adequate. Every IT organization should have a multiyear plan and an annual plan, although the level of detail is open for discussion. Every IT organization should have a mission or a vision statement, although both are not necessary in all cases. The decision to have goals, or to have objectives, or to have goals *and* objectives, is a little more subjective. However, it never hurts to have them all.

Some IT organizations have an official mission statement, but then let the staff create the rest. Having a contest to come up with the right goals and objectives is a good way of getting IT staff to think about IT's purpose,

Exhibit 3.18 Necessary Strategy Components

IT Strategy Component	Necessity
Mission and Vision	Have one or the other, but both are not always needed.
Goals and Objectives	Have at least one or the other. Have both if it helps IT management and IT's customers to better understand IT's role in the enterprise.
Multiyear Plan	Every IT organization should have one.
Annual Plan	Every IT organization probably does have one if it has been in business for more than a year. What it might not have, but does need, is a single, user-readable document.

what it ought to be doing, and how it might measure its success. And that, after all, is what an IT strategy is all about, isn't it?

SOME ADDITIONAL THOUGHTS

> *IT strategy.* Consists of the processes and deliverables that allow IT to demonstrate to the business that it understands the business strategy, recognizes its implications for IT, and knows exactly what IT must do (in the short and long term) to help realize it.

IT strategy has always been associated with aligning IT with the business, but it is much more than that. The benefits of an IT strategy also include:

- Defining and communicating IT's mission and goals to senior management, to its technology consumers, and to IT staff

- Establishing closer working relationships with the business, thus gaining a better understanding of what the business does, its issues and challenges, and where it wants to be in the future

- Becoming a part of the enterprise management team, if not as a decision maker, then at least as a first-hand observer, which results in closer ties to business decisions and the source of business information, the business decision makers

- Gaining a better understanding of the services IT should offer and the role IT should play in the enterprise

Most businesses would like to see their IT organization produce an IT strategy. They might not say it, they might not know exactly what it is, but if given the choice, they want one. Knowing what IT is doing and understanding the resources IT needs to meet business demand gives business staff a more comfortable feeling that IT is working with them.

Unfortunately, many IT staff, even some senior IT managers, feel that producing an IT strategy is a waste of time that could be better spent doing something more productive (and probably technical). The reality is that IT has little choice. Businesses are increasingly requiring IT to create longer-term plans showing how they intend to support the business. If IT has little choice, if it will have to produce a strategy, then it might as well do it right and get the full benefit from it.

IT STRATEGY	
DOs	**DON'Ts**
• Do ensure that IT has a specific audience in mind for all deliverables. • Do use the strategy as a communications document for senior management, consumers, and IT staff. • Do walk the report around—making one-on-one visits to senior managers, explaining the strategy, and building relationships.	• Don't let the lack of a business strategy deter the creation of an IT strategy. • Don't get bogged down in low-level and technical matters in the strategy. • Don't let the strategy get old. Keep the strategy updated, at least yearly, and more often if the situation warrants it. • Don't let annual plans drift from the strategy.

Moreover, a good IT strategy is an excellent way for IT to blow its own horn and let customers know that IT is on top of the situation, or at least *trying* to get on top of it. It allows the IT department to show that it listens to its customers, is concerned about what they are trying to achieve, and is on the team to make it happen.

It is also an opportunity to spend some quality time with senior business leaders, and discuss with them, not a bloated IT budget or another late or failed project, but their plans for the business—not an opportunity any serious business leader would want to miss.

REFERENCES

The following are some literature, Web sites, and organizations that might be useful:

Some Representative Literature

Broadbent, Marianne and Ellen S. Kitzis. *The New CIO Leader: Setting the Agenda and Delivering Results.* Harvard Business School Press, 2005.

Boar, Bernard H. *Practical Steps for Aligning Information Technology with Business Strategies: How to Achieve a Competitive Advantage.* John Wiley & Sons, 1994.

Cassidy, Anita. *A Practical Guide to Information Systems Strategic Planning.* CRC, 1998.

Labovitz, George and Victor Rosansky. *The Power of Alignment: How Great Companies Stay Centered and Accomplish Extraordinary Things.* John Wiley & Sons, 1997.

Lientz, Bennet P., and Lee Larssen. *Manage IT as a Business: How to Achieve Alignment and Add Value to the Company.* Elsevier Butterworth-Heinemann, 2004.

Lutchen, Mark D. *Managing IT as a Business: A Survival Guide for CEOs.* John Wiley & Sons, 2004.

Schubert, Karl D. *CIO Survival Guide: The Roles and Responsibilities of the Chief Information Officer.* John Wiley & Sons, 2004.

Ward, John, and Joe Peppard. *Strategic Planning for Information Systems.* John Wiley & Sons, 2002.

Some Helpful Organizations and Web Sites

Business Link is a British government Web site providing practical help for small businesses that includes some good advice on IT strategy. www.businesslink.gov.uk

CIO Magazine publishes a considerable number of articles on aligning IT with the business as well as IT strategy. Of particular interest is a series of articles in its May 1, 2004 edition. www.cio.com

TechRepublic usually has some good practical advice on a number of issues, including IT strategy. www.techrepublic.com

NOTE

1. Michael Porter, *Competitive Strategy: Techniques for Analyzing Industries and Competitors,* The Free Press, 1980, p. 3.

4

Portfolio Management

The available supply of every commodity is limited.
If it were not scarce with regard to the demand
of the public, the thing in question would not be
considered an economic good, and no price would
be paid for it.
—*Ludwig von Mises*

The race is not always to the swift, nor the battle to
the strong, but that's the way to bet.
—*Damon Runyon*

Economics is sometimes described as the study of scarce resources. They are scarce because the demand exceeds the supply, increasing their value. Economics is commonly divided into microeconomics and macroeconomics. *Microeconomics* deals with how individual organizations, such as a company or a household, make, buy, consume, manage, or sell scarce resources. *Macroeconomics* studies how collections of individual organizations deal with scarce resources.

Why is this important for portfolio management? The parallels between economics and portfolio management are striking. Information technology (IT) resources are scarce. Not everyone can have everything they want from IT, because IT simply does not have the resources to satisfy every demand. The traditional corporate project selection process is similar to the processes operating in microeconomics. Individual organizations compete for the approval of projects they want IT to undertake with its limited resources. Portfolio management, however, differs from the traditional corporate project selection process because it examines all project requests, calculates the total IT resources available, and then combines that information with how the company would like to see those resources fairly and equitably distributed. Only then does it decide which projects to approve.

81

Portfolio management appears closer to macroeconomics. With such prominent similarities, it is not difficult to believe that some of the processes and techniques applied in economics would work for IT.

THE PROBLEM

Every chief information officer (CIO) has felt the pressure from business managers or staff requesting services that IT cannot provide because of a lack of budget, time, or resources. This becomes a Hobson's choice of either angering a customer by saying no, or making the real mistake—call it Major Management Mistake Number One—of saying yes and then not meeting expectations. The one painful lesson CIOs learn early in their careers is to say *NO* when they cannot fit a new project into an already cramped schedule.

Obviously, the CIO would not have to say no if the company gave IT sufficient resources to cover all customer requests. However, this would be Major Management Mistake Number Two: Not all projects deserve to be implemented regardless of who asks for them. Studies have shown that little correlation exists between IT spending and enterprise performance. Companies that spent the most on IT did no better, or worse, than companies that spent the least. Researchers concluded that a successful return on an IT investment is not based on how much or how little is spent, but rather on how wisely the investment is made.[1]

The challenge in selecting which projects to fund and which to reject has three parts: (1) determine what the company really needs and can afford; (2) find and approve only the projects that meet that need; and (3) do it in such a way that, even if some customers are disappointed with the results, they at least feel that the process was fair.

Unfortunately, the challenge of selecting which projects to fund and which to reject is exactly where the senior business managers become uncomfortable. They are uncertain that the right technology choices are being made. They are not sure that IT has the ability, knowledge, or fortitude to make the right decisions. If the senior business managers are honest, then most will also admit that they are not sure that they could do any better. Given this situation, IT can provide a valuable service to the organization by creating an open, transparent, and impartial process so that business managers can be confident in the technology decisions that they, IT, or others make.

The core issue that must to be addressed is how to develop an equitable and objective process to assure all stakeholders that worthy projects are being approved, unworthy projects are being rejected, the budget is being honored, and customers will come away feeling that the procedure was fair and above board.

THE IT SOLUTION

Simply stated, portfolio management is the framework and set of processes that allow decision makers to analyze IT investment requests for the purpose of approving those that meet enterprise objectives and rejecting those that do not.

Using the governance model presented in Chapter 2, the portfolio management process starts with the special interest groups (SIGs) of the IT Steering Committee (ITSC). SIG members generate or uncover user requests for new or improved services and start the process of creating a business case for each. The ITSC councils monitor the business case creation of the SIGs. Those cases that show merit are passed on to the Executive Committee of the ITSC for consideration. The Executive Committee must decide which of the project candidates to approve and fund and which to reject.

Portfolio Management Process

Organization size, geographic disbursement, corporate culture, and other factors will determine to what extent and depth the company will need to go to analyze and select which project requests to fund and which to reject. Whatever level of complexity the process might need to satisfy individual enterprise needs, the basics are the same. This chapter uses the IT governance model introduced in Chapter 2. The process consists of a series of screens managed by the ITSC SIGs, the ITSC councils, and finally the ITSC Executive Committee.

Chapter 2 described the workings of the ITSC and its user councils. A key feature of the councils is its SIGs composed of people of similar interest, training, or position. They have three tasks: (1) they represent the interests of users in the enterprise; (2) they share information about business needs and technology use; and (3) they collect and prepare user requests for consideration as IT projects. The process starts by either users bringing potential projects to the attention of a SIG member or SIG members actively pursuing such projects through interviews with customers, understanding what competitors are doing, or their own knowledge of the subject matter.

Project selection is an iterative process of investigating the worthiness of potential projects. The ITSC process starts with SIG members discussing each potential project with other members in the SIG, rejecting those that do not make sense, and further developing those that do. Project requests with potential are documented in a preliminary business case that contains information on both the benefits and costs of the project (more on business cases later in the Business Case section of this chapter). When the preliminary business case is complete, and if the SIG still feels that the request has merit, the SIG passes the case on to the appropriate ITSC council as a recommended project. The role of the SIG in the project selection process is outlined in Exhibit 4.1.

Exhibit 4.1   Step One: SIG Project Screen

- Customer or ITSC member submits a project request to a council or to a SIG of the ITSC.

- The appropriate SIG assigns one or more of its members to conduct a preliminary investigation of the request.

- The investigator(s) reports to the SIG. If the SIG feels that the request has merit, it requests that a preliminary business case be created.

- The SIG reviews the preliminary business case; if the SIG concludes that the request still has merit, it passes the preliminary business case on to the full ITSC council. Those with insufficient merit are either rejected or returned to the team for further analysis.

The councils, which represent the major IT constituencies, further investigate potential projects passed to them by the SIGs. Those found wanting are rejected or sent back to the SIG for additional work, while those the council concludes have merit are further developed into full business cases (see Exhibit 4.2). When the full business case is complete, the council reviews the potential project again. If the council still feels that the potential project has merit, it forwards the full business case to the Executive Committee of the ITSC as a candidate project.

From SIG through the councils, the potential projects are evaluated strictly on their individual merit. The Executive Committee, however, must measure not only the worthiness of the individual candidate project, but also compare it with other candidates and approve only those that meet

---

Exhibit 4.2   Step Two: Council Project Screen

- The council reviews each preliminary business case, and if it concludes that the request still has merit, it assigns a team to expand the SIG-authored preliminary business case into a full business case.

- The council reviews the completed full business case. If it feels that the business case has merit, it recommends the project to the ITSC Executive Committee as a candidate project. Project requests not recommended to the Executive Committee are either rejected or sent back to the SIG for additional work or clarification.

Exhibit 4.3   Step Three: Executive Committee Project Screen

- The Executive Committee reviews each full business case submitted by the councils and either approves the investment, rejects the investment, or sends the business case back to the council for additional work or clarification.

- The Executive Committee gives approved projects to IT for implementation.

financial, budget, strategic, functional, and any other criteria established by the enterprise (see Exhibit 4.3). Approved projects are passed to IT for implementation.

Business Case

The enterprise needs a common vehicle to communicate a project's properties, as well as the results of any analysis or evaluation. The vehicle should not only be a document, but also function as a checklist to ensure that all project information is complete and properly reviewed. The project business case is designed to fulfill both of these needs. A business case is an argument or position paper detailing why a project should be approved and funded. Its components include the purpose for the project, the benefits, beneficiaries, costs, schedules, risks, and alternatives.

Exhibit 4.4 shows the main sections and components of a business case. The *Background* section includes the project name and a few sentences describing the project, what it is intended to do, and how it will do it.

The *Needs* section describes how the function is currently handled, its costs and benefits, and why it needs to be changed. What competitors are doing is always useful, particularly if they already have, or are working on, a similar application.

Next, the business case lays out the *End Product* section, describing how the system will work and detailing the benefits to the organization, such as revenue generated, costs alleviated, customers satisfied, or processes simplified. Although narrative examples are acceptable, and unavoidable in some circumstances, quantifiable benefits, particularly financial benefits, are preferred. Saying that the new system will cut the time to develop a widget by 20 percent is good, but not as good as saying that the cost to produce a widget will drop $300,000 per year. The business case should also be specific about who will benefit, such as customers, sales, or manufacturing staff. Most investment decisions are based on tangible benefits (e.g., costs reduced), but intangible benefits (e.g., increased brand recognition) are also important and should be identified.

Exhibit 4.4   Sample Business Case Outline

Business Case Components	Preliminary Business Case (To Pass The SIG Screen)	Full Business Case (To Pass The Council Screen)
BACKGROUND SECTION		
Project name	Required	Required
Project description	Required	Required
NEEDS SECTION		
How the function is currently handled	Required	Required
What the competition is doing		Project Dependent
END PRODUCT SECTION		
How the new system would work	Required	Required
• Costs		
• Benefits (tangible and intangible)		
Who the new system will support:	Required	Required
• Business users		
• Customers		
• Others		
Benefits	Partial	Required
• Tangible		
• Intangible		
REQUIREMENTS SECTION		
Costs (Implementation):	Partial	Required
• IT		
• Non-IT		
Costs (Ongoing):	Partial	Required
• IT		
• Non-IT		
Schedules	Partial	Required
Life of system		Project Dependent
Dependencies		Project Dependent
Implementation plan	Partial	Required
• IT		
• Non-IT		
Risks (financial, technical, project, functional, and systemic)	Partial	Required

Exhibit 4.4   *(Continued)*

Business Case Components	Preliminary Business Case (To Pass The SIG Screen)	Full Business Case (To Pass The Council Screen)
Costs of not doing the project		Project Dependent
Alternatives	Partial	Required
Similar systems or projects in the organization	Required	Required
VALUE SECTION		
Measuring success	Partial	Required
Cost/benefit analysis (ROI, ROE, Break-even, ROA, EY, etc.)	Partial	Required
SUMMARY SECTION		
Executive summary		Project Dependent

The *Requirements* section is the most detailed and difficult to pre-pare. Costs should be as specific as possible. They should include not just IT costs, but also the cost to the business of implementing the system, training staff, promotion, and any other project-related expenses the company will likely incur. To understand the costs, the business case also needs to include a proposed schedule, the projected life of the system after it is in production, its ongoing or operating costs, and any dependencies that could affect development or operating costs.

Known risks should be identified. Although the for-profits and the trade and academic literature contain numerous risk classification schemes, one of the simplest, yet most useful for IT, is described by Eric K. Clemons.[2] He identifies five kinds of risk: financial, technical, project, functionality, and systemic.

Financial risk is the possibility that the benefits of the project might not outweigh the costs. However, even if the benefits do outweigh the costs, there can still be a financial risk if the cost of the project is sufficiently high that it could significantly impair the health of the company, if some otherwise survivable business downturn occurs. During the dot.com era, many new businesses undertook make-or-break projects. Unfortunately, even the successfully run projects broke many of these companies when the economic bubble burst.

Technical risk is the possibility that the technology simply is not sufficiently developed or properly applied to allow the project to succeed.

California's Department of Motor Vehicles licensing system failed because it relied on a fourth-generation language that simply was not up to the task of supporting the application's heavy transaction volume.

Project risk is the chance that the IT organization cannot do the job required. The reason could be a lack of skills, staff inexperience, or simply insufficient numbers of available people to do the work. Other possible reasons might be the strain that an overly large or complex project would place on the IT department or too much reliance on consultants or system integrators to perform the critical work.

Functionality risk is the potential exposure when the project finishes but the application simply cannot accomplish the business tasks it was designed to perform. Functionality risk can also occur when the business changes during project development and the completed system cannot accommodate the changes the business made.

The last risk Clemons calls *systemic risk*. It is the possibility that the system is so successful, and changes the business so much, that the original assumptions about costs, prices, profits, and so forth are no longer meaningful. For example, electronic financial trading systems, which allow an individual investor to go online and buy or sell stocks and bonds, changed the entire dynamic of the business. Some of the changes were good for the industry, but others were not. For example, online trading inhibits the one-on-one relationship that existed between customers and stockbrokers. The relationship loss reduced the amount of advice stockbrokers gave to customers, which in turn decreased the revenue stream that advice generated.

These are just the most common risks. Others might exist, especially risks that are company-, industry-, or application-specific. The business case should mention all risks, including how they will be avoided or mitigated.

Clemons does a good job of classifying risk, but his work is not as useful for understanding what to do about it. Take the example of a project plan that includes using a new technology with which IT is unfamiliar. The risk is that the project will fail because of the team's inability to use the technology effectively. There are really only four approaches IT can take with such a risk:

1. *Ignore it.* This approach, which is the favorite for many IT organizations, implies, "what we don't acknowledge can't hurt us." Although popular in the short term, this approach is not a very good strategy for the long run.

2. *Confront it.* To confront the risk, the project plan should include resources to train staff, hire new knowledgeable employees, or obtain outside help from experts in the technology.

3. *Avoid it.* If the new technology presents a risk, then replace it. Find a way to execute the project using a different technology, one with which IT is more comfortable.

4. *Tough it out*. Recognize that the use of the technology will be a challenge, and add frequent and targeted monitoring to the plan to quickly alert management if the project starts to go awry. Including additional resources in the plan, ready to supplement those struggling with the new technology, is a good idea. Some organizations make this contingency part of the project plan; others might prefer to assign the contingency at the ITSC level, for use only if necessary. Even if resources are not allocated, at the very least, all stakeholders (IT, users, and senior business management) should understand the potential for schedule slippage and/or resource shortfalls.

Obviously, the first approach—to ignore the risk—is not a viable option. However, the business case should include a confront, avoid, or tough-it-out plan (CAT), consisting of one or more of the three remaining approaches for all identified risks. The business case should also include some discussion of the implications of not doing the project. It should identify available alternatives and/or what would happen to its costs, market share, efficiency, and so forth if the company did nothing.

Next, the business case should include a *Value* section. With the benefits defined, attention can be given to how the company should measure the success or failure of the project. Should success be measured as an increase in sales, revenue, or profits; or as a decrease in materials, labor, or production costs? Can the business expect market share to increase or sales per customer to rise? The business case should be explicit in how to measure the success or failure of the project. The criteria for success should be quantifiable and ideally independent of other events.

Deciding when the success measurement should take place is also important. Not every project hits the ground running. Some require a few months to get up to speed. The business case should explicitly state whether measuring the success of the application could take place right after the system is operational, or whether it should wait for six months, a year, or some other time afterward.

Once the costs, benefits, and the project success criteria are understood, the business case can now turn to the investment's more detailed cost/benefit analysis. The usual candidate cost/benefit measurements are *return on investment* (ROI), *return of capital* (ROC), *break-even analysis, return on equity* (ROE), *net present value* (NPV), *expected yield* (EY), and perhaps a few more. Some value measures are more popular than others, so it would be wise to determine, from the Executive Committee or the chief financial officer, which might be required.

A good business case for a medium to large project could run from 5 to 15 pages. Even this might be too long for Executive Committee members. If the business case goes beyond seven or eight pages, the author should include an optional sixth *Summary* section for Executive Committee members. The summary should be from one to no more than four pages long, summarizing the purpose, benefits, costs, schedules, value, and risks of the project.

How the Business Case and the Project Selection Processes Work Together

The project selection process is designed to work like a funnel or series of screens, as shown in Exhibit 4.5. Typically, most organizations receive many more project requests than they can afford to implement. Each screen (SIG, council, and Executive Committee) is designed to eliminate project requests that do not meet predefined criteria or ITSC member judgment. One could easily imagine a situation that involves 100 or more requests at the beginning of the process, reduced by more than half at each screen, until just a dozen projects are finally approved. For very large enterprises, each of these numbers could be an order of magnitude larger.

Producing business cases is a time-consuming process, but it also makes it obvious when the requested project lacks sufficient value for the enterprise. The process is designed to allow business cases to be gradually developed and expanded as the request moves from SIG to council to Executive Committee. Exhibit 4.4 indicates which business case components are recommended for the preliminary business case and which are recommended for the full business case.

Exhibit 4.5   The ITSC Project Screening and Approval Process

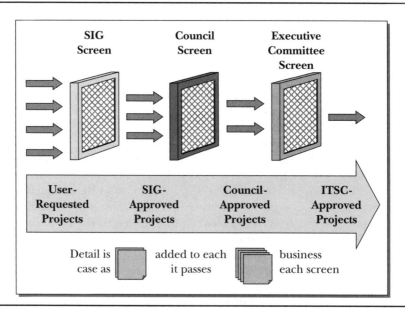

The multiple screens and the evolving detail of the business case serve two purposes. First, as pointed out previously, building business cases is hard work. Creating only 25 business cases for the most worthy candidates is far more efficient than creating 100 cases that include requests that council members know will never be approved. Second, as mentioned in Chapter 2, the Executive Committee members are busy senior executives who do not have the time to pore over hundreds of requests. Using the councils to reduce the number of cases to the few they think worthy of Executive Committee review is good business judgment. It is an efficient use of both the members of the councils and the members of the Executive Committee.

Creating an Investment Distribution Matrix

While the councils are developing the business cases, the Executive Committee should be developing a plan or matrix laying out how it would like to see project development funds distributed. The matrix outlines the ideal project budget distribution by IT constituency.

The traditional project prioritization and selection approach does not use any ideal distribution plan. Rather, it uses a simple list of candidate projects, sorted by value. Projects are approved, starting at the top, going down the list, until the money runs out.

Exhibit 4.6 displays all of the project candidates, sorted by the Value column. If the project budget is $7 million, then starting at the top, the process would approve projects going down the list until the $7 million is allocated. In this case, Warehouse Inventory, Sales Force Expenses, Distributor Performance, and Sell Through Analysis requests would be approved (those in bold), while the European Sales Training, Government Contract Compliance, and all those below would be rejected.

However, there is a problem with this selection process. Using this approach, only projects in the United States were selected, and, with the exception of one industrial business unit project, only consumer business unit projects were approved. The process rejected all projects for Europe and Asia, the government business unit project, and all but one of the industrial business unit projects. This might be acceptable for one or two years, but if this approach persists, eventually Europe, Asia, and a few business units are going to protest. It might be necessary to approve a less valuable project, at the expense of a more valuable one, to ensure that everyone gets a piece of the pie.

For example, the Executive Committee could decide that the IT project budget should be divided by geography. Based on some metric, let us say sales, it might decide that 50 percent of the budget should go to the United States, 30 percent to Europe, and 20 percent to Asia. For the $7 million budget, that would mean $3.5 million for the United States,

Exhibit 4.6 A Simple Prioritized Project List

Project Prioritization and Selection

Project	Business Unit	Geography	Cost	Value (ROI)	Running Total
Warehouse Inventory	**Consumer**	**US**	**$1,600,000**	**22.0%**	**$1,600,000**
Sales Force Expenses	**Consumer**	**US**	**$1,900,000**	**21.3%**	**$3,500,000**
Distributor Performance	**Industrial**	**US**	**$1,400,000**	**20.9%**	**$4,900,000**
Sell Through Analysis	**Consumer**	**US**	**$2,100,000**	**20.0%**	**$7,000,000**
European Sales Training	Consumer	Europe	$130,000	19.8%	$7,130,000
Govt. Contract Compliance	Government	US	$1,340,000	19.4%	$8,470,000
Credit Reporting	Consumer	Asia	$1,400,000	19.0%	$9,870,000
Customer Service Enhancements	Consumer	Europe	$800,000	18.7%	$10,670,000
Supply Chain Management	Industrial	Europe	$250,000	18.3%	$10,920,000
Rebate Analysis	Industrial	Asia	$800,000	18.2%	$11,720,000

$2.1 million for Europe, and $1.4 million for Asia. Exhibit 4.7 is an Investment Distribution Matrix (IDM) that shows how the budget could be distributed based on geography.

Using the IDM in Exhibit 4.7, the project approval spreadsheet would look like Exhibit 4.8. The United States now has only two approved projects, while Europe gets two approved projects, and Asia gets one approved project. This distribution was chosen even though two of the rejected U.S. projects have higher ROIs than the approved European and Asian projects.

To arrive at Exhibit 4.8, the budget was divided or segmented based on a category or dimension.[3] In this case, the dimension was *geography*, which consists of the dimension items *U.S., Europe,* and *Asia.*

There are still some problems with the example. Note that all of the approved projects but one, are for the consumer business unit. This could be corrected by adding a second dimension, *business unit*, with the dimension items *Consumer, Industry,* and *Government.* Exhibit 4.9 is an IDM that shows how the enterprise might ideally like to distribute investment funds over two dimensions (*geography* and *business unit*).

The IDM development process does not have to be limited to the dimensions of *geography* and *business unit*. Other dimensions could be *consumer type, growth areas,* or *corporate role,* to name just a few. This last dimension, *corporate role,* is of special interest because it can have the dimension items *Revenue Generation, Administration,* and *Infrastructure. Infrastructure* is a good example of the power of the IDM, because, left to their own devices, most users would not spend money on infrastructure projects. Using the *corporate role* dimension, the ITSC could agree beforehand that ideally it would like to spend 15 percent of the total investment budget on *infrastructure,* and that it would like to hold *administration* investments to no more than 10 percent, leaving 75 percent of the budget for *revenue-generating* projects.

The IDM process can accommodate as many dimensions as one wishes, with two qualifiers. First, there must be a sufficiently large pipeline of project requests so that all of the dimensions include an adequate number of choices to allow acceptable trade-offs. The other qualifier is that

Exhibit 4.7   An Investment Distribution Matrix

Dimension	Distribution	
Geography	Percent of Budget	Budget Dollars
US	50%	$3,500,000
Europe	30%	$2,100,000
Asia	20%	$1,400,000

Exhibit 4.8 A Segment-Adjusted Prioritized Project List

Projects (US)	Business Unit	Geography	Cost	Value (ROI)	Running Total
Warehouse Inventory	**Consumer**	**US**	**$1,600,000**	**22.0%**	**$1,600,000**
Sales Force Expenses	**Consumer**	**US**	**$1,900,000**	**21.3%**	**$3,500,000**
Distributor Performance	Industrial	US	$955,000	20.9%	$4,455,000
Sell Through Analysis	Consumer	US	$2,100,000	20.0%	$6,555,000
Govt. Contract Compliance	Government	US	$1,340,000	19.4%	$7,895,000

Projects (Europe)	Business Unit	Geography	Cost	Value (ROI)	Running Total
European Sales Training	**Consumer**	**Europe**	**$1,300,000**	**19.8%**	**$1,300,000**
Customer Service Enhancements	**Consumer**	**Europe**	**$800,000**	**18.7%**	**$2,100,000**
Supply Chain Management	Industrial	Europe	$250,000	18.3%	$2,350,000

Projects (Asia)	Business Unit	Geography	Cost	Value (ROI)	Running Total
Credit Reporting	**Consumer**	**Asia**	**$1,400,000**	**19.0%**	**$1,400,000**
Rebate Analysis	Industrial	Asia	$800,000	18.2%	$2,200,000

Exhibit 4.9   A Two-Dimension Investment Distribution Matrix

Dimensions		Distribution
Geography	Business Unit	Percent of Budget
US	Consumer	25%
US	Industry	15%
US	Government	13%
Europe	Consumer	15%
Europe	Industry	7%
Europe	Government	3%
Asia	Consumer	12%
Asia	Industry	10%
Asia	Government	0%

those creating and using the matrix must have the math skills to handle a three-, four-, five-, or more dimension table to represent the options.

The IDM needs to be *ideal* and *independent* of the project candidates. Ideal means that the IDM is no more than a way for the Executive Committee to come to an agreement on how it would *ideally* like to see the investment pot distributed. The word *ideal* is used to describe the matrix because it is optimal and theoretical but does not necessarily reflect the real world.

The IDM must also be independent. The value of the IDM—its impartiality and its fairness—is predicated on its being developed *before* the Executive Committee examines the business cases. Once the committee members see the business cases, they could be swayed in how they would like to see funds distributed. Letting the project requests drive the budget process is an undesirable approach to project selection. It is also one of the problems portfolio management was designed to remedy. Portfolio management works most effectively if the IDM and the business cases are developed *independently*.

Risk-Adjusted Valuations

A disadvantage of traditional value methods, such as ROI and ROC, is that risk is not taken into account when calculating a project's estimated return. Two potential projects, with the same ROI, are unlikely to be equally attractive to a project selection team if one has a higher chance of failure than the other. EY adjusts the expected return of a project based on historical success and failure rates for similar projects. It is a newer and slightly more complex valuation measure than traditional approaches, which is why few IT organizations have heard of it. Yet, it can be a powerful tool when used properly.

To calculate the EY of a project, three inputs are required. The first is the *loss* the business would experience or the incurred costs of the failed project. The second input is the project *NPV* if the project succeeds. The third input is the *chance of failure* of the project.

Finding the first two pieces of information is relatively easy: They should be part of the business case. Determining the *chance of failure* might be a little more complicated. If the IT organization stores information about past project successes and failures, then there should be no problem; the *chance of failure* can be derived from the IT project history database. If no enterprise IT failure rates can be found, then public benchmarks might be available, and can be used in the place of private data. For example, for a software development project, using publicly available information[4] and knowing the *project duration* in calendar months, formula (4.1)[5] can be used to calculate the *chance of failure*:

$$\text{Chance of failure} = 0.4805538 \times (1 - (2.718281828^{0.007488905}) \\ \times (\text{project duration}^{1.506090}) \tag{4.1}$$

If the chance of failure is 25 percent, the projected loss due to the failure of the project is \$100,000, and the NPV of the planned lifetime benefits of the project is \$300,000, then, using formula (4.2):[6]

$$\text{Expected yield} = (\text{loss} \times \text{chance of failure}) \\ + ((1 - \text{chance of failure}) \times \text{Project NPV}) \tag{4.2}$$

would result in a lifetime *expected yield* for the project of \$200,000.

The *expected yield* can be used in the Value column of the Prioritized Project List to prioritize projects.

Every organization is different, having its own way of working, moving at its own pace, and building its own success and failure history. Using an organization's own project success and failure record is best for predicting future success and failure. However, most organizations do not have sufficiently detailed historical data, or do not have the needed quantity of data, to make accurate predictions. This is where published data can be useful. Researchers have collected and analyzed project failure data for thousands of software development projects of varying sizes undertaken by hundreds of different organizations. This data can be used when private data is not available. Although not tailored to an individual organization, it has nonetheless proved effective at predicting project success. Unfortunately, published project data is currently only available for software development projects (categories include new development, maintenance efforts, and package modification for application and systems software projects). Extrapolating from software development initiatives to other types of projects, such as data center refurbishing or network deployment, where there is little historical internal or public failure data, is problematic and, most researchers believe, unwise.

Multiple Value Factors

The purpose of knowing a project's value is to be able to prioritize competing requests. ROI is the most popular measure to compare the relative value of the projects, giving a higher priority to those with a higher return on investment. However, one need not use ROI. Projects could be prioritized based on their NPV, their strategic fit, or both.

As in most enterprises, the example presented earlier in the chapter used only a single factor (ROI), but it could have used two, three, or more. A Meta Group study found that only 10 percent of the 2,000 organizations surveyed used more than one factor to evaluate candidate projects.[7] This is unfortunate, because a single factor is rarely enough to fairly appraise the value of a potential investment. It is not uncommon for one factor to indicate that the project request is very valuable to the enterprise, whereas other factors paint a less rosy picture. Using multiple factors gives a better overall assessment of the value of the project to the enterprise. Some senior executives are suspicious of projects with only one value factor. They suspect that the project managers went "benefit shopping," performing many types of analysis but only presenting the most favorable.

ROI can be supplemented with other numeric factors. Additional factors can be return on assets (ROA), ROC, cost/benefit ratio, payback, NPV, internal rate of return (IRR), and EY. Not all factors need to be financial or even numeric. Factors can also be subjective. This latter type can include strategic fit (alignment with company strategy), functional need, competitive advantage, ease of development or maintenance, or any other criteria that will help compare two candidate projects.

Prioritizing projects with multiple factors can be challenging. Does project A, with an ROI of 117 percent and an IRR of 96 percent, come before or after project B, with an IRR of 86 percent and an ROI of 127 percent? If more than one factor is used, then they might need to be combined to arrive at a single summary or aggregate value suitable for prioritization. The simplest solution is to give each factor instance a numerical value. If desired, the factors can also be weighed to reflect their relative importance to the enterprise. The various factors can then be combined into a single project value score.

Exhibit 4.10 shows how seven weighted factors can be combined into a single aggregate candidate project value to the organization.

Some projects are very difficult to value. The IDM *corporate role* dimension (with the dimension items *revenue generation, administration,* and *infrastructure*) is a case in point. Infrastructure projects rarely have a meaningful payback, and their value to the enterprise is difficult to quantify. If only financial valuations were used, phone systems would never be replaced,

Exhibit 4.10   Candidate Project Value Score

Multifactor Value Aggregation				
Project: Vendor Management System				
Factor	Fit	Numeric Equivalent	Weight	Score
Strategic Fit	Low	1	5	5
Business Need	High	3	4	12
ROI	Medium	2	3	6
IRR	Low	1	3	3
Payback	Medium	2	2	4
EY	High	3	5	15
IT Skills Available	Medium	2	2	4
Project Value				**49**

data networks would go unfunded, and human resource systems would be unsupported. Measures other than the traditional look at a project's costs and financial benefit are needed to prioritize competing infrastructure and administrative projects. Successful candidates include valuations such as strategic need or business impact, even if they can be quantified only as high, medium, or low.

Some projects cannot be valued at all. In the wake of several corporate and accounting scandals, the Sarbanes-Oxley Act of 2002 required U.S. companies to invest billions of dollars in IT to support new accounting and auditing requirements with no immediate payback, other than not going to jail. Tax law changes, stock exchange requirements, and regulatory agency directives can all require significant IT investment with no payback other than being allowed to operate a business. These projects need to be funded independent of any value calculation.

Prioritizing and Selecting the Approved Projects

Once the business cases are complete and the IDM is agreed upon, then the Executive Committee can begin the project selection process. If the councils did a good job on the business cases and the Executive Committee members agree on how they would like to see the investment funds distributed, then this task is rather easy. The Executive Committee prioritizes the candidate projects using the IDM. The higher-priority projects, within budget in each dimension, are selected for approval—maybe.

The IDM provides guidelines for selecting projects, but it should not make the decision. As in most decision-making situations, analysis, even numerical analysis, should provide input to the decision process, but should not replace it. In the example in Exhibit 4.8, the Asian Credit Reporting project was selected, while the European Supply Chain Management and the U.S. Distributor Performance projects were not, even though the U.S. project would provide a higher return. There would be nothing incorrect in the Executive Committee concluding that the supply chain application project was more important to the company than the credit reporting application, and in approving the former while rejecting the latter. Mechanized or procedural analyses only provide a starter set of information, to which management wisdom and discretion must be added.

If project prioritization and selection was totally automatable, then after creating the prioritized project list, the process would be over. However, despite technology advances, business decisions are still the responsibility of managers. No tools, frameworks, or processes will, or should, replace human decision making. Tools can only provide input to the decision makers. They are the start of the selection process, not the end.

Round one is very mechanical. The committee creates the prioritized project lists based on project value for each of the dimensions in the IDM and draws a line in the Running Total Column where the money would run out. Everything above the line would be funded and everything below it rejected. If the committee members are satisfied with the results, then the job is done. The committee has made its decision. If not, then the committee must go to round two.

Round two through round n are a little different. Rather than being mechanical like round one, rounds two and beyond consist of the committee members trading projects above the line for those below it. They might decide that, although the Australia employee beverage management system scored higher than the European heart transplant inventory, the European system should be funded before the Australian one.

After each round, the actual distribution should be compared with the ideal distribution. They will never be exactly the same, but unless there are good reasons agreed upon by all, they should be close. If there are good reasons to reject the IDM, then the committee should do so. If all are satisfied with the trade-offs, then the job is complete. If not, then the next round starts, and so on, until there is agreement.

Monitoring, Recording Actuals, and Collecting Feedback

ITSC responsibility does not end with selecting the approved projects. The projects also must be monitored during their development and for at least one year after they are in production. During development, the ITSC, as well as other interested parties, needs to be kept abreast of development progress, spend against budget, and any issues of a serious nature that may arise. The committee might be needed to help failing projects or, in the worst case, cancel projects that have no hope of providing value to the organization.

The post-implementation task is, in some ways, the simplest to begin but the hardest to finish. After the project is complete, it still needs to be tracked. If management is to know whether it got its money's worth, if the ITSC is to know whether its project selection process works, and if IT is to know whether its ability to manage projects and to estimate costs and benefits are accurate, then the actual business success or failure of the project must be measured and documented. Were the resource estimates correct? Were the business benefits as promised? Are stakeholders satisfied with the results? All of these questions and more need to be asked and answered, so that the business, the steering committee, and IT can continually improve their skills, their processes, and their expectations.

In practice, post-implementation reviews are almost never done. There are three reasons for this. First, project money is almost always gone by the time the implementation work of a project is complete. Most implementation project managers are likely to consume every dollar lying around to get the system out the door. If the ITSC wants a post-implementation review, it will probably need to fund it as a separate project. This is a difficult sell when new projects are waiting for resources.

Second, the best people to do the post-implementation review are those who worked on the project. Unfortunately, 6 or 12 months after implementation, those resources are likely to be staffed on other projects. Getting new staff up to speed on the completed project can be time consuming and expensive.

Finally, there can be considerable resistance to reviewing a completed project. Many project staff members may feel that no good will come from digging up the past. Often, successfully finishing a project means that the team members dodged another bullet. They got through another development effort without getting into trouble. Reviewing a project a year later opens them up to potential new criticisms they can live without. This is unfortunate, because reviewing past projects gives project staff, SIG, and council members the feedback useful for honing estimating and other project management skills. In addition, Executive Committee members can use the post-implementation review to evaluate and update their project selection process.

To be successful, post-implementation reviews need to exist in an environment of lessons learned rather than of stand by to witness punishment. Honest answers only come forward in a supportive environment. Dangerous environments produce cover-ups and lies. If the organization has a Project Management Office, then it would be the ideal organization to take on the post-implementation tasks, reporting results to the business, the ITSC, and IT. If there is no Project Management Office, then the ITSC councils or a disinterested third party should be given the job.

What is known about IT portfolio management is quite extensive, even if it is rarely well implemented. However, there is one area of managing projects that strikes fear in the hearts of most IT staff—RISK. It is an area that, when tamed, becomes a useful business tool. IT could learn a considerable amount from the for-profit business world about risk and risk management.

WHAT THE FOR-PROFITS CAN TEACH IT

IT has a strange relationship with risk. On the surface, IT is very risk-averse. A services firm recently created an IT mission statement, a few goals, and 20 objectives it called guiding principles. One of the principles was, "Take acceptable risks." Of all the guiding principles, the only one that raised objections from IT staff was the one about taking acceptable risks. Even the inclusion of the word "acceptable" did not mitigate IT's aversion to the R-word.

At the same time that IT seems to be totally risk-adverse, it ignores significant risk when it is obvious. When faced with major risks, IT tends to focus on minor risks. The Standish Group studied thousands of projects and found that "small projects are more likely to succeed than larger projects."[8] Its findings were that almost three-quarters of the projects costing less than $750,000 were successful. The success rate dropped to little more than a quarter for projects costing between $750,000 and $6 million. The Standish study found only 3 percent of the projects, in its sample costing more than $10 million that were successful (see Exhibit 4.11). In short, the larger the project, the greater the risk of being over budget, coming in late, not providing desired functionality, or being cancelled.

Exhibit 4.11   Project Success by Size of Project

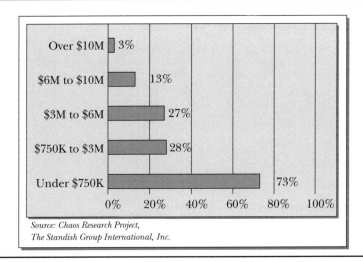

Source: Chaos Research Project,
The Standish Group International, Inc.

The good news is that project size can almost always be controlled by project management. The user community might push for one big project, but the judicious use of senior IT management intervention can usually turn that $5 million project into five $1 million projects. Project size is a major IT risk, but one that can be mitigated through the application of sound IT management. Yet, when IT executives are questioned, they see the majority of risks to IT projects coming from users and user management (Exhibit 4.12). The lack of user involvement is certainly a significant problem, but it is worrisome that of the top ten risks IT staff identified, only two are directly under project manager control.[9] Project size, which is a major, if not *the* number-one risk, identified by researchers, is under IT control, and it is not even on the list.

The business world tends to see risk differently than IT does, in that risk is often associated with opportunity. Apple Inc. already had the successful Apple II when it risked the whole company by introducing the Apple Macintosh. It took several years, but the risk finally paid off. Then Apple risked the company again with the iPod, and again the risk paid off. Business knows that there are risks to avoid and risks to embrace. The trick is to know which are which.

In the financial investing world, the word *risk* is often sitting next to the word *reward*. Increased risk can bring increased reward. Experts tell us that government bonds are typically safer than stocks. Fixed-income instruments usually have less volatility and are less risky than equities. But you will not keep up with inflation owning risk-free (or reduced risk) bonds.

Exhibit 4.12   Why IT Executives Think Projects Fail

1. Lack of User Input

2. Incomplete Requirements and Specifications

3. Changing Requirements and Specifications

4. Lack of Executive Support

5. Technology Incompetence

6. Lack of Resources

7. Unrealistic Expectations

8. Unclear Objectives

9. Unrealistic Time Frames

10. New Technology

Source: "The Chaos Report," The Standish Group International, Inc., 1995

Time proves that in order to stay ahead of inflation, you need to own stocks. Because of their higher risk, stocks need to compensate with higher returns. If you want to increase your return, you will need to increase the risk of the instruments you hold. If you want to increase safety, you will need to hold instruments that offer less return. Good investing is finding just the right balance between risk and reward. The same is true for IT.

What should the ITSC do if some project risks cannot be mitigated? Should the enterprise go ahead with the project? Presented earlier in the Business Case Requirements section of this chapter was the example of a project that planned to use a new technology for which the staff had no skill or experience. Imagine that the project only has a chance of achieving its benefits if the new technology is used. The question then becomes, do the potential benefits outweigh the risks? If the answer is yes, then go ahead. If the answer in no, then avoid the project.

> There is no trick to figuring out which horse is most likely to win a race. . . . It is the favorite. . . . Not that the favorite always wins, but it does so more often than other horses. . . . When the likely payout exceeds the perceived risk by a certain value, it is a good bet. So it is for projects: when the payback at a given level of resources allocation exceeds the cost at a certain level of risk, it is a good plan for that project.[10]

Does the reward exceed the risk? This is a very difficult question to answer at the project level. At the portfolio level it becomes easier.

Modern Portfolio Theory

In the early 1950s, an economics graduate student at the University of Chicago came up with an interesting theory—so interesting, in fact, that he won the Nobel Prize for it. The traditional way of building a financial portfolio was to examine each individual financial instrument (stock, bond, CD, etc.), calculate its risk and its reward, and then decide whether to purchase it. Harry Markowitz discovered that if investors replaced the traditional way of examining individual securities, and instead looked at all of the instruments as a whole (a portfolio), and calculated the aggregate risk and reward, they could increase the overall return of the portfolio without necessarily increasing the risk.

By holding a portfolio of instruments, the investor can introduce diversification that can reduce the overall risk of the portfolio. How? Take two high-risk investments: Each on its own might be rejected as too risky, but together the risk of one can mitigate or compensate for the risk of the other, reducing the overall risk of the portfolio. If the portfolio contains all computer company stocks and the computer industry is hurt, then the entire portfolio is hurt. However, if the portfolio contains computer, consumer, financial, entertainment, and travel stocks, then the downturn of just the technology sector will not hurt as much. With an overall lower portfolio risk, the investor can then buy otherwise riskier instruments, potentially receiving higher aggregate returns.

Modern portfolio theory (MPT) involves three variables: risk, reward, and what Markowitz calls *covariance*, although it can be thought of as the degree of independence. For a security, reward is the interest or dividend it pays plus any price appreciation. Its risk is more complicated. Markowitz equates security risk with volatility. Volatility is how much the price of the security swings up or down compared with the market as a whole. If stock A's up-and-down swings are greater than those of stock B, then stock A is said to be more volatile and riskier than stock B.

Covariance is the level of independence of the instruments, or more appropriately, the level of independence of the factors that affect the instrument. Instruments with a high covariance behave similarly in a given situation. Those with low covariance, or high independence, react differently to the same stimulus. For example, two computer stocks are both dependent on how the technology sector is doing, which means that they have a high covariance and low independence. A computer stock and a coffee company stock do not have a high covariance, because an upswing in one has little effect on the other. If the technology sector takes a hit, it is not surprising that both computer stocks decline while the coffee stock is unaffected. Markowitz's diversification requires that the securities in the portfolio be independent of one another.

For IT, portfolio theory is seen as a way of increasing overall IT performance while managing risk, allowing IT managers to better allocate scarce resources across the portfolio.[11] The idea was adopted by the U.S. government in the Clinger-Cohen Act of 1996, which requires that U.S. government agencies adopt a portfolio approach to IT investments.

Diversity can be incorporated into project selection dimensions by ensuring that the portfolio does not consist exclusively of U.S. projects, or projects that rely on a single technology or just one vendor or system integrator. Patrick McKenna gives the example of the U.S. Department of Veterans Affairs and its use of MPT techniques for its Information Security Program. The VA used MPT to determine which projects would provide an acceptable return based on their individual and portfolio-level project risk.[12]

> The [project] used scientific methods to analyze the degree that IT security investments would reduce the frequency and severity of IT security related incidents that cause fraud and loss of productivity. . . . The strengths [of the process] were the investment analysis that quantified costs, benefits, and risks.[13]

The take-away from Markowitz is to diversify the portfolio, something that can be accomplished with the Investment Distribution Matrix. Many portfolio management tools now incorporate MPT into their software. However, it is possible to take modern portfolio theory too far. Projects do not behave like securities. Securities are liquid; they can be traded over the phone or on a PC in just a few minutes. If the risk, reward, or independence of a security changes, it can be sold almost instantly. Not so with projects. Short of canceling it, once a project is started, IT is stuck with it. Also, it is doubtful that projects can be as independent as securities. Even Markowitz has his doubts. In an interview he stated:

> I would be cautious about applying MPT [modern portfolio theory] to corporate projects as though these are liquid assets. There are different constraints regarding projects, like management expertise, human skill sets, physical production capabilities and other factors that come into play. I'm not sure that the constraint side of the project portfolio problem has been properly modeled. Understanding how an organization's experience in one product area may be applicable to other markets is not very clear.[14]

Although some interesting research is still being done on using MPT in IT (e.g., in mitigating the independence issue),[15] for the time being, the lessons of MPT should probably be limited to the use of diversification and simple risk assessment, both of which can be achieved by the proper use of the IDM.

By the Numbers

The value of MPT for the financial investment world is that it gives the investor insight into a portfolio that is not available at the instrument level. Along with this insight are opportunities to act to increase portfolio return, without increasing risk, over and above what was achievable at the instrument level. Conversely, the investor could choose to reduce risk at the portfolio level without reducing the return, an option not possible at the instrument level. One could call this increased return—or decreased risk, achievable over and above the aggregate instrument return, or risk—the portfolio premium. In other words, by using MPT, one can achieve, at the portfolio level, a premium over and above what is achievable at the instrument level.

As has been shown, this portfolio premium is more problematic for IT. While IT struggles to use MPT as a process, its real value might turn out to be as a goal. MPT could encourage research into information one can know and actions one can take at the project portfolio level that are not knowable or actionable at the individual project level.

Researcher Chris Verhoef of the Department of Computer Science, VU Amsterdam,[16] and later with R.J. Peters,[17] takes the best from recent work in software development quantitative project assessment and portfolio management and marries it to the best quantitative financial management used in, for example, the banking industry. Building on the work of Boehm,[18] Jones,[19] Parr,[20] Putnam,[21] and others, Verhoef constructs a way of quantifying and monetizing software development project costs, benefits, and risks.

Exhibit 4.13 illustrates how, by using publicly available information about past projects, IT can predict the likely outcome of a planned project, including its risk. Recent research has shown that it is also possible to calculate the impact of scope creep (adding functionality after the project starts) and time compression (shortening the project schedule without shedding functionality)[22] has on project schedules and project costs, as well as the overall project return.

Most of the values uncovered at the project level can be aggregated to the portfolio level. For example, the planned project development costs for the individual projects can simply be added together to determine the

---

Exhibit 4.13   Sample Quantitative IT Software Development Investment Analysis

Given:

Fully loaded daily rate for a developer:	$1,000
Total net benefits of the project (gain):	$8,745,341
Project size in function points:[a]	1,000

The following can be calculated from public sources:[b, c]

1. Calendar months required for development:	14.8 months
2. Average staffing required for development:	6.7 FTEs
3. Average staffing required for maintenance after development:	1.3 FTEs
4. Total cost of development:	$1,646,532
5. Total annual maintenance cost:	$329,306
6. Application total life:	5.6 years
7. Minimal cost of operations:	$1,501,957
8. Chance of failure:	17 %
9. Chance of being late:	18 %
10. Expected (risk adjusted) Yield:	$5,928,946

[a]A function point is an end-user business unit of work where the effort to design, program, or test it is essentially identical to the effort required to design, program, or test any function point given the same conditions. Function points were created by Alan Albrecht. A.J. Albrecht, "Measuring Application Development Productivity," *Proceedings of the Joint SHARE/GUIDE/IBM Application Development Symposium*, 1979, pp. 83–92. One of the best books describing functions points is J. Brian Dreger, *Function Point Analysis*, Prentice Hall, 1989.

[b]C. Jones, *Applied Software Measurement: Assuring Productivity and Quality*. McGraw-Hill, 1991; C. Jones, *Estimating Software Costs*. McGraw-Hill, 1998; and C. Jones, *Software Assessments, Benchmarks, and Best Practices*, Addison-Wesley, 2000.

[c]*FTE = Full time Equivalent*

planned portfolio development costs. The same is true for the planned annual maintenance costs, the planned benefits from the projects, and even the monetized risk.

The project risk described previously should not be confused with project contingencies. If IT project managers are doing their jobs, then contingencies are built into the plan. Good project planning calls for creating a budget and schedules based on the best-educated conclusions regarding the real cost and time required to complete a project, including contingencies for the normal hazards and roadblocks projects routinely encounter. Without contingencies, a project plan represents the best possible cost, schedule, and benefits that can be achieved. Because the best is rarely achievable, contingencies move the plan from the best possible case to the more likely case, in the project estimator's mind. The risk presented in Exhibit 4.13 is risk over and above that already in the project plan. It is the risk identified, not by IT's best project estimating skills, but statistically by examining past projects and how often those projects were actually late, actually over budget, or did not come in at all. The words *plan* and *forecast* are useful to differentiate these two concepts. While the best IT project *plan* says that a project will cost *x*, including contingencies, statistics *forecast* that the project will likely cost *y*.

At the project level, forecast information is of limited use because it is, in most cases, unactionable. There are at least two reasons. The first reason risk is unactionable at the project level is because of the nature of statistics. Although the average life expectancy in Malaysia in the year 2000 was 64 years, what that says about an individual Malaysian is limited. The average Malaysian may live past 100, or he may die at 50. It is only when considering Malaysians as a group that the statistic becomes meaningful. As with all statistical data, its value increases as the number of subjects increases. Likewise, information about the risk of a single project being late is also limited, although still valuable (e.g., for comparative purposes). However, what statistics say about a portfolio of projects is far more meaningful.

A second reason that project-level risk is unactionable relates to the question of what IT should do with the risk information. If IT's risk calculations show that a project will probably take longer and cost more than planned, then why not just add the additional cost to the budget and time to the schedules now, and be done with it? IT could always put another contingency in place on top of the existing project contingencies to, hopefully, mitigate the statistical risk. Most IT project managers agree that this would be a mistake. The reason is simple. If a project manager is given additional resources because there is a 10 percent chance the project might run into unanticipated trouble, then there is an almost 100 percent chance that those excess resources will be consumed.

At the portfolio level is a different story. Assume that the plan says that the 10 projects in the portfolio will cost a total of $10 million to develop and that the benefits they generate will total $20 million. Using a better understanding of risk, IT could forecast that development costs will probably not be $10 million, but $12 million, and that the expected yield of the portfolio will not be $20 million, but $14 million. At the portfolio level, this information becomes actionable. IT, or the business, could decide to set aside additional funds, at the portfolio level, but not at the project level, for potential overruns. These funds would function as a portfolio-level insurance premium against the risk of any particular project going over budget.

If the projects in the portfolio are interdependent, perhaps forming some larger business program, then, using the portfolio-level information, the senior business managers could decide not to fund the portfolio at all, or at least not until some of the risks are reduced. They could even calculate exactly how much risk will need to be reduced in order to make the portfolio profitable. The good news is that a portfolio premium exists. Further, it turns out, there are actions that IT can take to improve performance at the portfolio level that it cannot take at the project level.

And the Winner Is?

Academics and practitioners have been working for years to understand the dynamics of projects. Serious scientific studies of project portfolios are more recent. Unquestionably, there are techniques available right now to help the IT manager better understand and manage portfolios. Equally unquestionable is that this subject is still in its adolescence. Presumably, and hopefully, there should be some significant advances in portfolio science and practice in the next few years. The astute IT professional should keep an eye on this area.

SOME ADDITIONAL THOUGHTS

> *Portfolio management* is the set of processes and deliverables used by senior representatives from the business and IT to objectively, equitably, and transparently analyze and categorize IT investment requests. This analysis allows them to identify, approve, and fund the development and implementation of projects the enterprise should invest in, while avoiding those it should not.

The goal of portfolio management is to define and apply a fair and equitable process for approving project requests. More than that, this process needs to be transparent so that all constituents can observe how it works. This will help take the mystery out of project portfolio planning, which is good because mystery in IT is usually perceived by IT's customers as arrogant, arbitrary, or unfair.

Portfolio management also assigns responsibility to the right parties. IT can design and oversee the project selection process, but it should not decide how the business will invest in its future. The business cannot abdicate its responsibility to IT, and IT cannot expect the business to understand the intricacies of project planning. The two groups need to work together to decide how IT can best help the business grow and prosper.

PORTFOLIO MANAGEMENT	
DOs	**DON'Ts**
• Do create a formal, business-driven, transparent process for investment selection. • Do give every part of the enterprise the opportunity to suggest investments. • Do create a set of investment guidelines that articulate, ideally, how the investment pie should be equitably shared.	• Don't let the business off the hook. Investing in the business should be a business and not an IT decision. • Don't let a formal and fair process evolve into petty politics; keep the process strong. • Don't let the fear of risk deter sound business judgment.

Todd Datz summarized portfolio management fairly well when he said:

A strong portfolio management program can:

- Maximize value of IT investments while minimizing risk

- Improve communication and alignment between IS and business leaders

- Encourage business leaders to think "team," not "me," and to take responsibility for projects

- Allow planners to schedule resources more efficiently

- Reduce the number of redundant projects and make it easier to kill projects[23]

Doing portfolio management right is difficult, and the work required by IT and the business can sometimes seem tedious and overwhelming. However, the results can be impressive. Better project selection, more efficient use of IT, happier users, and, finally, the feeling that IT is charting a course that is not only understood by the business but developed in partnership with it, can make all the difference in the world.

REFERENCES

The following are some literature, Web sites, and organizations that might be useful:

Some Representative Literature
Business Case

> *Inside Tips for Building a Business Case for IT Investment*, Hitachi Consulting Corporation, 2003.

> Mullaly, Mark E. "Business Case Benefits." Gantthead.com, July 21, 2004. www.gantthead.com/article.cfm?ID=218742

> Mullaly, Mark E. "Business Cases 'R Us." Gantthead.com, May 17, 2004. www.gantthead.com/article.cfm?ID=217630

> Turbit, Neville. "Vision, Business Problem, Outcome, Objectives and all that stuff . . ." Project Perfect, June 27, 2005. http://www.projectperfect.com.au

Cost/Benefit Analysis

> Trotta, Ray. "Whiteboard: Hot to Determine the Value of a Project," *CIO Insight*, November 12, 2002. www.cioinsight.com/article2/0,1540,675256,00.asp

> Pisello, Thomas. *IT Value Chain Management – Maximizing the ROI from Investments*, Alinean, LLC, 2003.

IT Portfolio Management

> Clemson, Eric K. "Evaluating Strategic Investments in Information Technology."*Communications of the ACM*, January 1991, Vol. 34, No. 1, pp. 23–36.

> Datz, Todd. "Portfolio Management: How to Do It Right." *CIO Magazine*, May 1, 2003.

> Harder, Paul. "Learning From Your Uncle Sam." Gantthead.com, July 31, 2002. www.gantthead.com/article.cfm?ID=137387

> Harder, Paul. "Under New Management . . ." Gantthead.com, May 1, 2002. www.gantthead.com/article.cfm?ID=112880

> Kersten, Bert, and Chris Verhoef. "IT Portfolio Management: A Banker's Perspective on IT." *Cutter IT Journal*, April 2003.

> McGaughy, Cameron. "Gartner Shines the Light on PPM." Gantthead.com, August 18, 2004. www.gantthead.com/article.cfm?ID=219526

Winters, Frank. "Project Portfolio Management: A Primer (Part 1)." Gantthead.com, February 16, 2005. www.gantthead.com/article. cfm?ID=222787

Risk

Armour, Philip G. "Project Portfolios: Organizational Management of Risk."*Communications of the ACM*, March 2005, Vol. 48, No. 3, pp. 17–20.

Bernstein, Peter L. *Against the Gods: The Remarkable Story of Risk.* John Wiley & Sons, 1996.
   An historical look at risk. Not directly useful for IT, but a great read.

Glass, Robert L. *Facts and Fallacies of Software Engineering.* Addison-Wesley, 2003.
   Glass likes to wander in the rubble. His books focus on IT disasters and how they might have been avoided.

Glass, Robert L. *Software Runaways.* Prentice Hall, 1998.
   More of the same, though interesting.

Hall, Elaine M. *Managing Risk: Methods of Software Systems Development.* Addison-Wesley, 1998.

"Mitigating Risk in Technology Investments Through Information Technology Portfolio Management. An Interview With Mark Jeffery," *Technology Portfolio Management Series*, Teradata.com Executive Center.

Kiel, Mark, Paul E. Clue, Kalle Lyytinen, and Roy C. Schmidt. "A Framework for Identifying Software Project Risks." *Communications of the ACM*, November 1998, Vol. 41, No. 11, pp. 76–83.

Levine, Harvey A. "Risk Is a Four-Letter Word, But Denial Is Our Biggest Enemy." Gantthead.com, March 12, 2001. www.gantthead. com/article.cfm?ID=17457

Smith, John M. *Troubled IT Projects: Prevention and Turnaround.* Institute of Electrical Engineers, London, 2001.

Turbit, Neville, "Basics of Managing Risk," Project Perfect. www. projectperfect.com.au

Verhoef, C. "Quantitative IT Portfolio Management." *Science of Computer Programming*, Vol. 45, October 2002, pp. 1–96. www. cs.vu.nl/~x/
   Verhoef is a prolific writer. Some of his articles are longer and contain more useful information than many books. His focus is on quantitative project and risk assessment.

Modern Portfolio Theory

Markowitz, Harry. "Portfolio Selection." *Journal of Finance,* Vol. 7, No. 1, 1952, pp. 77–91.
This paper is not for the mathematically faint of heart. Even for those who are comfortable with math, its interest for IT will be largely historical.

McClure, Ben. "Modern Portfolio Theory: An Overview." Investopedia.com, March 14, 2006. www.investopedia.com/articles/06/MPT.asp

Applying Modern Portfolio Theory to IT

Dickinson, Michael W., Anna C. Thornton, and Stephen Graves. "Technology Portfolio Management: Optimizing Interdependent Projects Over Multiple Time Periods." *IEEE Transactions on Engineering Management,* Vol. 48, No. 4, November 2001, pp. 518–527.
A very technical paper, but useful for seeing the direction some are taking in applying MPT to IT.

Harder, Paul. "A Conversation with Dr. Harry Markowitz," Gantthead.com, May 21, 2002. www.gantthead.com/article.cfm? ID=119883

Harder, Paul. "What is Project Portfolio Management?" Gantthead. com. www.gantthead.com/content/articles/114344.cfm

McFarlan, Warren F. "Portfolio Approach to Information Systems." *Harvard Business Review,* 1981, Vol. 59, No. 5, pp. 142–150.

McKenna, Patrick. "Modern Portfolio Theory: Driving Project Portfolio Management With Investment Techniques." *IBM,* August 15, 2005. www.128.ibm.com/developerworks/rational/library/aug05/mckenna/index.html

Teach, Edward, and John Griff. "Analyze This."*CFO Magazine,* December 1, 2003.

Project Management Office (PMO)

Gliedman, Chip, and Forrester Research. "The Portfolio Management Troika." *CIO Magazine,* October 18, 2004. www2.cio. com/analyst/report3010.html

Hoffman, Thomas. "How to Ease Tension with PMOs." *Computerworld,* February 16, 2004.

"Project Management Office Charter of the Lawrence Berkeley National Laboratory." Lawrence Berkeley National Laboratory. www.lbl.gov/DIR/OIA/PMO/

Rosenfeld, Sue-Rae. "PMO and Portfolio Management." The Advisory Council, Inc. 2006. http://www.tacadvisory.com

Santosus, Megan. "Why You Need a Project Management Office." *CIO Magazine,* July 1, 2003.

Some Helpful Organizations and Web Sites
Chris Verhoef is a professor in the Department of Computer Science at VU Amsterdam. This Web site contains some interesting portfolio management papers he has published. www.cs.vu.nl/~x.

Gantthead.com: A consulting firm with some useful information on its Web site. www.gantthead.com.

Project Perfect: An Australian consulting firm with some useful information on its Web site. www.projectperfect.com.au.

NOTES

1. Thomas Pisello, *IT Value Chain Management: Maximizing the ROI from Investments,* (Orlando, FL: Alinean, LLC, 2003), 3–4.
2. Eric K. Clemson, "Evaluating Strategic Investments in Information Technology," *Communications of the ACM,* (1991), 34: 23–36.
3. A dimension is the set of objects sharing a distinguishing characteristic, such as geography, business unit, industry, country, and so forth. A dimension item is a member of a dimension. For example, *Latin America, Europe,* and *Asia* are all dimension items of *geography.*
4. C. Jones, *Applied Software Measurement: Assuring Productivity and Quality,* (New York: McGraw-Hill, 1991); C. Jones, *Estimating Software Costs,* (New York: McGraw-Hill, 1998); and C. Jones, *Software Assessments, Benchmarks, and Best Practices,* (New York: Addison-Wesley) 2000.
5. C. Verhoef, "Quantifying Software Process Improvement," 2004. Available at www.cs.vu.nl/~x/spi/spi.pdf.
6. *Ibid.*
7. *IT Investment Management: Portfolio Management Lessons Learned,* The Meta Group, 2002.
8. "Chaos: A Recipe for Success," The Standish Group International Inc., 1999; and James H. Johnson, "Micro Projects Cause Constant Change," The Standish Group, 2001.
9. Mark Kiel, Paul E. Clue, Kalle Lyytinen, and Roy C. Schmidt, "A Framework for Identifying Software Project Risks," *Communications of the ACM,* November 1998, Vol. 41: 78; "The Chaos Report," The Standish Group, 1995; and "Extreme Chaos," The Standish Group, 2001.

10. Philip G. Armour, "Project Portfolios: Organizational Management of Risk," *Communications of the ACM*, March 2005, Vol. 48: 19.
11. F. Warren McFarlan, "Portfolio Approach to Information Systems," *Harvard Business Review*, 1981.
12. Patrick McKenna, "Modern Portfolio Theory: Driving Project Portfolio Management with Investment Techniques," IBM, August 15, 2005. www-128.ibm.com/developerworks/rational/library/aug05/mckenna/index.html.
13. *Lessons Learned on Information Technology Performance Management: Applying the Balanced Scorecard and Applied Information Economic to Federal Information Technology Techniques*, Community of Practice for IT Performance, Federal Chief Information Officers Council, Best Practices Committee.
14. Paul Harder, "A Conversation with Dr. Harry Markowitz," May 21, 2002. www.gantthead.com/article.cfm?ID=119883
15. Michael W. Dickinson, Anna C. Thornton, and Stephen Graves, "Technology Portfolio Management: Optimizing Interdependent Projects Over Multiple Time Periods," *IEEE Transactions on Engineering Management*, Vol. 48: (November 2001) 518, 527.
16. C. Verhoef, "Quantitative IT Portfolio Management," *Science of Computer Programming*, 2002, Vol. 45, No. 1, pp. 1–96. Available at www.cs.vu.nl/~x/ipm/ipm.pdf; C. Verhoef, "Quantifying Software Process Improvement," 2004. Available at www.cs.vu.nl/~x/spi/spi.pdf; and C. Verhoef, "Quantifying the Value of IT-Investments," *Science of Computer Programming*, 2005, Vol. 56, No. 3. Available at www.cs.vu.nl/~x/val/val.pdf.
17. R.J. Peters and C. Verhoef, "Quantifying the Value of the Optimal IT-Investment Portfolio." Available at www.cs.vu.nl/~x/opt/opt.pdf.
18. Barry Boehm, *Software Engineering Economics*, (Englewood, NJ: Prentice-Hall, 1981).
19. C. Jones, *Applied Software Measurement: Assuring Productivity and Quality*, (New York: McGraw-Hill, 1991); C. Jones, *Estimating Software Costs*, (New York: McGraw-Hill, 1998); and C. Jones, *Software Assessments, Benchmarks, and Best Practices*, (New York: Addison-Wesley, 2000).
20. F.N. Parr, "An Alternative to the Rayleigh Curve Model for Software Development Effort," *IEEE Trans. Software Engineering*, (May 1980) 291–296.
21. Lawrence Putnam and Ware Myers, *Measures for Excellence: Reliable Software on Time, Within Budget*, (Yourdon Press Series), (Englewood, NJ: Prentice-Hall, 1992).
22. R.J. Peters and C Verhoef, "Quantifying the Value of the Optimal IT-Investment Portfolio." Available at www.cs.vu.nl/~x/opt/opt.pdf.
23. Todd Datz, "Portfolio Management: How to Do It Right," *CIO Magazine*, May 1, 2003.

PART TWO

LEARNING FROM THE BEST

5

Customer Management

Spend a lot of time talking to customers face to face.
You'd be amazed how many companies don't listen to
their customers.

—*Ross Perot*

The customer is the only one who can fire us all.

—*Sam Walton*

Willie Sutton, the famous bank robber, was asked why he robbed banks. His reported answer was, "Because that's where the money is." Sutton was an intelligent guy despite his unfortunate career choice. He escaped, or at least almost escaped, from prison more than nine times, once remaining free for more than three years. He also managed to be paroled despite his two life terms "plus 105 years" sentence. He finished off his life consulting to banks on how to avoid being robbed. What did Sutton know that information technology (IT) could learn? Willie knew that you can not wait for things to come to you; you have to be proactive and go out and get them. IT departments could stand to learn that to be successful, they have to get off their corporate duffs and get out to where the customers are.

THE PROBLEM

Right or wrong, front-line users see IT as an ivory tower that is disengaged from the trials of those who spend each day in the corporate trenches working for a living. Fat, dumb, and happy, though unkind and inaccurate, is not an uncommon description of IT, at least from the self-proclaimed technologically disadvantaged. The fat, dumb, and happy (FDH) label is location dependent. The farther away you are from corporate headquarters, the fatter, dumber, and happier IT appears to be.

The FDH label is a manifestation of the same problem that the IT strategy, IT governance, and portfolio management concepts introduced earlier are designed to help correct. However, the benefits of strategy, governance, and portfolio management are primarily experienced by senior management—IT's clients. They are remedies that IT's consumers, such as the first-line supervisor in manufacturing or the order entry clerk in customer service, care little about. Technology consumers want their applications up, running, and able to keep up with their daily workload. They want solutions that enhance their day-to-day business lives.

This is one problem for which both types of IT customers—senior management clients and technology consumers—can sometimes agree on a solution. IT, they feel, needs to be decentralized. It should be carved up by geography, or line of business, or some other scheme, with control of the local IT organization passed to the local senior business manager. If IT is already decentralized, then it should be even more decentralized. This attitude conflicts with the trend over the last two decades to centralize IT, which has been driven by corporate's desire to manage costs. The real problem is not centralization or decentralization, but disenfranchisement. Users feel ignored by the IT organization that is supposed to serve them.

THE IT SOLUTION

It is unlikely that decentralization, or more decentralization for already decentralized IT organizations, will do much to reduce disenfranchisement. Although breaking up IT does satisfy the desire for local ownership, users can still feel underserved. The underlying problem is not where IT hangs its hat, but where it spends its time.

Willie Sutton had the answer—go where the users are. Senior managers, first-line supervisors, and clerks from Omaha, Nebraska, to Jackass Flat, Australia, want support, help, and attention, even if it is only to complain about how hard they have to work. IT needs to engage its user base for the same reasons any business needs to engage its customer base—to keep its customers loyal to the brand.

Would You Like a Placebo with That?

In 1927, Harvard professor Elton Mayo wanted to study the effects environment had on workers. Did changing conditions such as lighting, number of breaks, or pay (later studies included music and management style) increase or decrease productivity? He carried out a series of experiments in the Western Electric Company Hawthorne Plant in Cicero, Illinois.

He discovered that when the plant increased lighting, productivity went up. When the company added music, productivity went up, and it went up again as the amount of time the music was played increased. However,

Mayo also found that when the plant decreased lighting, productivity went up, as it did when they decreased the amount of music played. In fact, when almost anything changed, productivity went up. Why? Attention. The more attention management paid the workers, through such activities as changing the work environment or surveying them about their work habits, the more positively workers responded, increasing their productivity with each change. In short, the workers were so pleased that management was paying attention to them, giving them a feeling that what they did was important, that morale jumped, and so did productivity. This finding became known as the Hawthorne Effect.

Although much of the science of the original study has been recently brought into question (e.g., control groups were not used), the fundamental principle remains. It is seen today in medicine as the placebo effect. One study group is given an experimental medicine while a second study group, the control group, is given a sugar pill (called a placebo) that they believe is the real thing. Regardless of what the medicated group experienced, the placebo group almost always reports an improvement in their health. The sugar did not cause the improvement, but the attention paid the subjects did.

Politicians have known this for years. Shaking hands and kissing babies, an interaction measured not in minutes but in seconds, pays off. Even people who do not like politicians wait in line for hours to spend three seconds shaking a politician's hand. The guy they consider a bum Monday through Friday is suddenly a hero when he visits their small town on Saturday.

IT should learn from these examples and get its leaders out of their offices and interacting with users, even if it is not much more than a "How are you doing?" and a handshake. Hewlett-Packard calls it *management by walking around* (MBWA), others talk about "showing the flag," while the more militaristic refer to "trooping the line." Whatever it is called, it involves IT management getting out and meeting users in order to understand their needs and to show users that IT cares about satisfying those needs. Meetings can be formal, informal, just walking around visiting cubicles, or doing all three.

Meeting customer needs is not just pro forma management behavior. Although the IT Steering Committee is an excellent way for chief information officers (CIOs) to learn what customers want, it is not the only way. Another good avenue to understanding what people want is to ask them directly. While most of the suggestions or recommendations coming from customers might be unactionable (because they are too expensive, inconsistent with corporate policy or strategy, or just short of a science fiction award), there are the occasional few that are not only reasonable but also downright good ideas.

Moreover, visiting the troops can cool the intensity of known hot spots. IT might know that the new order entry application is slow or burdensome to use, but talking first hand with those who use it every day can help put the problems into context and illuminate exactly how difficult it is to use and how much it affects productivity. When Hurricane Katrina hit the southern United States in 2005, those in Washington, D.C., could easily obtain quantitative data about the effects of the storm without leaving their offices. However, to truly understand the magnitude and implications of the storm's destructiveness required going there and experiencing it first hand. No numbers, no matter how detailed or accurate, can convey what seeing something first hand can reveal.

Unfortunately, senior management interaction with customers will be occasional at best. Any executive who can spend a lot of his or her time with users is fodder for the next cost-cutting exercise. But while most CIOs and IT directors cannot spend a lot of time roaming the halls looking for staff to impress, some managers and junior staff can.

Account Managers

The sales staff differs considerably from technology vendor to technology vendor. Some salespeople are technically competent, understanding not only their products but also how they can be used in each IT shop to that organization's best advantage. These salespeople seem to be technologists first and salespeople second, or at least coequal. Many more are just the reverse: salespeople first, with technical skills a close or distant second. Whether IT vendors hire professional salespeople because they think they sell more, or because they cannot hire enough technically competent sales staff, is probably vendor dependent. The fact is that many vendors supplement their sales staff with technical experts to bolster the professional sales team and to minimize the technical trouble the latter can get into.

Going by names such as sales support, technical support, systems engineer, and so forth, these technicians have the job of understanding the product, being able to answer technical questions about it, helping customers figure out how to use it to their best advantage, and acting as a conduit if they need technical support that can only be provided by staff in the home office. For some companies, technical support staff are the only ones who can talk to both the customer and internal development or operations staff, ensuring that customer questions are properly routed, while limiting the disruption to developers and data center staff.

Some IT departments have successfully copied these technology vendors, creating a position modeled after the sales support function. Called a customer service manager, IT liaison, relationship manager, or account manager, each supports a region, line of business, or some other IT customer segment. The account manager needs to be knowledgeable in all of the IT services provided to that customer base. His or her job is to spend considerable time with users, understanding how they use technology and resolving problems.

Each account manager should be a seasoned IT professional who has shown an aptitude and desire to work closely with IT's customers. He or she

Exhibit 5.1   Commonwealth of Virginia Relationship Manager Role

Customer Relationship Management

The Virginia Information Technology Agency's (VITA) Customer Relationship Management (CRM) directorate was launched in November 2005 to directly support VITA's vision of becoming a model service organization.

CRM is tasked with improving communication with our customers and helping better align with them strategically. VITA's direct customers are the executive branch agencies, institutions of higher education, localities and other governmental entities throughout the Commonwealth.

The ultimate goal of the CRM directorate is to continually improve services and add value in order to benefit citizens of the Commonwealth.

Primary CRM functions:

- Understand the business needs of VITA's customers

- Advocate for excellent customer service across VITA

- Coordinate effective communication to customers and other stakeholders

- Identify opportunities to improve government service through collaboration and enterprise solutions

- Assist with effective integration of technology into customers' strategic plans

- Promote awareness and use of VITA's statewide technology contracts

- Conduct marketing research and analysis, including customer satisfaction and service quality surveys, and integrate results into VITA's strategic plan

- Create service partnerships through business user groups and other strategies

- Customer relationship management is the responsibility of the VITA Enterprise Business Director (EBD). EBDs are the primary business contact for each customer, and focus on ensuring that VITA understands the customers' requirements and is exceeding their expectations.

Source: Commonwealth of Virginia Web site: www.vita.virginia.gov/about/crm/index.cfm.

Exhibit 5.2   Stanford University Internal IT Account Management Role

Account Management

The account managers build and maintain partnerships with clients who use the services we provide. They provide a single point of contact for those clients, help them navigate the many available services provided by the different groups in IT Services, and negotiate clear and reasonable service level agreements. Process and Account Management also supports a liaison program that, in maintaining relationships with schools and business offices, promotes open communications as well as an understanding of their business plans and campus IT needs and requirements.

The group's primary goal is to ensure two-way communication between IT Services and its clients. Outreach efforts help clients understand the services that can help them meet their goals. Connecting clients to the appropriate IT Services resources helps reduce confusion and provides faster solutions. Soliciting input on client needs helps IT Services to develop and refine services clients will use and from which they will benefit.

Source: Stanford University Web site: www.stanford.edu/dept/its/organization/processaccountmgmt/.

---

needs to be able to sit down with senior business management, discussing IT's long-term plans one day, while patiently working with frustrated users who cannot get the help desk or IT to resolve technology problems the next. Studies have shown that 40 to 55 percent of IT professionals are not suited to working closely with customers, so IT will need to ensure that the right people are selected.[1]

Account managers are not a super or advanced desk-side support function. They are IT's ambassadors. They help customers plan and use IT, and even assist department heads in budgeting for IT resources. They represent IT at gatherings or individually in customer offices, and collect information to help IT understand how it can better support its customers.

Exhibit 5.1 describes the account manager position for the Commonwealth of Virginia's VITA, while Exhibit 5.2 does the same for Stanford University. Both descriptions emphasize the role of the account manager as the catalyst for interaction between IT and the user community.

Account Management Benefits for IT Customers   Account managers provide an IT presence wherever they go. They are the local IT franchise supporting a subset of IT's entire customer base and all the IT services relevant to that subset. Account management provides at least six customer-related services:

1. *Quick and local response to IT problems.* An IT manager who is close to the problem can usually address technical issues more quickly and more accurately than someone who is far away. Having a resource nearby is also comforting to many customers, even at a time when the remote remediation of problems is becoming more prevalent. Local, of course, can be relative. The enterprise might only have one IT account manager for all of South America, potentially placing the account manager thousands of miles from some of his or her customers. However, the very fact that there is an account manager in South America can give customers a feeling of closeness they might not have if their account manager was headquartered in New York and had a Brooklyn accent.

   Close can also have a nongeographic meaning. Close can mean that the account manager is close to the business issues that are most important to customers and IT management. It can mean that he or she regularly attends regional business meetings (even if by conference call) and participates in regional discussions. Close can mean that he or she knows the people and is on a first-name basis with them. Most important, close can mean that the account manager has a genuine relationship with his or her customers, and that they feel that he or she is one of them.

2. *Single source of IT information.* Any centralized organization can seem bureaucratic if your primary contact is a phone directory. This can be painfully true when you have an immediate need, such as answering a question or trying to resolve a problem. Customers should not have to know who to call in IT for each different type of problem they encounter—a particularly daunting task if IT is a large organization. An account manager represents all of IT to a customer. This is not to say that the account managers can answer every question about IT, but if they cannot answer the question, they can locate someone within IT who can. Account managers function much the same as librarians: They know the answer to the question or they know where to find it. More important, each account manager is a person with a name and is the one customers know to call with a problem.

3. *Business-knowledgeable conduit into IT, cutting through layers of interfaces.* As mentioned previously, the account manager can locate within IT the information the customer needs. But he or she can do more. Because the account manager knows the customer's business, the search can be performed in context. For example, if the customer needs information on cellular connectivity, it makes a difference whether the customer is a manufacturer in just one state or province,

or in sales and travels throughout the world. Knowing the customers and knowing how and where they work, the account manager can get an answer not just to the question the customer asked, but to the question the customer *should* have asked.

4. *Business advocate inside IT.* IT is constantly making decisions about products to buy and services to offer. The challenge is not just finding the right technology, but finding technology that fits a niche or fulfills an individual customer need. The account managers can play a very important role in this decision process. They work with customers daily and should have the best knowledge within IT about what users want, what they need, and how what they want and need might differ. It is to the customers' advantage to have someone within IT who has firsthand knowledge of their business, someone who can represent them at internal IT meetings, and can present their point of view to IT decision makers.

5. *Help for customers to plan and manage their own technology assets.* Customers' plans and budgets are not independent from IT's plans and budgets. The two should coordinate what the local technology customers must provide with the products and services IT must provide. Coordinating customer and IT plans and budgets can reduce inconsistencies, limit redundancies, and lower costs. The difficulty is making each organization aware of the other's plans. The account managers are best suited to help customers acquire and operate locally managed IT that is consistent with corporate policy and leverages enterprise–vendor relationships and negotiating power. It is also an excellent way to keep IT informed of user technology acquisition plans and budgets.

6. *Personal service.* The help desk does an efficient job of supporting a customer's use of IT's services. However, there are times when a customer's technology problems do not line up with IT service offerings. While traditional support is product- or service-focused, account management is customer-focused. The account manager works closely with customers to resolve their problems, regardless of exactly in which technology bucket they may reside. More than one CIO has been surprised to have an account manager praised by a senior business manager for his or her support in selecting a cell phone or PDA.

The help desk, end-user or desk-side support, the account manager, and the considerable resources in IT headquarters are all responsible for building and maintaining the customer relationship. All support the customer when things are not going according to plan. However, as Exhibit 5.3 points out, who should take the lead in a given situation depends on the type of customer and the type of problem. If executed correctly, there is little overlap, yet great synergy, among the various roles.

Exhibit 5.3 IT's Ability to Support Customers

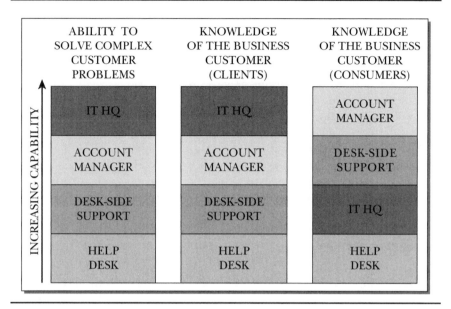

ABILITY TO SOLVE COMPLEX CUSTOMER PROBLEMS	KNOWLEDGE OF THE BUSINESS CUSTOMER (CLIENTS)	KNOWLEDGE OF THE BUSINESS CUSTOMER (CONSUMERS)
IT HQ	IT HQ	ACCOUNT MANAGER
ACCOUNT MANAGER	ACCOUNT MANAGER	DESK-SIDE SUPPORT
DESK-SIDE SUPPORT	DESK-SIDE SUPPORT	IT HQ
HELP DESK	HELP DESK	HELP DESK

(vertical axis: INCREASING CAPABILITY)

Account Management Benefits for IT   The benefits generated by account managers are bidirectional. Done right, IT has as much to gain from account managers as do IT's customers. The following are nine ongoing benefits to IT, but the list could easily be longer:

1. *Improves customer satisfaction.* Customers can feel dissatisfied dealing with a large, distant, and seemingly disinterested organization. Whether IT is centralized or decentralized, it can rarely be located close to all of its customers. Even if nothing else changes, having someone who customers can meet and interact with can significantly improve customer satisfaction. Unfortunately, that interaction will most likely have to take place at the customer's location. An insurance company found that help-desk complaints about system response time decreased after it placed account managers in the larger offices, even though the account managers had no impact on response time. Having someone who customers felt was on their side, who they could talk to about problems, was sufficient to reduce complaints and improve customer satisfaction.

2. *Reduces customer interactions with central IT.* Small vendors, such as software developers, quickly learn that you cannot have customers calling and interrupting operators or programmers to ask questions about their systems. Nothing would get done. After selling just a few systems,

vendors quickly learn to have customers call a set of professionals who do nothing but answer customer questions. If the support person does not know the answer, he or she knows who in the organization to ask.

Help desks provide the same function. Rather than having hundreds of people calling network administrators each time they think their systems have gone down, IT has created an organization whose role it is to answer questions, record problems, and escalate only those they cannot resolve, thus freeing up production staff to do what they were hired to do.

However, help desks cannot resolve all issues. More serious issues, or in some cases those involving senior managers, have to go to corporate IT, unless there is someone who knows the customer situation and has the knowledge, experience, and influence with corporate IT, and trust of the customer, to resolve the problem locally. This is the account manager, a knowledgeable and senior IT professional, who can quickly resolve problems in the field, consistent with local culture, often without having to involve corporate IT.

3. *Personalizes IT services.* The help desk is an effective and cost-efficient way of resolving small IT issues. The downside of help desks is that they are rather impersonal. While customers might be comfortable having the help desk solve their personal computer (PC) problem, they are not as agreeable to having them work on planning, broader support, or purchasing decisions. For these issues, customers, particularly business managers, feel more comfortable dealing with IT management. While corporate IT has the power to resolve major IT issues, they are sometimes too far away and too busy with other issues. Their involvement can sometimes seem as impersonal as that of the help desk.

The account managers fill a role between the help desk and senior IT management. Unlike the sequestered help desk, which might be on a different continent, account managers can be on the ground at customer locations. While the help desk solves transactional IT problems, the account manager can deal with the managerial issues of support coverage, technology rollouts, and IT planning. Unlike senior IT management, the account manager focuses solely on one region or business unit, giving full attention to its questions and concerns.

One of the most important functions of the account manager is to provide a human face for IT. While the help desk might appear as an amorphous toll-free telephone number, and corporate IT managers as disembodied voices on a conference call, the local account manager is someone people can learn to know and trust. If the account manager does a good job, he or she can easily become one of the family. It is not uncommon for customer senior managers to want to deal only with their account manager and have little to do with corporate IT.

How to Keep Account Managers from Going Native

Saint Jude Airlines' information technology (IT) department put an account manager program in place five years ago, with good results. IT's internal customers are very pleased with the account managers IT has assigned to them. The account managers participate in local planning, attend local manager meetings, help with thorny technology problems, and have become one of the family. A few have even been given regional or business unit excellence awards.

Then the cracks started to show. At corporate IT meetings, a few of the account managers had harsh words for some of IT's actions. Communication between corporate IT staff and the account managers started to decline, and what remained was formal and business-like. One manager threatened to quit and work directly for the business unit. Bottom was hit when, at a corporate executive committee meeting, the chief information officer (CIO) discovered that an account manager leaked some confidential internal IT memos to a business unit head.

What happened? Something that vendors and consulting firms have known about for years. The account managers went native. If staff spend most of their time with customers, if they work with them every day, eat meals with them, and even socialize with them, they can start to identify with them. They suddenly realize that they are more customer than they are IT. Worse, they start to see IT as "them." Going native is a sort of IT version of the Stockholm syndrome. (The name was given by Swedish criminologist Nils Bejerot to the psychological state where hostages started to emotionally identify with, and defend, their captors, after a Stockholm bank robbery in 1973, where four hostages were held captive for six days.)

The tightrope IT needs to walk, but one that has been mastered by many vendors and consultancies, is keeping IT staff working with the customer but still identifying with IT. IT needs to develop a program to ensure that account managers, and any other staff who spend considerable time away from other IT staff, still feel part of IT. Such a program would require periodic trips to the corporate or larger IT offices, special reward programs, IT social events, lots of T-shirts and coffee cups, considerable interaction with IT staff (e.g., visits, calls, memos, e-mails, etc.), and all of the other sundry items that remind staff what team they are on.

---

4. *Increases IT's understanding of customer satisfaction.* Surveys are a useful tool for measuring customer satisfaction. However, the effective CIO rarely wants to rely on only one means of measuring success. Account managers can provide another avenue to understanding what satisfies customers and what does not. Account managers can put meat on the statistical bones that surveys provide, relaying tales of customer elation and distress.

Customers' reaction to their account managers can also be a barometer of IT success. The director for account management at a European financial institution complained that the Asian business unit head kept interrupting the IT internal staff assessment and promotion process pushing for a larger-than-approved raise for his account manager. A friendly consultant pointed out that, although the business unit head's interference was disruptive and unwanted, it did show his level of support for his account manager and IT.

5. *Improves IT's understanding of customer business and technology needs.* It is a staple of business books that IT needs to do all it can to understand what the business needs from IT. The IT strategy and IT Steering Committee were created to do just that. However, understanding the customer's business and knowing how technology can help is sufficiently important that IT should pursue every avenue that can help. The account manager is the best-positioned IT person to understand IT's customers, their business, what technology they have, how well it is working, how satisfied they are with it, what technology they could use, and how they could use it. The account manager should be part of every discussion concerning the customers or business units he or she supports.

6. *Validates the service offerings.* IT is always moving. New technologies are brought to market at an amazing speed. It is not just technology that changes, but the business also changes, requiring new products and services delivered to new markets and new customers. IT must constantly be testing and confirming that the services it offers to its customers are the right ones. Do changes in technology provide an opportunity for IT to improve its services? Are there changes in the business marketplace that mean IT is no longer providing the right services to its customers?

Account managers, with their role of bridging IT and the business, are uniquely positioned to help validate that IT is providing the right services to its customers. They know, firsthand, which IT services users are happy with and which they struggle with. Good account managers even know what competitors are doing. They are an invaluable source of assessing IT services.

7. *Provides a vehicle for customer technology education.* Getting training in headquarters is rarely difficult. Materials are at hand, training space is usually easily acquired, and trainers are available. If there are difficulties, often a corporate training function can help with coursework, space, materials, and trainers. However, on the other side of the state, country, or world, the situation is often more problematic. It is important to have someone on the ground, such as the account manager, who can coordinate these efforts, and even function as the trainer if needed.

Moreover, the account manager knows the local users, and the best and worst times to offer the training, as well as which parts of the training will be more important to the customer. Finally, training sponsored by a corporate unit might not get the attention and attendance that the same course offered by one of their own would get.

8. *Provides input to the IT planning process.* The IT Steering Committee, and in particular its councils, are a prime input into the IT planning process, but they are not, and should not be, the only source. Account managers are ideally positioned to report on what is currently happening in the field (the state of the business and how current IT service offerings are meeting demand) and changes on the horizon (e.g., market forces, competitors, products, and technology requirements).

9. *Builds relationships.* Support areas, such as the help desk, do an excellent job of educating customers about how to use IT services or repair them when minor problems occur. Help desks are less successful at building a relationship with the customer. By design, they are efficient and factual and, as a result, rather bland. Account managers, particularly by supporting the customers in all technology areas, regardless of their relationship to a specific service offering, do a better job of bonding with the customer. The personal service they can provide can result in the customer associating all of IT with excellent service. The account manager is the only formal position that gives IT an opportunity to provide customized service to its customers. It would seem unlikely that any IT shop could be considered a provider of exceptional service if it did not have an account management function.

Account Managers and Business Analysts

There are many similarities between account managers and business analysts. Both positions are responsible for bridging the gap between information technology (IT) and IT's customers. Both need to have a good knowledge of the business, of IT, and of company culture. Both need strong interpersonal skills and a desire to work with users, helping them get the most out of technology.

However, there are also significant differences. Business analysts are part of the application development group, and their knowledge of the firm and of IT centers around the application development department, application development's services, and application development's customers. Business analysts' work is usually project oriented, where the workload increases or decreases based on application life cycles. Most business analysts are located together as a group in IT headquarters.

Account managers are responsible for all of IT's services, not just those provided by application development. Although account managers are assigned to a subset of the total IT customer base, that subset is determined by geography, line of business, or some other mechanism, but never by product or service. Their work is ongoing and rarely project related. Account managers are either collocated with their customers or spend considerable time at customer locations.

Shadow Spend   In a perfect world, all IT staff and IT assets are in the IT department, the IT plan, and the IT budget. Likewise, all finance staff and finance assets are in the finance department, the finance plan, and the finance budget, while all human resource staff and human resource assets are in the human resources department, plan, and budget, and so on. But this is rarely the case. IT management might decide that it needs some finance people of its own to handle budgeting, contracts, and that thousand-page phone bill. Finance management needs a programmer-analyst to create some special reports for corporate management or regulators that IT cannot do right or do on time. The IT staff in finance are known as IT shadow staff, and the IT items in the finance budget are known as the shadow IT budget. In many companies, the combined shadow IT budgets can rival the real IT budget.

Why is this important? First, it hides the total cost of IT. Most chief executive officers (CEOs) would like to know that while the IT budget is $100 million per year, the total company IT spend is actually $200 million. The bigger surprise often comes when you look at the second $100 million. It is not uncommon to find that the company has multiple contracts with the same vendor, each perhaps paying for licenses or services covered by the other. Shadow spend can also mitigate volume discounts as well as clout, with vendor management. Worse, some contracts could be with different vendors that work against each other. Over- or underspending is another problem. How does central IT estimate next year's network demand if it does not know how many PCs the Asia region is buying?

Periodically, about once a decade or so, senior management might try to rationalize shadow spend by transferring all staff who perform an IT function to IT, all staff who perform a finance function to finance, and so forth, under the guise of reducing duplication of effort and costs. This is usually a good move for the staff, because an employee performing IT functions in finance will probably not get the needed training or have the career mobility of one in IT. But inevitably, after an appropriate period of compliance, IT will begin hiring finance people again, finance will hire its own IT staff, and so forth, and the cycle starts again.

Some shadow spend is unavoidable. For any number of reasons, including, but not limited to, local tax laws, import and export laws, corporate policy, or organic growth, many business units are forced to own and manage IT assets. It might be just PCs, print supplies, or local phone service. Business units budget and purchase up to 40 to 50 percent of a large multinational's total IT spend.[2] Unfortunately, many of them are not prepared to do an adequate job deciding between technology options and vendors, or acquiring products compatible with corporate standards.

While probably inefficient, shadow spend is also here to stay because it provides a necessary service. However, some of the shadow spend downside can be mitigated by the effective use of account managers. The account manager can help coordinate a region's or business unit's shadow spend with IT's own budget. Should the region upgrade current PCs or plan on buying new ones in a year or two? Does the IT budget reflect the planned staffing increase in Latin America? Do service and parts contracts match headcount or PC count? These questions are difficult to answer without knowing what is happening in the region, as well as what is planned for the corporate unit. The account manager not only has the IT budget know-how, but also understands local needs and customs. No one is better positioned to provide a win-win for both the region and corporate.

Importance of Being Local   Most IT professionals have heard something like this during their careers: "IT is a bunch of idiots, but Bob, our local IT guy, is okay." Bob might be, in fact, a moron, but because he is "one of us,"

Should it be Centralized or Decentralized?

There are four drivers of the decision to centralize or decentralize any function:

1. *Corporate organization or strategy.* There is a policy decision, coming right from the top, to either centralize or decentralize services. If the chief executive officer (CEO) decides that the organization will be decentralized, then it will probably be decentralized. Celebrity CEOs often run very centralized organizations, while consensus CEOs lean toward a more distributed model.

2. *Culture.* The decision can be predestined when it is woven into the fabric of an organization. Many accounting firms are decentralized because of regulatory restrictions that were placed on them. When their consulting units split off, most stayed decentralized, even though they no longer faced the accounting industry regulatory requirements. Their culture was such that they just feel more comfortable being decentralized.

3. *Logistics.* Decentralization can help when the resources consumed or the customers to be served are dispersed across the country or globe. Centralization can help if resources or customers are concentrated.

4. *Sovereignty or regulatory reasons.* Companies are often decentralized when the law says they have to be. Some countries require certain types of business to be run locally or even be locally owned.

There is no rule or study that says centralization always works better than decentralization, or the reverse. Success or failure comes down to the environment in which the company exists and how well the company is managed. This does not mean that one structure does not work better than the other in a specific set of circumstances, only that neither one nor the other predestines success or failure. All of the principles presented in this book work equally well with both types.

he is considered okay. The distinguishing factor is often not whether Bob is a moron, but *whose* moron he is. If he is *our* moron, then he is okay; if he is *your* moron, then he is a jerk. Such is the world of mine and yours.

IT can be the greatest organization in the world, but if it does not exist *here*, then it is nowhere. This sentiment probably started 10,000 years ago, when the first business opened its second location. Corporate never understands what we do here in this . . . (pick an example from one of the following categories: location, business unit, department, floor, cubicle).

There is some truth to this. They do things differently in Brazil, in the consumer business unit, in manufacturing, on the third floor, and in the vice president's office. An effective IT group is one that melds local practice with corporate policy and local knowledge with central efficiency. The account manager is the sole individual who has the opportunity to bridge this gap. Organizations that have implemented an account management program and have collocated their account managers with customers all have stories of customers saying that the local IT guy is (1) okay and (2) theirs. However, if the account manager spends the majority of his time at IT headquarters, his IQ suddenly drops 50 points, and he is one of them. The lesson is clear: Account managers need to be either located with their customers, or, at the very least, spend the majority of their time with their customers.

IT is moving in the right direction with the implementation of account management programs, but many of these programs still resemble the Department of Motor Vehicles when it comes to service. Sometimes unresponsive, occasionally unavailable, and always stiff, IT and IT's account managers could both learn a few things from their for-profit counterparts.

WHAT THE FOR-PROFITS CAN TEACH IT

It is debatable whether customer service in the for-profit sector is improving or getting worse. The past two decades of cost cutting have introduced interactive voice-response units, those pesky "press one for account balance" telephone options, and self-service checkout lines, which let consumers experience what it is like to have a minimum wage job, if only for a few minutes per week. However, even at their worst, for-profit businesses do a better job of managing customer relationships than do most cost centers. Even as we see customer service waning in the outside world, organizations like IT can still learn a few things by looking at some revenue-generator tricks of the trade.

Stop, Look, and Listen

What should IT staff talk about when they visit customers? Maybe they should not talk at all. In the 1980s, a new sales technique was leading the business book parade. It even became the focus of one computer company's advertising campaign. It was to listen. Yes, listen. Now, listening was not new in sales training, but it experienced a major resurgence in the 1980s as companies, particularly technology companies, tried to reconnect with customers. They found that customers were getting tired of being preached to about solutions for problems they did not even have. (The previous popular technology vendor sales gimmick was to say that they did not sell computers or software, but solutions.) The frustration fumed and boiled until some smart promoters recognized that what customers wanted was for company representatives to shut up and listen to what their real problems were.

As a result, the sales staff was subjected to listening training classes, where they listened to their instructors talk about listening. Advertisements for technology giants bragged about how they listened more than their competitors listened. Everyone wanted to hear what the customer had to say. And the customers? Did customers see through this thinly veiled scheme to sell more punched cards and paper tape? No, they ate it up with a spoon. It was a very successful campaign, vestiges of which still exist today. Salespeople are still trained in listening (although a number of them could use a refresher course), even if the fanfare has been toned down.

Many internal users have similar feelings. They want IT to give it a rest, and just listen. They recognize that there might not be technical solutions to their problems, but unless they get a chance to sit down with someone from IT and tell them what those problems are, they will never know.

There is an old adage, "Be silent and be thought a fool; speak and remove all doubt." A good tactic is for IT managers to meet with senior business managers or groups of business employees and listen to their questions, concerns, and frustrations. On-the-spot answers are not always necessary and definitely to be avoided if they are not well thought out. It is far, far better to shut up than to come across as someone making it up on the fly or being defensive. After the meeting, IT staff can always follow up with a memo or e-mail reiterating questions and concerns, and providing any answers or resolutions that might be possible.

Prepare a Road Show

Sometimes listening is not enough, and IT has to communicate with customers about its plans, successes, and failures. Rather than every IT manager writing a presentation for each meeting he attends, IT should consider creating standard road show documents that tell the story IT wants to convey.

Getting a presentation right is difficult. Amassing the facts about completed initiatives or information about planned projects can be time consuming. Telling a coherent and interesting story is even more difficult. Getting the wording just right requires considerable trial and error.

It is reported that Jay Leno, the host of NBC TV's *Tonight Show*, would try out his jokes on local audiences before he ever told them on the air.

At night, after taping his show, he would go to the Los Angeles comedy clubs and test his new material. Jokes that were well received were on the air the next night. Those that were not well received were either rewritten or abandoned. Getting the wording of the joke correct sometimes required multiple edits after multiple trials. Not until a joke was just right was it used on the show.

Presentations are the same; rarely are they just right the first time. Only after they have been presented multiple times, and then edited to reflect the questions and lessons learned from each audience, are the diagrams and the wording effective. For most IT organizations, that means the presentations will need to be shared among the senior IT managers and account managers, each giving them to an audience and then improving them based on the audience's reception.

This works out well for three reasons:

1. Few IT managers, senior or account, have the skill to create a good presentation the first time, and fewer will present it enough times to get sufficient feedback.

2. Sharing a presentation reinforces presenting the same message. Contradictions can be virtually eliminated by creating and using an official IT presentation. More difficult to control are inconsistencies that can crop up simply by including one issue and not another. These can also be virtually eliminated by having a standard road show document.

3. In order to have a standard presentation, IT will need to review and update the document at least quarterly, with accomplishments, changes in policy, and new initiatives. The rigor of the required updates is good discipline for IT to review what it promised to do last quarter, articulate progress, and lay out the next quarter's initiatives.

Using a corporate communications group to create and edit the IT presentation is a good idea, but it does not change any of the previous suggestions. Even with professional presentation help, the message will still need to be honed over multiple meetings with various audiences.

Joint Planning

The bank advertisement presented a strong case. Banks, it said, offered a great investment in tax-deferred annuities, but there was one drawback: too much paperwork. No problem, the ad said, come in and the bank's staff would fill out the forms for you. All you have to do, besides forking over the money, is sign on the dotted line. Clever idea. If potential customers are scared away by stacks of insurance company and government paperwork, have the bank staff fill it out for them.

As stated earlier, for any number of reasons, many business units are forced to own and manage IT assets. This is particularly true for multinationals, where local tax or import laws sometimes dictate who can purchase and own local IT assets. However, purchasing and owning IT assets might be a responsibility for which the local business staff are neither trained nor prepared. A good solution is for the business and IT to plan and budget together to ensure compatibility and the maximum benefit from volume pricing. This might require IT and dozens of business units coordinating their planning and purchasing—a daunting task.

However, IT can take a cue from the bank and help the businesses with their plans. IT could prepare a how-to guide with formatted and partially filled spreadsheets for local IT planning and budgeting that lists the corporate budget line items, and the cost drivers for each line item (see Chapter 3 for a discussion of cost drivers), preferred vendors, and the business projections (growth, headcount, sales) that will drive the plan.

IT staff, in particular the account manager, could then help business unit staff fill out the guide that will determine their budget. The result should be separate business and IT budgets that are driven by the same business projections, use the same cost drivers, and acquire products and services from the same vendors, while achieving the same maximum discounts.

More work for IT? Maybe for some organizations, but for others there might actually be less work than there would be when struggling all year with incompatible or poor-quality equipment or services. Even if there is more work for IT, there is significant value in the goodwill gained.

SOME ADDITIONAL THOUGHTS

> *Customer management.* The organization and processes IT uses to maintain a technically competent, customer-knowledgeable, and helpful presence in all areas of the enterprise. Account managers represent IT, and all of IT's services, to a subset of IT's total customer base.

Internal overhead organizations have always struggled with customer management. A few cost center staff point to a captive audience as a reason that customer service is not needed. It's not a reason; it's an excuse. IT customers suspect, sometimes correctly, that IT takes them for granted just because they are a captive audience.

The reality is that most cost center staff do try to provide good customer service, but they simply do not know how to do it right. Worse, the incentive is questionable. Regardless of corporate mission statements or annual reports, cost cutting, not customer service, is the message that is coming across from senior management. For example, cost management, and not customer service, drives the move toward centralization. What can sometimes be forgotten is that technology, which allows centralization, can also provide the cost savings that permit IT to invest in good customer service.

CUSTOMER MANAGEMENT	

DOs	DON'Ts
• Do create a team of personable and technically knowledgeable staff who can represent IT with customers. • Do empower account managers to resolve customer complaints while helping customers effectively use technology. • Do encourage the joint development of IT and business plans and budgets. • Do listen to customers even if there is no practical solution for their problem.	• Don't let account managers function as a super help desk. • Don't let account managers go native by aligning themselves with the customer and against IT. Constantly reinforce that they are an important part of IT. • Don't let senior IT managers ignore customers simply because there are account managers. All senior IT management should develop relationships with (remote) customers.

Account managers can help with the perennial senior management question: Should IT be centralized or distributed by geography or business unit? Account or relationship managers provide the best of both worlds. They allow a centralized IT organization to provide many of the benefits and advantages of a decentralized one. Embedded IT staff, aligned either by geography, region, or both, are a microcosm of corporate IT, but with a local flavor. The account manager should be *their* IT point person, explaining, answering, coordinating, advocating, intervening, and expediting what the local organization needs to do its job. At the same time, IT has a disciple, preacher, ambassador, agent, intelligence source, and problem fixer close to the customer—a good deal for both IT and the customer.

The account management position does not exonerate senior IT management from interaction with customers. IT senior staff need to listen to what the users have to say, and tell them what is happening, what is expected to happen, and how it will affect them. They should explain IT's structure, governance, and processes, and how customers can participate in its workings or influence its decisions. Most important, senior IT managers need to let users know that IT is aware of their contribution to the enterprise and that IT is there to help them achieve their goals.

REFERENCES

The following are some literature, Web sites, and organizations that might be useful:

Some Representative Literature
Hawthorne Effect

Franke, R.H., and J.D. Kaul. "The Hawthorne Experiments: First Statistical Interpretation."*American Sociological Review,* 1978, Vol. 43, pp. 623–643.

Gillespie, Richard. *Manufacturing Knowledge: A History of the Hawthorne Experiments.* Cambridge University Press, 1991.

Landsberger, Henry A. *Hawthorne Revisited.* Cornell University Press, 1958.

Account Management

Adair, Kate. "Embedded IT."*Information Age,* October 2005. http://www.information-age.com/article/2005/october/embedded_it

Hightower, Trenton. "Everybody's in Sales."http://www.vccs.edu/Workforce/Everybody'sinSales.doc

Mateyaschuk, Jennifer. "Relationship Managers Gain Strategic Role."*InformationWeek,* February 22, 1999. http://www.information-week.com/722/relate.htm

Cramm, Susan H. "The Demand Management Primer."*CIO Magazine,* February 18, 2004. http://www.cio.com/research/leadership/edit/la021804_demand.html

Conant, Robin. "Relationship Management in Higher Education Information Technology."*Research Bulletin,* Educause Center for Applied Research, Vol. 2003, Issue 13, June 24, 2003.

NOTES

1. Jennifer Tucker, Abby Mackness, and Hile Rutledge, "The Human Dynamics of IT Teams," *CrossTalk: The Journal of Defense Software Engineering* (February 2004), http://www.stsc.hill.af.mil/crosstalk/2004/02/0402Tucker.html.
2. There is considerable anecdotal agreement, although little actual data, to support the claim that for the large multinationals, 40 to 50 percent of total IT cost can be shadow spend. However, it is the author's experience that the number has never been challenged by large multinational IT or corporate finance groups. The assertion is also in the range of what McNeese, Hayes, and Bonneau report as shadow headcount. (Cindy McNeese, Owen Hayes, and Scott Bonneau, "Shining the Light on Shadow Staff," *CIO Magazine Online,* http://www2.cio.com/consultant/report2085.html.)

6

Market Intelligence

If one is only to talk from first-hand experience,
conversation would be a very poor business.
—*C.S. Lewis*

Human beings, who are almost unique in having the
ability to learn from the experience of others, are also
remarkable for their apparent disinclination to do so.
—*Douglas Adams*

Yoshi Koyama is like many Japanese information technology (IT) managers approaching retirement. In 1975, he was recruited by a large bank right out of college. He worked his entire professional life for the same employer, thanks to the bank's lifetime employment policy. Lifetime employment was a common benefit at large Japanese companies in the 1970s, so Yoshi could count on decades of reliable work and a decent retirement from the bank at the end of his career. Policies of hiring right out of school and lifetime employment meant that turnover at large Japanese companies was almost unheard of.

The bank used mainframe computers from a single Japanese computer manufacturer that supplied almost all of the IT equipment at the bank. The computer company also was the primary source for all IT training. Knowing that it would have a customer for life, the computer company was ready and willing to make a significant investment in training bank staff. Much of the training was free or bundled into the price of the hardware and software. When training was not free, the cost was very reasonable. Yoshi and his fellow workers spent many days per year being taught by their vendor how to use and get the most out of the vendor's products and services. As a result, Yoshi learned a considerable amount about the bank's computers, but he learned almost nothing about other computer companies' products, the equipment other banks relied on, or how they used it in the running of their business.

Things have changed over the years. Many Japanese companies had to formally give up the commitment of lifetime employment in the economically tough 1990s, although few have had to act on it in any significant way. Japanese companies now rely on more technology vendors, particularly for non-mainframe processing. Even so, a primary vendor still significantly influences large Japanese IT organizations, and training is still vendor-dominated, with primary vendors investing heavily in their customers. However, what has not changed is that turnover is still low, with most IT professionals never seeing the inside of any other IT department.

THE PROBLEM

In the West, things are a bit different. Europe and North America rely much less on vendors for staff training. Instead, IT training has become big business in its own right, leading to fierce competition among vendors and companies specializing in training.

Just a few years ago, the average IT department might have supported two mainframes, probably from a single vendor. It might have two or three application development languages, one, or at most two, telecommunications languages, and two or three file and database management systems. Today, the average IT department has hundreds of servers, probably from a half-dozen vendors (particularly if you count the specialty servers such as gateways, firewalls, etc.). IT shops today might have anywhere from a half-dozen to a dozen operating system versions; a dozen or more programming languages, report writers, and development environments; and four or more file and database management systems. Unless a department is large, the number of products to know can exceed the number of people who have to know about them. Programmers, network, and data center administrators need to be fluent in multiple products, perhaps from multiple vendors. Training has become a time-consuming and expensive necessity.

Vendors are of limited help. They are uncomfortable spending much money training client staff, as they do in Japan, and then having the client use that skill with competitor products. Rather than using training as a way to sell products and services or to keep customer satisfaction high, Western vendors use training as a second, and very profitable, revenue stream.

Conversely, IT organizations are uncomfortable placing all of their training eggs in just the vendor's basket. They would rather rely on multiple suppliers. To supplement vendor training, the West has developed a lucrative third-party training market, where IT organizations can acquire vendor-specific, vendor-neutral, or cross-vendor training at premium prices.

Another way IT in Europe and North America differs from IT in Japan is that the IT industry in the West has traditionally suffered higher turnover than in Japan. Double-digit numbers have been the norm in IT, although there have been some exceptions. Just before the dot.com bubble burst in 2000, turnover was much higher than average, topping 30 percent per year in some U.S. organizations. After the dot.com bust, turnover nearly disappeared, with single-digit turnover numbers down to zero, and remained so for the next three or four years. A frustration of IT during the heyday of the dot.com era was paying handsomely to train staff, only to have them leave and go elsewhere after acquiring a new technical skill.

The training problems persist to this day. Current training programs do not provide IT with the quantity and quality of knowledgeable staff it requires. IT needs additional ways to expand its knowledge base with information about the latest and best products, services, processes, and techniques for running an effective and efficient IT organization. Because training budgets are at their limits, any new way of gaining IT knowledge has to be very cost effective.

THE IT SOLUTION

The solution pursued by many IT organizations in the United States makes the best of a bad situation, although its overall effectiveness is questionable. Faced with high training costs (tuition as well as loss of work during training) and a poor staff-retention rate, some shops have used turnover as a method for acquiring new skills. Rather than recruiting to replace a worker, skill for skill, they use turnover to change the skill base of the organization. Lose a COBOL programmer, and replace her with a new hire who knows Visual Basic; have a Solaris expert quit, and replace him with a Linux expert. Sometimes shops have artificially increased turnover, pushing out workers with less desirable skills and replacing them with those possessing more needed ones, not as a means of restoring headcount, but rather as a way of supplementing the department's skill base.

Using turnover as a way to supplement missing or inadequate skills has another advantage over training: It provides a window into how other organizations use technology. Experienced technicians who have worked for other companies can bring with them more than just their technical skills. They can also bring experience using different processes, knowledge of the effectiveness of different policies, new ways of negotiating with vendors, and knowledge of different organizational structures, as well as technical tricks that might be unfamiliar to the new employer. These experiences do not have to be success stories. Learning what was tried and did not work elsewhere might be as valuable as learning what did work.

Unfortunately, the problem with using turnover to acquire needed skills is that it is an uncertain and unpredictable foundation for a staff development program. The time it takes to recruit new resources can be quite long. It is not uncommon for some technical positions to remain unfilled for a year before someone suitable is found and brought on board.

Moreover, the turnover rate required to gain all of the needed skills is often too high to provide a real knowledge solution for IT. Even when bundled with a vigorous training program, a turnover-based skill enhancement program cannot give IT the sustainable resources it needs. Worse, letting go of good and loyal workers, just because IT needs to hire someone with skills that are more recent, is bad for morale and bad business. As the saying goes, "The worst use of a soldier is to shoot him." Likewise, trading a good worker for an unknown new hire simply does not make sense. It is much harder to develop a good worker than it is for that worker to learn to code SQL. IT needs a method that is more stable and less destructive to staff morale for acquiring new skills at the pace they are needed, and at the price IT can afford.

WHAT THE FOR-PROFITS CAN TEACH IT

One of the very first jobs for new hires at any of the hundreds of management consulting companies around the world is the telephone interview. Their job will be to interview not their client's staff, but individuals outside their client's company. Sometimes they will question their client's customers or people in other industries, but eventually they will have to perform a competitor interview.

Competitor interviews are calls to employees at a company that is a direct competitor of the consultant's client. The consultant's job is to gain competitive intelligence for his client by asking the competitor's employees about their organization. There is nothing dishonest about this. The consultant identifies himself and the client for which he is working, and asks the competitor employee if he or she will answer a few questions. Sometimes the client lets the consultant share results with competitors as an inducement to participate; other times the client will not. Sometimes the client wants to remain anonymous, and sometimes the interviewee wants to keep his or her name or the company's name anonymous from the client. In both cases, the consultant must honor these requests.

Making the first call can be difficult for a new consultant who can easily imagine being cursed at and hung up on. Sometimes that happens, but rarely. Not everyone participates, but a surprising number do, and even those who do not participate are rather gracious about it. The higher up you go in the competitor organization, the easier it is to get an interview. Junior managers rarely talk to outsiders, middle managers do so about half the time, but senior managers are willing to talk most of the time. One reason is that they know that their company commissions similar studies, so a general environment of cooperation is useful for all.

Competitor cooperation occurs all the time. Chief executive officers (CEOs) often meet with competitor CEOs—maybe not during working hours, but dinners and golf outings give CEOs the chance to meet with, and size up, the other person, and learn what he or she is doing.

Noncompetitive interviews are even easier for consultants. Imagine a client in the clock manufacturing business who is thinking of buying a supply-chain management software package. The client might want to know which packages major manufacturers are using, how they are using them, and their level of satisfaction with the product. Many companies who do not make clocks use supply-chain management software. It will not be difficult to find people at an aircraft manufacturer, or a furniture company, or a kitchen utensil supplier, who are willing to help a clock maker with its supply-chain management questions. The information gained about non-competitors is often called *market intelligence* to distinguish it from *competitive intelligence*.

Interviewing employees at nonclient companies is one of the ways consultants learn how IT deals with technology, technology staff, senior business management, government regulations, and customers. It is a very effective way of learning what has been tried and what has not been tried, what works and what does not work. Better yet, the cost of gaining this knowledge is cheap—sometimes just the price of a phone call. No wonder consulting companies consider it one of the most important weapons in their consulting arsenal.

There is nothing that these management consultants do that the average IT professional cannot do. IT staff could contact IT people at other organizations and interview them about how the interviewee's company provides services, increases customer satisfaction, or reduces costs. The manager of the e-mail team could interview the managers of e-mail teams at other companies. They could compare procedures, discuss products, and commiserate on problems dealing with spam. The discussions can be a two-way street, with the interviewee gaining as much information as the interviewer. The e-mail managers do not have to come from companies in the same industry; in fact, it might be better if they do not, because there will be less concern about helping a competitor. The e-mail team manager of an insurance company could be interviewing the e-mail team manager of a nonprofit organization, while a network administrator for the state motor vehicle department could be interviewing a network administrator from a consumer products manufacturer.

The subjects of these discussions can be diverse. The breadth of useful information gained can range from the most technical issues down to lifestyle questions on work/life balance. Gathering market intelligence by interviewing colleagues at other companies is an easy, inexpensive, and potentially ongoing way to keep staff up on the best products, processes, and practices in IT. It allows technicians and managers to share the good and the bad in a nonjudgmental environment, all while exercising and expanding interpersonal skills.

How a Market Intelligence Program Works

A market intelligence program gives IT staff an opportunity to gain technical and business, as well as interpersonal, skills, without formal training. Although it should not replace a formal training program, it can easily be incorporated into the IT department's staff development program, as well as its staff performance appraisal processes. Following are some of the details for how a market intelligence program could be implemented in an IT department.

Participants   The ideal candidates for a market intelligence program are IT staff members who have sufficient maturity and experience to:

- Construct a set of interview questions.
- Contact and set up a meeting with staff outside the company.
- Communicate the questions to the interviewee (beforehand, if required).
- Share experiences with the interviewee.
- Compare, in a meaningful way, interviewee experiences with the interviewer's organization.
- Communicate the similarities and differences between the two companies to fellow IT staff.

These requirements probably limit participation to staff who have a few years of experience and are managers, experts, or near-experts in one or more technical fields. Junior managers are the ideal candidates because they:

- Are just starting to understand what they do not know.
- Have demonstrated some level of communication skills.
- Have a need to develop interpersonal skills more than they ever did before.
- Are looking for ways, not to manage the technology, but to manage the people who manage the technology.

The interviewers are not the only participants in this program. Senior manager facilitators will also be needed, especially in the early days of the program. They can help with one of the biggest problems in getting the program kicked off—the *freshman mixer syndrome*. The first freshman mixer or dance can be quite a daunting experience. The boys are bunched up against one wall of the gym, and the girls against the other, with the center of the room empty, each group reticent about making a move toward the other, for fear of rejection. Many IT staff members are similarly afraid of calling someone they do not know at another company and asking to interview them. The fear of rejection is so high that some will be in a near panic.

Market Versus Competitive Intelligence

Competitive intelligence is information gleaned about competitors. Market intelligence is information gained from organizations regardless of their industry. Most of the literature deals with competitive intelligence because for-profits are concerned with what their competitors are doing. They want to know about their competitors' customers, the products those customers are buying, and the price they are paying for them. In addition, for-profits want to know their competitors' costs and how the competitors produce or acquire their products. In short, they want to understand the competitors' entire value proposition. The aim of competitive intelligence is to win at the expense of the competitor.

Market intelligence is more benign. No one need lose and, in fact, it can be a win-win situation. Sharing information and experiences with noncompetitors can allow both companies to survive and prosper.

IT senior managers, acting as program facilitators, can help get the program started. They can contact senior managers at other companies (e.g., friends, acquaintances, or total strangers), explaining the program to them, getting agreement from them on its value, and obtaining from them the names of potential interviewees. (The potential interviewees should know that they might be called about an interview.) Most senior IT managers will welcome the chance for their staff to share knowledge with others, as long as the exchange is bidirectional.

There is a second area where senior managers can help. Most new interviewers and interviewees will have some concern about what they can say about their own company and what they cannot say. There will be a fear of giving away company secrets or sensitive information. Senior managers should hold discussions with the staff about what can be shared and what should not. Staff members should be informed that if they are unsure of what the policy is on a particular topic, they should simply avoid it.

In reality, this is rarely a problem. Senior managers should be sure that the participants understand the distinction between genuinely sensitive information and embarrassing information. Very little information the average IT manager can share is genuinely company-sensitive. Of greater concern to some IT managers and staff are the things that might make them look bad. The wise thing to do is to share both the good and the bad. IT has a lot to gain and learn from coming clean about its failures as well as its successes.

Market Intelligence Alpha Release

For many vendor organizations, an alpha release is the first distribution of a software system after testing has been completed. However, the recipients of the software are limited to in-house staff. For example, a word processing vendor's alpha release of a software package would only be distributed to company employees. If the package does well in its alpha release, it then progresses to a beta release, where it is given to selected customers who know that the software might or might not be ready for prime time.

The alpha release concept could be applied to market intelligence as well. In many IT organizations, more than half of the current staff came from other employers. Before interviewing people in other companies, IT staff could practice interviewing fellow IT staff members about their former employers. When the interview is over, the interviewee could brief the IT interviewer about the session from the interviewee's perspective. The debrief could include a discussion of what the interviewer learned about the interviewee's former employer, as well as what the interviewer failed to learn because he or she did not ask the right questions or follow up where needed.

Interviewing test subjects could be part of the market intelligence training program, giving trainees a real-life opportunity to test newly acquired interviewing skills. It could also function as a market intelligence training program final exam.

The facilitators should also ensure that the program is run efficiently, that staff are properly trained and prepared, that they conduct their interviews, and that interview notes are properly created and shared.

Senior IT management can be more than just facilitators; they can be interviewers as well. Senior managers, directors, and even chief information officers (CIOs) can benefit from seeing first hand how other organizations are run, the processes they developed, the management techniques they use, and their assessment of what worked and what did not work.

Interview Subjects One of the first areas interviewers will want to know about is the technology other companies use. However, after the program gets underway, it is not uncommon to find that the areas with the most impact are not those centered on technology, but on the processes, policies, and practices other companies put in place to manage their own technology, vendors, customers, and themselves.

At the beginning of the interview, discussions usually focus on *things* (e.g., hardware, software, vendors, etc.). Early information sharing will be centered on successful uses of hardware and software. After a short time, as each side (interviewer and interviewee) becomes more comfortable, discussions will shift to what was tried but did not work. As the comfort level continues to increase, the topics will shift from technology to policies, working

---

Exhibit 6.1   A Few Market Intelligence Interview Topics

- Technology
  - The strengths, weaknesses, and suitability of technology vendors
  - The features, strengths, and weaknesses of technology products
  - Using the products effectively
  - Workarounds and other methods of increasing product usefulness
- Processes and procedures
  - Processes and procedures the department uses, has used, or is thinking of using (internal to IT, customer facing, outside expertise (ITIL, CMMI, etc.))
  - Process strengths, weaknesses, and effectiveness
- Management
  - Management techniques, styles and approaches, and their effectiveness
  - Management training and evaluation
- Staff
  - Staff development programs (training, conferences, internal opportunities)
  - Staff assessment and advancement programs
  - Staff work environments and morale

---

environment, and eventually to more personal areas, such as morale. Discussions will also shift from organizational successes and failures to individual successes and failures.

It is not uncommon for both interviewers and interviewees to come away from a meeting with the desire to experiment with some new products, services, processes, or programs. Exhibit 6.1 gives a few examples of useful interview topics.

How It Should Work   Staff should take the initiative to find people to interview.

Identify interview candidates

The ideal interview candidate is someone who is at approximately the same level in his or her organization as the interviewer is and has the same or a similar job, but in another company. They can be from the same industry (competitors) or from a very different industry. Although the type of industry is not important, size is. Candidates from IT organizations of about the same size or slightly larger organizations are best. To find candidates, staff can talk to managers, friends, co-workers who still know people at former employers, and vendors. Other sources can be trade shows and conferences, user groups, professional association directories, and school alumni associations. Vendors are a good source because they not only know staff at other companies, but they can function as a go-between, making the first contact with a potential interviewee and asking whether the individual would be willing to participate.

Set up a time and place for the interview
The interviewer should call the interview candidates and ask whether they would be willing to be interviewed. The interviewer should set up the first meeting as a phone call or as an in-person get-together at either company, or at a neutral location such as a restaurant. Interviewers should explain that they would be willing to answer as many questions about their organization as the interviewee does. If the interviewee wishes, the interviewer should share the questions that will be asked in advance of the interview. The interviewer should not press for an immediate answer but allow the candidate time to think it over or to talk to a manager.

Create an interview guide
An interview guide is simply a statement of the goals of the interview and the questions to be answered. Some interviewers like to share the interview guide with the interviewee beforehand; others wait for the visit or call. If the questions are predominantly numerical (e.g., transaction volumes, number of help desk calls, etc.), then the interviewee will need some time to collect the data before the interview. If the interview questions are more subjective than numerical, advanced notice is not as important.

There is a tendency for some interviewers to ask for too much. The interview should not require more than 20 minutes' preparation by the interviewee. Request more, and the interviewer might get nothing. The interviewer should start slowly, asking the easiest questions first. Save the tough questions and ones about money for last.

Conduct a friendly interview
The meeting should be light and informal; it is not an interrogation. The interviewer should ask open-ended questions that get the interviewee talking, and not questions that can be answered with a simple yes or no, or with just a sentence or two. An interview of less than 20 minutes will probably glean little information, but one of more than 45 minutes might wear out a welcome, unless the interviewee is interested in continuing. The interviewer needs to remember to give as much as he or she gets. This should be a

Swot Analysis as an Interviewing Technique

There is a strategic planning technique that some have found useful when interviewing business or technical staff. It is called SWOT analysis (*strengths, weaknesses, opportunities,* and *threats*). It was developed in the 1960s by Marion Dosher, Otis Benepe, Albert Humphrey, Robert Stewart, and Birger Lie at the Stanford Research Institute. Strengths and weaknesses refer to the characteristics of the organization's internal environment, whereas opportunities and threats refer to the external environment. SWOT is usually represented diagrammatically as a two-by-two matrix (see Exhibit A).

Exhibit A   SWOT Diagram

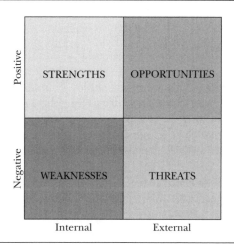

SWOT was designed to analyze an entire enterprise, but the framework can be applied equally well to an IT organization. For market intelligence purposes, it is only important to remember to ask the interviewee about the IT organization's internal strengths, internal weaknesses, external threats, and external opportunities. Those four questions can generate a wealth of information.

good experience for both participants, so they will want to repeat it in the future.

One or two interviewers, but no more, should conduct the interview. More than two people asking questions can be intimidating and can stifle free discussion. The amount of information in an answer is often inversely proportional to the number of people in the room. The same is true for interviewees. More information is often gained from one or two interviewees than from four or five. Having co-workers in the room can limit some discussion.

However, particularly in the beginning, both interviewers and interviewees might feel more comfortable with some support. Two interviewers should help allay interviewer fears, and two interviewees should help allay interviewee fears. Try, at all costs, to avoid having an interviewee's supervisor in the interview. Nothing shuts up a worker faster than having a boss in the room.

Write up and share the interview notes
The information gained from the interview needs to be published if the IT organization is to gain from it. The interview questions and answers should be written up and shared with other IT staff. A shared directory, internal Web site, or hard-copy report of the notes from each interview should be available to all participants, if not all IT staff. Publishing interview notes not only shares potentially useful information but also, in most cases, increases the quality of the notes.

When the Program Should Take Place   Market intelligence interviews can take place any time, but best results are achieved when they are part of a formal, scheduled program. For example, senior IT management could set up an annual program that consists of identifying the IT staff in the program for the coming year and determining how many market interviews they are to complete in that time frame. For example, each participant could be required to complete and write reports on three interviews during the calendar year.

Market intelligence and interview training might be needed for some staff members who are new to the program. They should be taught techniques for creating interview guides, conducting the interviews, and writing up their interview notes afterward. Integrating the market intelligence program with the staff appraisal process can be easily achieved by simply evaluating the interviewers' notes as part of their annual appraisal or review.

Once or twice a year, all of the participants in the program should meet and review all interview notes from the past period. They should then select the best ideas from the notes and present them to IT management as change recommendations. These recommendations for IT could be to acquire, modify or experiment with new products, services, policies, processes or projects. This group should also review the market intelligence program, identifying any changes they feel that are warranted.

Benefits of Market Intelligence

At the end of a year, even a moderate-size IT organization could have completed dozens of interviews at several external companies. Singly, the information gained is useful, but collectively, it can paint an interesting picture of real successes and failures in similarly sized or slightly larger IT organizations. Benefits are most common in four areas:

1. *Technology.* The most obvious benefit of a market intelligence program is an increase in institutional knowledge about technology products, services, and vendors. The IT department will have an additional source of information about the hardware, software, and services, and the companies that peddle them.

2. *Operations.* A second benefit centers, not on technology, but on its use. IT organizations can gain insight into new ways to develop, deliver, and support the services they provide to their customers. Some of this insight will affect customers directly through better customer service, help-desk support, and applications. Other benefits will be internal to IT, such as improved data center operations, change management, and use of staff. In all cases, IT will gain information that it is very difficult to acquire in any classroom.

3. *Staff development.* A third benefit will be the increased interpersonal skills of the IT staff participants. IT staff need good interviewing skills when hiring new staff, interviewing vendors, or meeting with internal customers. Although interview training is not uncommon in many companies, the opportunity to practice the skill is often insufficient to keep it at the necessary level. The market intelligence program is ideal for developing interviewing skills, keeping them up-to-date, providing sufficient opportunity for use so that they do not atrophy, and doing it in a friendly, nonjudgmental environment, with little downside.

   Insufficient interviewing skills can have disastrous consequences when hiring or purchasing IT products or services. Hiring a Charles Manson fan for the help desk or purchasing your hardware from Bob's Computers and Screen Door Company can cost the firm dearly. Blowing a market intelligence interview with a programmer at the Midwest Farm By-Products Company will likely have few repercussions. The benefit of having staff train on the latter before attempting the former: priceless.

   Getting out and meeting peers, interviewing them, and posting the interview reports for all IT staff to read can help build confidence as well as skills. Staff who are more comfortable interacting with external peers are also more comfortable dealing with internal customers, vendors, and management.

4. *Management.* The fourth benefit is learning about new and different management techniques, the good as well as the bad. IT managers are known to be innovative; they are also known to be ineffective. IT is often the first department to try something new, such as an innovative recognition or reward program. They have more interesting and enjoyable off-site meetings that many other departments envy. Single-handedly, IT shops worldwide have kept the T-shirt and coffee cup industries prosperous.

Competitive Intelligence Training When You are Shy

Do you want competitive intelligence but are afraid to call a competitor? Could information technology (IT) staff use a few competitive interview dress rehearsals before hitting the big time? Talk to IT staff and internal customers who have worked at competitor companies. People who worked in a competitor's IT department can give their current IT employer insight into how the competitor's IT department worked when they were there.

Interviewees do not have to be IT people; staff from any department will do. Non-IT employees who worked for competitors can report on how well the competitor's IT department was perceived by its employees. Both groups can give valuable insights into how the two IT departments compare. This technique has the added advantage of letting some of IT's customers know that IT is actively trying to learn more about their business issues.

IT is reputed to have some of the worst management on the planet. Maybe IT management problems are the result of a lack of training, or poor IT manager role models, or even the fact that IT staff may be more difficult to manage than are non-IT people. Certainly, a major reason is that IT has many managers who did not really want to be managers, or did not know what the job entailed, but took on the role to increase their salaries. Whatever the reason, IT does not do well in the manager sweepstakes. Given the opportunity to learn what other IT organizations have tried successfully is invaluable. Learning about failures is also valuable. Knowing that certain techniques did not produce the desired results might just save IT from forking over a lot of money for that circus tent and those clowns it planned for its next IT meeting.

Market Intelligence Benchmarks   There can also be some derivative benefits from a market intelligence program. A recognized way of measuring IT performance is by using benchmarks. Comparing a company's costs with the costs of similar companies, or comparing one company's services with the services of others, can be an effective way of demonstrating where IT is strong, as well as identifying where it needs improvement. However, accurate and useful benchmarks are often difficult to obtain. The major failing of the benchmarks from journals or research firms is not the numbers, but the definitions. These organizations do a good job of collecting numbers such as revenue, headcount, and costs, but do a less thorough job of defining *revenue, headcount,* and *costs.*

Accountants know that no two companies define *revenue* the same way, even though, as a consequence of government and tax regulations, revenue is one of the most common and shared concepts in business. Even slight differences in a definition can significantly skew a comparison between two companies. The only way to make numbers comparable between two organizations is to ensure that the definitions are exactly the same. This is an almost impossible task for journals and research firms.

A derivative of a robust market intelligence program, particularly if senior IT management is heavily involved, will be the relationship created between IT departments at different companies. This relationship can lead to sharing data at a more senior level. The most commonly shared senior-level IT data is benchmark data, which organizations use to try to understand their costs relative to others. The most critical part of sharing benchmark information is the definition of the data.

If two IT departments want to share, for example, the cost of supporting a personal computer (PC), the IT finance staff of each firm will probably need a few days working together just to create comparable information categories. Gathering useful benchmark information will always be an onerous task, but to make it meaningful requires a level of sharing of internal information that can only occur between two organizations that have established a level of trust.

Moving from Interviews to Forums

Is your market intelligence program working well? Are both the interviewer and interviewee gaining from the experience? Ever think of making it permanent? Many research companies find it very profitable to hold forums where information technology (IT) peers can congregate and share knowledge and experiences. These forums can be expensive for participants, but many IT senior managers consider the cost worthwhile.

Although not a replacement for professionally run forums, IT shops can set up their own forum based on a successful market intelligence program. If the security staff has profited from interviewing its peers in other local companies, it might make sense for a group of them to meet once or twice a year and expand the benefits. The companies could share hosting the meeting, perhaps on a rotational basis, with the host setting up the agenda and chairing the meeting.

If the IT staff is event planning challenged, a vendor might be willing to do the job for them. Contact Microsoft or Oracle or any vendor who is dominant in an area—and makes a lot of money off local companies—and ask them to host (not run) the meeting. The forum might have to give the vendor a 20-minute selling spot, with an agreement that there is no selling in the other parts of the meeting. If possible, it is best if the vendor is not a player in the subject area (e.g., it might be better having Symantec host the application development forum and Dell the security forum).

Two rules should apply: (1) the chair sets the agenda and makes the others keep to it (to avoid the meeting sliding into a recap of Sunday's game), and (2) the vendor does not run the meeting; its representatives just provide the resources. They can sit in, but they have to keep quiet until, and if, they are given the floor.

One of the intangible, but very real, benefits of a program like market intelligence is that it enables the IT technician to see first hand how IT serves the business.

A More Modest Proposal

The previous sections focus on a market intelligence program for junior through senior IT managers. Its goal is to (1) gain information about the successes and failures of other organizations, and (2) help IT staff gain the skills needed to interview and interact with other professionals. The nature of the program dictates that it be of a sufficient size and ongoing. A more humble approach, which could coexist with the more formal market intelligence program or function in place of it, could achieve many of the more robust program's objectives.

At the very least, IT should be in contact with the company's human resources department to learn the employment history of all IT and non-IT new hires. Then, after the new employee has worked at his or her new job for six months or so, IT staff should conduct an interview. The objective of the interview is to learn how the new employee's former employer used IT and how the IT service at the former employer compared with the IT service provided in the current job.

Some of these new employees will have come from competitors, but others will not. Some will be in IT, while most will not. Regardless of where they came from, this is an excellent, painless, and inexpensive way for IT to learn what other organizations are doing and how well IT compares with them. The drawbacks to this approach are the smaller number of people who can be interviewed, not having the choice to target certain companies, and losing the first-hand knowledge IT staff can gain from visiting and talking with peers from other companies.

SOME ADDITIONAL THOUGHTS

> *Market intelligence.* A program that enables IT staff to learn from IT professionals in other organizations about their experiences in attempting to satisfy their IT customers. Other benefits include improved IT staff interviewing skills and the broadening of IT staff professional networks.

In most product- or service-oriented training classes, participants have three questions:

1. How does this product work?
2. Who else is using it?
3. How are they using it?

Exhibit 6.2   Knowledge Acquisition Effectiveness

	Training	Recruiting	Market Intelligence
How does this product work?	Excellent for training multiple staff	Very good for gaining one person with expertise	Good
Who else is using it?	Ancillary, discussed as a sidebar	Good for information about previous employer only	Excellent, purpose of exercise
How are they using it?	Rarely discussed in any detail	Good for information about previous employer only	Excellent, purpose of exercise

A training class is an excellent way of answering question one because it is the purpose for the class. However, classes are less effective for answering question two because this information usually comes either from the instructor's or the students' personal experience, and not the training material. Question three is the most difficult for a class to answer because, in most cases, neither the instructor nor most of the students will have the answer.

As Exhibit 6.2 shows, recruiting new staff is very effective at gaining one, two, or, at most, a few people who know how to use a product or service. Unfortunately, relying on the new experts for knowledge transfer to other staff members is often disappointing. Outside hires know what

MARKET INTELLIGENCE

DOs

- Do set up a formal program requiring managers and experts to interview peers at other companies.

- Do require that the interview notes and recommendations be published within IT.

- Do consider making the market intelligence program part of the staff performance appraisal process.

- Do leverage the information gained by the program, experimenting with new services, processes, and tools.

DON'Ts

- Don't throw staff out into the market intelligence world without proper training and preparation.

- Don't let senior IT managers leave the program to itself. Make sure they prepare the way with other companies and support staff when necessary.

- Don't ignore the results and recommendations coming out of the program. Reward good ideas.

products or services their former employers used and how they used them, but their knowledge rarely goes beyond these former employers.

Market intelligence is not very good at understanding how a product or service works, other than at the highest levels. However, because multiple sources are interviewed, market intelligence is excellent at informing IT about who is using a product or service, how they are using it, and their successes and failures with it.

Beyond technology, market intelligence is an excellent way to learn about the successes and failures of processes and techniques others have tried. Unvarnished by marketing departments, editors, or consultants, market intelligence is a glimpse into the true-life adventure of running an IT organization.

Market intelligence has ancillary benefits. It allows IT staff members to pick up some interpersonal and interviewing skills that will benefit IT and themselves personally for the remainder of their careers.

There is always the risk that when program participants visit other organizations, some might resign and move to the firm where they conducted the interviews. That is always a problem with well-trained or highly experienced staff. However, as it is with training, the benefits of a market intelligence program significantly outweigh the drawbacks.

REFERENCES

The following are some literature, Web sites, and organizations that might be useful:

Some Representative Literature

Beatty, Richard H. *Interviewing and Selecting High Performers: Every Manager's Guide to Effective Interviewing Techniques.* John Wiley & Sons, 1994.

Brady, John. *The Craft of Interviewing.* Random House, 1977.

Greiner, Larry E., and Robert O. Metzger. *Consulting to Management.* Prentice Hall, 1983.

Perlich, Martin. *The Art of the Interview: A Step-by-Step Guide to Insightful Interviewing.* Empty Press, 2003.

Ruben, Herbert J., and Irene S. Ruben. *Qualitative Interviewing: The Art of Hearing Data.* Sage Publications, 2005.

Stewart, Charles J., and William B. Cash. *Interviewing: Principles and Practices*, 11th Edition. McGraw-Hill, 2005.

Some Helpful Organizations and Web Sites

Interviewing Tips

Monster.com, one of the largest job Web sites, has some simple interviewing tips posted on its homepage, although they are from the perspective of the interviewee. http://hr.monster.com/articles/tips/.

Interviewing tips from Michigan State University. http://ed-web3.educ.msu.edu/digitaladvisor/Research/interviewing.htm.

Interview Guides

The National Science Foundation offers a sample interview guide at: www.nsf.gov/pubs/1997/nsf97153/c3app_b.htm.

Case Western Reserve University offers a sample interview guide at: http://worldbenefit.cwru.edu/inquiry/files/WIInterviewGuide 2006.pdf.

Bates College's interview guide is at: http://abacus.bates.edu/career/interview/index.html.

SWOT Analysis

12Manage is an interesting potpourri of management information, including SWOT analysis: http://www.12manage.com/methods_swot_analysis.html.

Mind Tools is an interesting site providing skill development aids in a number of areas. The link below is for SWOT analysis, but the site also has information on project management, decision making, and problem solving, to name a few. http://www.mindtools.com/pages/article/newTMC_05.htm.

7

Service-Offering Management

We have company think, not consumer think. . . .
What we make is not what they want.
—*C. K. Prahalad*

If I'd asked my customers what they wanted, they'd
have told me, "a faster horse."
—*Henry Ford*

There is an old marketing tale about the pet supply company that introduces a new premium dog food. Despite its upscale image, sales are miserable, so the company hires a top-notch marketing consultant to help them. The company executives explain to the consultant that they conducted an extensive advertising campaign, ran nationwide store promotions, and even went as far as to gain celebrity endorsements, but the dog food still did not sell. The consultant then asked a single question, "But do the dogs like it?" The stunned executives looked at one another for anyone who had an answer. None did. There are many versions of this story, all of questionable veracity. Yet, within this tall tale is one of the most important lessons any purveyor of a product or service can learn: Make sure that the dogs like it.

THE PROBLEM

As has been stated in other chapters, customers question whether they are getting their money's worth from information technology (IT). They report dissatisfaction with the services IT offers, the way they are delivered, and the cost. For some, it is not so much that the technology is wrong or is not acceptably delivered and supported, but that it is just not exactly right. Solutions for user problems are there, but they do not do the job completely, or the way users perceive they should. Regardless of the precise problem, or its complete articulation, somehow, some way, IT got it wrong.

159

Users, like the dogs, just do not like it. The fundamental problem is that the methods IT uses to select and deliver products and services for users are driven primarily by what is available, not by what is needed.

THE IT SOLUTION

IT's problem is not for want of trying. Overall, IT has been diligent in researching, acquiring, and delivering new technology for its customers. Conferences introducing new products, new versions of old products, or new ways of using existing products, are sellouts with IT staff, who are always on the lookout for something new, better, or faster for their customers. Most IT organizations deliver new releases of software to their customers relatively quickly after those products are deemed secure and compatible. IT shops take seriously user suggestions about products or services that might do a better job than existing ones. Overall, IT deserves an "A" for its efforts in trying to provide the best that the industry has to offer. Most users recognize IT's desire to help, which can be seen by their willingness to attend user conferences with their IT coworkers. Still, IT seems to always come up short when evaluated by its customers. Something is missing.

Despite all of IT's sincere efforts, service development is still supply, and not demand, driven. IT provides the newest and latest, but not necessarily the most needed. IT's current service acquisition process, which starts with the vendor and ends with the customer, needs to be reversed so that IT starts with the customer and ends with the vendor.

WHAT THE FOR-PROFITS CAN TEACH IT

For vendors, success is getting the right product or service, to the right customer, at the right price. If they can do that, then the venture will probably be successful. Having the right product or service is obvious, but having the right customer is a little more complicated.

Imagine that after seeing those "Greatest Hits" classical and doo-wop music albums advertised on TV, you come up with a great business idea. You notice that no one is offering CDs of gangsta rap's greatest hits. You might make a fortune if you could get the current owners of those Death Row Records hits, such as *Murder Was the Case, Christmas on Death Row, Necessary Roughness, Dead Man Walkin,* and *I Can Getcha Block Knocked Off Volume 1,* to go along with your scheme. Next is the marketing question. The vendors of the classics and doo-wop albums did very well advertising in *AARP The Magazine,* the official publication of the American Association of Retired Persons, but you are not sure if this advertising avenue is right for your venture, and for good reason. While AARP readers have bought truckloads of the classics and doo-wop albums, a gangsta rap album might not be their cup of tea.

Your bright nephew suggests advertising the album in *Vibe* magazine. Why? *Vibe* readers are different from *AARP* readers. The former are younger and more interested in contemporary music, especially gangsta rap, than the latter. What your nephew knew was that there is more than one type of customer and that different types of customers want different products and services.

Mass marketing is the assumption that the world consists of one large market and that a product or service that is right for one customer is also right for any other. This one-size-fits-all philosophy works well for commodity items, such as bathroom tissue, table salt, and can openers, but for most products and services, different groups of customers want different things. The AARP crowd likes classical music and the doo-wop sound of the 1950s. Young urban youths like rap music, and some of them like gangsta rap. This latter group does not read *AARP The Magazine*, but it might read *Vibe*.

Selling to a specific subset of a mass market is called target marketing—you target a subset of the mass market for a product or service. Target marketing recognizes that there are different types of customers who have different wants, and that the products or services they are willing to purchase need to be tailored to those wants.

For IT, getting the right product or service to the right customer involves understanding who IT's customers are and then determining what they want. The for-profits have various names for this, but one of the most descriptive is *service-offering management*.

Service, Service Offerings, and Service Components

Service offering is one of those phrases that does not have a universally accepted definition. Many business authors prefer not to define it at all, although they use it extensively. Those who do define it posit varying definitions, but there are common themes. Finding useful definitions for *service* is almost as difficult. For clarity, this book uses a few simple working definitions.

To understand a service offering, one must understand the relationship between a *product* and a *service*, and between an *offering* and a *component*. A *product* is a material thing produced by one or more processes. The concepts of *offering* and *component* distinguish the *product* that is the whole (the offering) from the *products* that are the parts of the whole (the components). Most *products* are made up of other *products*. The steel mill considers the steel sheeting and steel bars it sells to the automobile manufacturer as its products. The battery company considers the battery that goes into the car as its product, as do the light bulb manufacturer and the radio manufacturer. The car is what the dealer is offering to sell (the *product offering*) to the customer, while the battery, radio, tires, as well as the hundreds of other products that constitute the car, are the components (*product components*) of the *product offering*.

A *service* is a nonmaterial product. A *service* can be part of the *product offering*, such as the warranty or road service the dealer extends to the car buyer. When a *service* is part of a *product offering*, it is a *service component*. A *product offering* is a customer-recognizable and purchasable material item, consisting of one or more *product components* and zero or more *service components*.

Service is a generic term that can refer to a *service offering* or to a *service component*. A *service offering* is a customer-recognizable and purchasable nonmaterial item, usually consisting of one or more *service components* and zero or more *product components*. In other words, a service offering is a primarily nonmaterial package, consisting of any number of integrated components (products and services), which is purchased by a customer or in some other way changes hands.

For example, IT can offer its internal customers e-mail as a *service offering* consisting of Microsoft Exchange, Symantec's antivirus software, and McAfee's antispam software as *product components*, bundled with support (*service components*) from all three vendors plus IT. From the IT customers' perspective, they only purchased one thing: the *service offering* e-mail.

Chapter 5 dealt with the subject of *personal service*, which is the service given to a customer that is not directly related to a specific product offering or service offering. All three are services (service offering, service component, and personal service), yet all three are different.

Service-Offering Management

Service-offering management (SOM) focuses on customers (current or potential) and the products and services they want and need. For IT, SOM can be encapsulated into five steps: (1) understand IT's customer base, including its various members' similarities and differences; (2) determine the services IT should be offering to satisfy its customers; (3) create and deliver the needed services; (4) measure service-offering performance; and (5) establish service-offering management as the key contact point for all IT services. Each step will be looked at in turn.

Understand IT's Customer Base   Saint Jude Airline had a rough start until it recognized that it had different types of customers. The services that regular airline customers, such as CEOs and senior business executives, want, expect, and are willing to pay for are very different from the services senior citizens may be willing to pay for. The executives want amenities such as tablecloths, good wine, sleeper seats, constant attention, and nonstop service. However, senior citizens usually want the cheapest fares they can find, even if the seats are small, the meals inedible, and they have to make three stops in South Dakota.

Saint Jude recognized that these two customer types, or customer segments, wanted different services at different price points. This recognition raised an important question: Are there just these two customer types, or are there more? *Customer segmentation* (sometimes called market segmentation) is the aggregation of individual customers into groups that share the same wants and needs. Segmentation tries to uncover natural groupings of customers who share characteristics that drive service differences. However, although the customers are similar within a group or segment, there are significant differences in needs and how to resolve those needs across segments; a product or service solution for one segment might not be appropriate for another.

The airline commissioned a customer segmentation exercise to investigate whether there were other customer segments wanting different services. What Saint Jude found was interesting (see Exhibit 7.1).

Although the airline might have tens of thousands of customers, they all fit into one of six categories or segments.[1] Each segment has distinctive characteristics in terms of what it requires from an airline, what is not important for it, and what it is willing to pay for a ticket. For example, spending time and funds providing expensive meals for Students, Vacationers, and Senior Citizens might be a waste of money, because these passengers would probably rather forego the meal to get a lower ticket price. However, many Executive Travelers and Large Company Business Travelers would want you to skip the cheap wine and put out the expensive stuff, even if it would add to the price of the ticket. Each segment can become a target for a unique marketing approach—a target market.

Not only can segment characteristics be tracked, but also segment profitability; and once the airline has profitability information, it can then formulate decisions about which segments to support. For example, analysis might show that even with all of the demanded amenities, not enough Executive Travelers and Large Company Business Travelers fly the airline. Contracts between large corporations and national carriers might preclude Saint Jude Airline from ever making a profit from these two segments. As a result, the airline could decide to be a low-cost carrier, no longer targeting the Executive Travelers and Large Company Business Travelers segments. It might be more profitable for the airline to rip out the first-class seats, sell the wine cellar, throw away the tablecloths in favor of cheese sandwiches and nachos on paper plates, and focus the airline on the Small Company Business Travelers, Vacationers, Senior Citizens, and Students as its target markets.

Segmentation is important because it divides the customer mass market into groups of similar individuals with similar needs who can be satisfied with similar solutions, making it the ideal audience for a particular product or service. The customer segment becomes a target market. This marriage of target market and segment allows vendors to produce products for a group containing a known number of people who share common and known needs.

Exhibit 7.1   Saint Jude Airline Customer Segmentation

Customer Segment	Segment Attributes
Executive Travelers	• First-class service (food, wine, attention) • Large seats with sleeping capability • Nonstop service required • Cost not an issue
Large Company Business Travelers	• Above-average service (food, wine, attention) • Larger seat with extended recline • Nonstop service important • Volume discounts required
Small Company Business Travelers	• Moderate service (food, attention) • Aisle seats when possible • Nonstop service important • Price sensitive
Vacationers	• Price conscience • Minimal amenities required
Senior Citizens	• Price conscience • Nonstop not important, but a direct flight is (so they do not have to change planes) • Personal assistance with luggage and boarding
Students	• Price driven • Will put up with almost any hardship, such as off-hours, flying standby, connections

How many segments should there be? For the most part, the diversity of the market determines the number of segments, although manipulation can play a role. The extreme is designating every individual as a segment—everyone is so different that each person needs a unique solution created just for him or her. A market of 1 million people would translate into 1 million market segments, requiring 1 million products. This is just

---

Customer Segmentation versus Market Segmentation

This chapter focuses on customer segmentation, but most of the available literature, including the material mentioned at the end of this chapter, deals with market segmentation. For this book, there is no difference between market and customer segmentation, but that does not mean there are no distinctions between the two. For-profits see two main differences between marketing segmentation and customer segmentation: scope and use.

Markets consist of customers and potential customers, so a market is much larger than a customer base. If one is selling a teen fashion and celebrity magazine in the United States, the market is the 35 million American girls between the ages of 11 and 17. But that does not mean the magazine will have 35 million customers. Most magazines would jump up and down with joy for one-tenth of that for a customer base. The reality is that the scope of a market always exceeds the scope of the customer base.

Markets can be segmented just as customer bases can be segmented, but they are often used quite differently. For our magazine example, the segments could be Daddy's Little Girls (teens 11 to 17 in households with family incomes over $125,000, who live in California and the Northeast); Affluent (teens in households with family incomes over $125,000, who do not live in California or the Northeast); Home Landers (teens with family incomes over $30,000 but below $125,000); and Dreamers (teens with family incomes below $30,000). A difference between market and customer segmentation is that a business could decide not to target a particular market segment. For example, the magazine could decide not to target Daddy's Little Girls because research shows that this group buys adult fashion magazines instead of teen magazines. The magazine can decide not to target (use) some segments.

For IT, the market base *is* the customer base—few IT organizations have the luxury to decide who their customers are. The processes for customer segmentation are essentially the same as for market segmentation. So for IT, there is little practical difference between market and customer segmentation.

---

as impractical as having only one or two segments, which would hide important differences. Most businesses find that four to eight segments works best.

Who are IT's customers, what do they do, and what do they want from IT? If the answer is something like, "Our customers are the employees of Ship Bottom Boat Works and they want PCs to do their work," then IT has just made one of the great marketing blunders. The one-size-fits-all philosophy of mass marketing does not work for IT. As the for-profit businesses know, to sell high-end products or services, such as IT solutions, requires products or services targeted to the customers' needs. If Ship Bottom Boat Works has salespeople who need computing and communication capability on the road;

accountants, designers, and business analysts who crunch numbers and create detailed plans; and clerks who enter orders, monitor manufacturing progress, and oversee supplies and raw materials all day; then one size will *not* fit all.

For Ship Bottom, target marketing is much more appropriate. The salesperson will need a light, portable laptop that can communicate with the home office. The accountants and analysts will need spreadsheet or even multidimensional analytical software and computers with considerable memory and speed to run the applications. Designers will need resource-intensive computer-aided design (CAD) software and hardware that can run a CAD application. The order entry clerks can use lower-power machines, but they will need fast Ethernet connections to allow them to communicate with the order processing servers.

How should IT's customer base be segmented? The easy answer is probably the wrong answer. Segments based on title or geography, such as manager and clerk, probably miss the mark. This is also the case with segments such as the United States, Europe, and Latin America.

The best way to derive IT customer segments is to hire a company that does customer segmentation. They have staff who can survey IT users and interview senior business managers, and statistical packages that can pore over help-desk calls, all to come up with a set of customer segments. Other IT shops might be able to use the corporate or business unit marketing departments that do segmentation for the business units. Unfortunately, for many IT shops, there will be no money to hire an outside marketing company or internal staff ready to take on the challenge. They will have to go it alone with little or no segmenting experience. For these IT organizations, the best way to segment their customer base is to meet with users and ask them what they do and how automation helps, or could help. They can then use this data to create a list of the functions users perform and their suitability for automation.

Because interviewing all customer staff is often impractical, IT can supplement the interviews with surveys to gain a good picture of customer needs and preferences. Interviewing need not be limited to end users, but can include IT Steering Committee members, account managers, and even vendors. Exhibit 7.2 contains a sample list of Ship Bottom Boat Works' users and the functions they perform. Segments can be formed by grouping users who perform similar functions together, as in Exhibit 7.3.

The result for Ship Bottom Boat Works is four customer segments: Road Warriors, Overseers, Agents, and Specialists. This is only the first cut. Customer segmentation should be an iterative process of researching what the user does and realigning the segments. Several passes are often needed to come up with a useful picture of the customer base.

For-profit marketers usually assign names to segments that cannot be confused with titles, departments, products, or other existing labels. For example, in the mid-1990s, Dell Inc. divided its market into four segments. There were the unsophisticated techno-to-go buyers who wanted a simple,

Exhibit 7.2   Ship Bottom Boat Works Customer Segmentation Analysis

Sample Functions	Users
Need to communicate with servers	All staff
Create and read financial and text reports	Managers, analysts, sales, executives, designers, secretaries, clerks, technical staff
Connect to firm from anywhere in country	Sales, executives
Collaborate with other staff	Executives, managers, designers, technical staff
Conduct online research at internal and external sites	Executives, analysts, technical staff, designers
Fill out and submit time sheets and expense reports	All staff
Analyze data and create graphics of the results	Analysts, technical staff, designers
Store and retrieve vendor, material, manufacturing, product, and customer data	Order entry, manufacturing, materials, vendor, and customer support staff, clerks, managers

Exhibit 7.3   Ship Bottom Boat Works Customer Segments

Segment	Description
Road Warriors	Staff who travel extensively and enter/modify orders and communicate with others, while they are on the road (executives and sales)
Overseers	Those who oversee the operations of the company and company staff (managers, analysts, and personal assistants)
Agents	Data entry and support staff who connect with the customers, suppliers, manufacturing, etc. (order entry, materials, and manufacturing clerks, customer support staff)
Specialists	Technical and design staff who need to do research, create products, and collaborate with others (technical staff and designers)

affordable home computer ready to use right out of the box. The techno-wizards were sophisticated home computer users who buy hot components from computer magazines. The techno-criticals were high-end corporate buyers interested in advanced features and productivity. Lastly, the techno-teamers were price-sensitive corporate buyers who wanted connectivity and reliability. [2]

Actual Customer Segmentation Examples

Segmentation became an integral part of the Internal Revenue Service's (IRS's) reorganization. The IRS, the federal taxing authority for the U.S. government, was organized around the tax filing process: prefiling, filing, collections, compliance, and so forth. In 2000, Commissioner Rossotti reorganized the agency into four customer (taxpayer) segments: individual, small business and self-employed, large business, and tax-exempt. Rossotti believed that the change was needed to better serve both the taxpayer and the government.

Source: Charles O. Rossotti, *Many Unhappy Returns*. Harvard Business School Press, 2005.

In 2002, Sony Corporation organized its entire operation into seven customer segments: Affluent, Early Adopters, Zoomers (age 55 and greater), SOHO (small office and home office), DINKS (double income, no kids, ages 25 to 34), Families (ages 35 to 54), and Gen Y (ages below 25).

Source: "New Approach: Sony Marketing Aims at Lifestyle Segments," *Advertising Age*, March 2002.

The Ship Bottom segments are one-dimensional, meaning that they consist of one set or domain, in this case, functionality, to differentiate customers. However, differentiation by more than one dimension might be needed. For example, a geography dimension might be needed if not all Ship Bottom staffers work out of their Ship Bottom, New Jersey, headquarters. If IT concludes that the needs of Road Warriors in Latin America or Asia are different from those of the Road Warriors in North America, then the segmentation should be expanded to reflect this additional domain. Regardless of the number of domains or customers, the end results should be somewhere between four and eight segments. Fewer segments is too close to a mass market, whereas more becomes uncontrollable.

Determine the Services IT Should Be Offering   Once the customers are identified (the customer segments) and what they do for a living (the functions) is understood, then IT can start to describe what customers could use to do their jobs more efficiently and effectively. By examining the functions, IT can begin to see the problems (or opportunities) that it can help resolve (or exploit).

IT probably does this now, but the difference is looking at the opportunities and the solutions by customer segment. This will allow a more detailed and crisp description of the problem and of the potential solution as well.

For Ship Bottom Boat Works, this examination means looking at the Road Warrior functions, understanding the problems or opportunities they face, and then developing solutions just for them. Then IT should do the same for the Overseers, Agents, and Specialists. This is called *needs analysis*, the determination of what customers need or want.

Determining what a segment needs is not as simple as just asking the members of that group. Sometimes customers do not know what they need, are not aware of what is available, or do not understand how a given technology or service can benefit them. What is required is not just needs analysis, but *intelligent needs analysis*, which goes beyond the simple answers customers give, to research how changing customer products, services, or procedures can improve their lot.

Akio Morita, cofounder and former chairperson of Sony Electronics, knew that the Walkman would be a hit even though no customers were asking for it. The 1980s were not filled with millions of teenagers asking when text messaging would be invented. 3M's Post-It® note was an oddity that no one was looking for. In each case, innovators knew what customers needed even before the customers did. (Of course, there are far more failures than successes in the innovation history books—a fact intentionally, but respectfully, ignored to make my point.)

What Do Customers Want?

There are two rules for understanding what customers want. *Rule 1*: Ask them. *Rule 2*: Assume customers do not know what they want and figure it out for them.

Information technology (IT) training, particularly for business analysts and systems analysts, pounds into students' heads that they have to ask users what they want. This is because, at least in the past, some IT organizations did not see much need for involving users in buying or building systems for them. The "ask users what they want" campaign was created to reverse this destructive trend. But asking users what they want only works if customers know what they want, understand the options, and can accurately articulate the need in terms of the options. Many cannot.

The Sony Walkman was not introduced to satisfy a customer want. Customers had no idea what a Walkman was. The same is true of the iPod, personal digital assistant (PDA), and the spreadsheet program. All were developed, not because of customer clamor, but solely based on the insight of the developers. Sometimes you cannot just focus on the solutions the customers say they need, but the problems they are facing. Good solutions often require more than browsing through a vendor catalog.

There are three sources of input for intelligent needs analysis. First, customers, through interviews, surveys, problem reports, and so forth, can tell IT what they are having problems with and what they feel they need. Second, industry sources, including the IT industry and the users' own professional community (such as accounting, manufacturing, and finance organizations) and external sources, such as marketing research firms, can all provide useful information on what users need. The third source is analysis of IT's own customer segment data.

Interviewing and surveying customers was discussed in earlier chapters. Users are the best source of information about what they need or what they could use to improve how they do their job. However, they are not the only source of information about enhancing the customer's lot.

Industry and external sources can provide considerable information. IT journals periodically focus on what IT is doing for specific industries, such as pharmaceuticals and airlines, or professions such as finance and accounting. Other professional communities occasionally focus on IT and what IT is doing for them. For example, *CFO* magazine and *IndustryWeek* are good examples of industry publications that occasionally devote articles to IT issues and successes. Other sources of information are research firms such as the Gartner Group and Forrester Research. Lastly, do not overlook the research internal IT staff have accumulated as part of the market intelligence program mentioned in Chapter 6. Their interviews with external IT staff can provide valuable information about what other companies are doing to support sales staff, comply with new governmental regulations, and so forth.

A third source of information is the analysis of the data IT probably already collects. Help-desk calls, trouble reports, system or network performance information, project management status reports, and a host of other current data resources and reports can reveal a considerable amount about the service IT provides its customers.

Although all of these sources of information are valuable, they are even more valuable when analyzed by customer segment. Take the simple customer satisfaction survey many IT shops already use. Exhibit 7.4 shows that 70 percent of Ship Bottom's IT customers are satisfied with the service they receive. If Ship Bottom did not survey customers by segment, then this would be the only information IT would have. Seeing 70 percent satisfaction, IT might conclude that it is doing a good job. However, looking at the satisfaction ratings by customer segment shows that, while the Agents are very satisfied (90 percent), the Road Warriors are not (only 30 percent satisfied). IT seems to be doing a good job for the Agents, but it has a significant problem supporting the company's traveling sales and executive staff. Further interviews or analysis of data, such as help-desk calls, can probably determine the exact cause of the dissatisfaction.

Other analyses might show how server and network priorities affect the time it takes Agents to complete a customer transaction or the backup

Exhibit 7.4   Ship Bottom Boat Works Customer Satisfaction by Customer Segment

Segment	Segment Size (Headcount)	Staff Satisfied with Service	Percentage Satisfied with Service
Road Warrior	130	39	30%
Overseer	200	130	65%
Agent	450	405	90%
Specialist	220	126	57%
Total	**1,000**	**700**	**70%**

problems Specialists encounter. These analyses could augment company efficiency and profitability by identifying new services, or improvements to existing services, that should be implemented.

Thinking should not be limited to the here and now. A common mistake is to ignore solutions that are currently not technically available or within the customer's price range. It is far better to identify functions IT should provide, but currently cannot, than to ignore them. Noting them provides future goals that IT can realize as new technology becomes available or as prices change.

The results of step two (*Determine the services IT should be offering*) should be a picture of the solutions both the customers and IT feel the business should have now, or in the near future.

Create and Deliver the Services   Once IT knows what its customers need, it can then decide how and by whom these needs should be met. The question becomes, should IT, or some other organizations, provide the service?

When IT Should Not Provide the Service
It might sound strange that one of the first tasks in creating a new service is to decide whether IT should offer it at all. The unfortunate truth is that many IT shops get in trouble by becoming involved in what they should avoid. There are two reasons why IT should not provide a needed service: (1) it is not an IT core competency, and (2) it is not within IT's charter.

Not an IT Core Competency
The 1950s and 1960s saw the rise of the conglomerates, huge companies that, it seemed, could do anything. Manufacturing companies turned to retailing, heavy industry corporations created consumer products divisions, telephone companies bought bakeries, and car manufacturers decided to build boats. The theory was that a combination of economies of scale and good management could overcome knowing little about a particular business.

By the late 1960s, the craze was largely over when investors realized that the conglomerates did no better, and sometimes considerably worse, than their smaller and more specialized counterparts. As important as MBAs and economies of scale are, they cannot eclipse a lack of fundamental knowledge about the business. The death of the conglomerates had a direct impact on the later business philosophy, still in force today, of companies focusing on their core competencies. (Core competencies will be discussed in greater detail in Chapter 9.)

Core competencies are important for IT as well. Should IT provide graphics support for the business? Who should be responsible for office wiring in Burrumbuttock, New South Wales, Australia? Should the business unit offices or IT run video conferencing? There are no fixed answers. It all comes down to who else can do the job, where the skills lie, and, not the least of all, a balance between bravado and timidity. The right, but tough, decision might be for IT to say, "Sorry, but that is just not a service we provide. You would do better to look elsewhere for someone who could do a better job than we could." IT might take some hits for the decision, but probably fewer than by assuming responsibility for something IT does not know, does not have the resources to do, and might have little interest in doing. The better solution is for IT to stick to what it knows best and to be the best at providing those services.[3]

Not within IT's Charter

The second reason IT should not provide a service is if the service is inconsistent with its mission and goals. Although it might make sense for IT to provide wireless PC support, it might not be reasonable for IT to supply paper for all office printers or install toner in fax machines. Even services that might make sense in one context could be inappropriate in another if, for example, they conflicted with corporate culture, enterprise strategy, or government regulations. For example, in some countries, telephony is part of IT because of the belief that data is data, whether it is encoded or voice, digital or analog. However, in other countries and cultures, telephony has been kept separate from IT. In some cases, this differentiation is due to telephony's roots (the national post office offered telephony) or how it is configured (individual call billing is an internal finance issue).

When IT Should Provide the Service

Once IT concludes that it should provide the service, the next question is how. IT has three options: (1) build the service, (2) integrate components produced by others, and (3) contract the work to others. However, some preparation is needed before addressing this question.

Value Chains

A supply chain is the system or process of moving products or services from raw materials to the finished goods in customers' hands. In the process, goods pass through manufacturers, distributors, and retailers before winding up with the eventual consumer.

In the 1970s, Michael Porter noticed that the supply chain was more than just a distribution network. He observed that at each link in the chain, features were added to the product or service, increasing its value.[4] Value is not all that is added, so is cost. Further, one could measure the value each link in the chain adds to the product or service and the costs incurred in doing so. Porter turned the supply chain into the more robust value chain.

One can see value chains at work almost everywhere. The mining company digs up the mountainside, extracting the valuable iron ore that it sells to the steelworks. The steelworks adds value to the iron ore by turning it into steel bars and sheets. The car company buys the steel bars and sheets from the steelworks and turns them into sport utility vehicles (SUVs). The car dealer buys the SUVs from the car manufacturer and adds value through showrooms, advertising, pre- and post-sales service, and providing day-old coffee to customers. Every link in the value chain purchases materials from its suppliers, adds some value to the product or service, and then sells it to the next link in the chain, hopefully at a profit. With the exception of the first and last links of the chain, each is both a customer (of the previous link) and a supplier (to the subsequent link).

Looking internally at an organization, Porter used the value chain model to highlight the value and cost of each step in the company's internal processes, including support activities such as human resources (HR), finance, administration, and IT. Materials, information, and even people can be seen as entering the company at one end, passed from department to department, or position to position, each adding value and cost to it. Just as the iron ore becomes an SUV in manufacturing, the customer inquiry becomes a payment in the payment-processing department, while the trainee becomes an experienced professional in the professional development program. Understanding the value and costs each link in the chain adds can help companies maximize profitability.

Businesses took to Porter's value chain theory like a politician to a golf junket. The musty old supply chain became the strategic value chain, with each link scrutinized for the value it adds. Because each link also adds costs, those that did not add sufficient value to mitigate their cost were dropped or replaced by a link that could.

What happens when a link gets weak? It is cut out or replaced. Dell decided that it did not need the retail store link in its value chain if it could sell PCs directly to the consumer. Carmakers, computer manufacturers, and many others decided that, although the American worker added value to the value chain, he or she did so at too high a cost. Korean, Chinese, and Indian labor, they felt, could add the same value at a lower cost, so they moved their operations overseas. Porter's message is clear: business needs to be constantly looking at its place in the value chain, assessing the value, as well as the cost, the organization adds to the product or service.

Exhibit 7.5   Service-Offering Value Chain

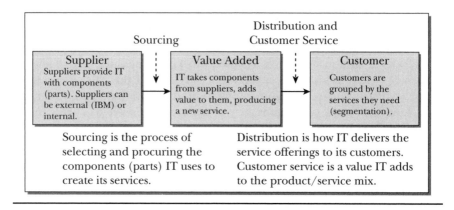

Exhibit 7.5 shows a simple value chain. The *value-added* box is important because it is the place in the value chain where IT needs to be. IT purchases products (from raw materials all the way to finished goods) from suppliers. It then adds value and passes the service on to its customer—at least ideally. We say "ideally" because not all IT organizations add value to the products and service they purchase from suppliers and pass on to their customers. If IT does not add value, then the obvious, legitimate, and perhaps unfortunate, question is, "Why do I need IT?"

Computer-based applications are the easiest value-added service to understand. IT buys computers and system software, hires programmers and operators, and then gives the enterprise an order entry system. The programmers add value to the hardware, compilers, and file systems when they create the order entry application. Operations adds value when it runs the application, delivering the functionality to the data entry clerks and reports to management.

A little more difficult to understand, in a value-added context, are the networks, PCs, and security procedures IT provides. This becomes clearer if you look at IT's position in the value chain. Like car dealers, supermarkets, and airlines, IT is situated near the end of the value chain, next to the customer (see Exhibit 7.6). Most manufacturing goes on at the beginning of the chain, where the raw materials are processed. The front end of the chain does the heavy lifting while, in most cases, the back end provides service.

Auto dealers do not manufacture cars, supermarkets do not grow corn, and airlines do not build airplanes. Auto dealers provide a service by finding buyers, taking the orders, arranging financing, acquiring the car in the right color, providing predelivery service, and fixing things that go wrong—all in your hometown. Supermarkets establish relationships with hundreds of food suppliers (so the consumer does not have to), move the

Exhibit 7.6   IT's Position in the Value Chain

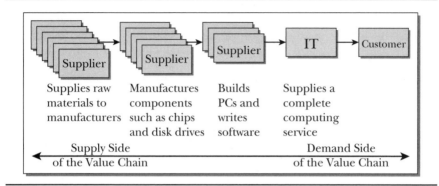

Supplier	Supplier	Supplier	IT	Customer
Supplies raw materials to manufacturers	Manufactures components such as chips and disk drives	Builds PCs and writes software	Supplies a complete computing service	

Supply Side
of the Value Chain
←

Demand Side
of the Value Chain
→

stock to a convenient store, offer a satisfaction warranty, provide the stock in a pleasant atmosphere complete with elevator music, and, just sometimes, offer discounts. Airlines do not build the planes, they operate them, going where you want to go, more or less when you want to go there—with peanuts included. All right, talking about airlines providing service might be a stretch, but the concept is valid.

This uncovers IT's fundamental problem: IT sells technology, but customers buy service. This disconnect is perhaps the major cause of user dissatisfaction with IT. More than anything else, it is the primary reason why IT and customers sometimes do not see eye to eye.

Anyone who has spent the night before a child's birthday trying to assemble a bicycle, swing set, or computer components knows that buying the best product available can be almost as frustrating as getting the worst. Face it, for most people, a BMW you have to assemble yourself is less useful than a Yugo ready to go. The same is true with IT customers, who want their IT department to supply them with solutions to their problems and not a Rubik's cube on a power cord. The common IT skill, knowing technology, is important, but it needs to be supplemented with the less common IT skill of knowing how to make technology useful for customers.

The number-one message of this book is that IT is a provider of services and not of technology products. Most IT customers can get technology products on their own. AT&T is willing to sell them a cell phone; CompUSA will sell them a computer and software; and strange little guys driving PT Cruisers or VW bugs are willing to come to their office or home and fix their PCs. Why IT? Why IT indeed!

Because IT is probably not going to manufacture its own brand of computers, and it is not going to pull cable below Cleveland's streets, and it is doubtful that it has its own satellites, then what exactly does IT do that anyone would want? In most cases, the answer will be that IT's value added is the service it provides to its customers bundled with the products

IT purchases from its own suppliers. Dell might provide the PC, but IT will load the needed software onto it, test it, deliver it to the customer's desk, explain how to use it, fix it when it breaks, upgrade it when it is outdated, and replace it when its life is over. To do that, IT needs suppliers, staff, tools, training, and a clear vision of what value they add to the value chain. In the final analysis, IT is not a technology organization, not even a product organization, but a service organization. Virtually everything else users can get from others at a cheaper price.

This will be a surprise for IT staff who see themselves as delivering technology. Some see IT as performing high-testosterone activities, such as making technology conform to standards and corporate policy. For them, bending bits and beating bauds into submission is an arduous task made all the more difficult by whiney users. The macho view of IT does not see IT as a service organization, even if service is something IT must (perhaps reluctantly) provide. However, the reality is that if IT has any place at all in the corporation, it will be as a service provider, not as a bit bender.

Many chief information officers (CIOs) know this reality. More than one IT chief has discovered that the loved and trusted telecom supplier, or enterprise software vendor, has gone over the CIO's head, trying to sell products or services directly to the business unit leaders or the CEO (see Exhibit 7.7). These vendors argue that the user can get the same or better service at a cheaper price by cutting IT out of the value chain. This is called *disintermediation*—a supplier tries to sell directly to the customer, cutting one or more other links (called middlemen because they exist in the middle of the value chain) out of the value chain. When is this sales ploy successful? When IT does not supply sufficient value added to cover its own costs.

Not all is lost. IT can not only survive in this value theory environment, but it can do quite nicely. However, first IT needs to sit down and examine every product or service it provides to users to determine exactly the value IT adds to that product or service. Then IT needs to calculate the costs it incurs providing that value and add it to the final price the enterprise must pay for it. That $1,200 PC from a vendor might end up costing $3,200 when the IT labor, parts, facilities, costs of purchasing, storing,

Exhibit 7.7   Disintermediation of IT

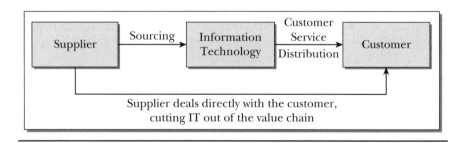

preparing, testing, and delivering it to the user are added in. This is a time for brutal honesty: Does IT really provide a worthwhile service to its users when it writes word processing scripts? Could users get better and cheaper clip art from an outside source? Does backing up user PCs to the corporate data center make more or less sense than using an outside, and perhaps local, service? IT has to be ruthless when it asks these questions because the business units and corporate management certainly will be when they eventually ask—and they will. Maybe not today, but sometime soon someone in Elephant Butte, New Mexico, or Moose Jaw, Saskatchewan, or in corporate headquarters will get the idea to use an outside vendor for some service currently provided by IT.

IT should now be prepared to address the question raised earlier about how IT should provide a service. To reiterate, there are three options: (1) build the service within IT, (2) integrate components produced by other organizations into an IT service, or (3) contract the work to others.

Build the IT Service within IT

If the service customers need is something IT can do, and if IT can do it better and or cheaper than anyone else, then IT is the right candidate to produce that service. For example, a help desk, particularly for a small or specialized set of customers, might be best supplied by IT. Although there are companies who do a good job providing help-desk support, they are not always economical for small organizations. Start-up costs and needed infrastructure can drive third-party per-seat support costs into the uneconomical realm. IT, however, might be able to handle the small incremental resources needed if the service can be provided with its existing infrastructure.

Specialized support is another area where IT might be a better choice than looking outside. While it is relatively easy to find outside firms to support Microsoft products, the same vendor would have to train its staff to support applications developed by the customer company. The question, which is cheaper, training outside parties to support an application or using in-house resources, is a math contest that IT might just win.

Integrate Components Produced by Other Organizations into an IT Service

Integrating vendor components is the most common solution for providing IT customers with new and improved services. In this scenario, to create new and better services, IT buys the materials it uses from vendors. In most cases, this consists of bundling the products from one or more vendors into a new whole, perhaps held together with IT customer service as an integrating glue.

Presented earlier in the chapter was the example of IT purchasing hardware and software from vendors, writing computer code, and producing an application unique to the organization. However, the concept of integrating components into a new whole can go even further. Telephony is perhaps one of the most finished products used by IT's customers. Users have phones at home, have used them in other companies, and, therefore, need little training or support from IT. Yet, IT plays an important role by managing the telephone providers (and for international companies, there are many of them), dealing with service outages, handling internal services (e.g., wiring, new handsets, voice mail, etc.), and finding alternatives when vendors come up short.

IT's position next to the customer in the value chain should be exploited. IT staff have a better knowledge of the enterprise, its users, and what they do for a living than any vendor. By exploiting its knowledge of the company, the user, and the functions the user performs, IT can provide tailored services with which no outside vendor can compete.

The integration model is the best example of IT playing a significant role in the value chain. IT employs others to provide service-offering components when and where they can do a better job than IT, and reserves the role of providing service-offering components from IT where it can do a better job than anyone else.

Contract the Work to Others

If IT cannot add value to the value chain, then it should not provide the service. The third alternative is for IT to find someone IT can enter into a contract with to provide users with the service. The contractor can be internal or external to the enterprise.

As an example of an external contractor, take the case of Ship Bottom Boat Works setting up a new four-person office in North Piddle, Worcestershire, England. IT traditionally provides all Ship Bottom employees with telephone service, PC and printer support, and centralized backup. That might not make sense in North Piddle. A better solution might be for Ship Bottom to contract with a local service bureau for North Piddle IT support. IT could screen companies, interview vendors, select a company to use, and then send the selected vendor Ship Bottom policy and procedure manuals. The service bureau would be servicing the North Piddle office, but the service bureau's customer would be IT. From the perspective of the North Piddle staff, IT would be providing the service.

An internal contractor could be some other department within the enterprise. For example, take report printing: If hard-copy reports are still required, then IT could shift printing from the data center to the mailroom. Having the printers in the mailroom should provide faster distribution and lower cost, because this method requires one less handoff, and mailroom staff are usually less expensive than IT staff.

Putting It All Together

The traditional way of providing new or expanding existing services to users is to study what's new from suppliers. Making the latest gizmos from vendors available to users is supply-driven value creation. The alternative is

Exhibit 7.8   Demand-Driven Value Creation

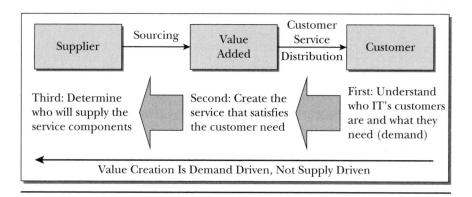

to look at what users need, or in economic terms, what they demand, and then try to meet that demand. This is demand-driven value creation and is depicted in Exhibit 7.8.

Demand-driven value creation starts with the customer, not the supplier, and works backward. First, the demand needs to be understood, then the value IT can add needs to be analyzed, ending with a decision about who should supply the service or the service components. By working with customers to understand the demand, IT gains the proper perspective for evaluating the value it can add as well as the value others can provide. Only then can IT determine the most effective and efficient solution for the enterprise.

Measure Service-Offering Performance   *Tempus fugit* (time flies) Virgil tells us, and with time, things change. Business conditions, internal processes, competitors, and staff expectations all change over time. In addition, new vendors appear with new solutions, and existing vendors provide better solutions to available products. All combine to bring into question whether the solution that IT developed yesterday is still the right solution today.

Doing SOM right means that IT must constantly assess the effectiveness of each IT service offering in satisfying IT client and technology consumers' needs. To do this, IT must periodically, if not continually, reassess its customers and its services. The reassessment should examine the following areas:

- *Customer segments.* IT should ensure that its customer segments continue to accurately describe legitimate customer aggregates. IT should understand the needs of each segment and how those needs might be changing.

- *Customer satisfaction.* IT should know how satisfied each customer segment is with IT's service, how well it helps them do their jobs, how the satisfaction might be changing, and what customers would like to see different.

- *Business environment.* IT needs to understand how well the business is doing and any planned changes for the future, such as new or modified business unit products or services, organizational shifts, internal process changes, or new regulatory requirements.

- *Competitive pressures.* What competitors are doing, how well they are doing it, and how their IT organization is supporting them is important for IT to know.

- *Service offerings.* IT needs to examine its service offerings to truly understand both customer satisfaction and how well IT is meeting its own goals. How good are its service offerings? What do customers think of them? How are they the same or different from those offered by outside (third-party) competitors? How do costs compare with competitors? How will changes in the business environment drive the need to change service offerings?

- *Sources.* Change affects not only IT and IT's parent organization, but IT's suppliers as well. IT should understand how well its suppliers are doing, what they could be doing better (functionality, quality, cost), who their competitors are, alternative sources if IT decides to change suppliers, and how IT could use them more effectively.

- *Existing and emerging technology.* New technologies, new uses of existing technologies, or new technology cost structures can provide opportunities for new or enhanced existing IT services.

- *IT's role.* IT needs to continually assess its value added by asking three critical questions: What does IT provide that no one else can? What does IT do better than anyone else does? What can others do better or cheaper than IT can?

Most IT organizations have a good understanding of available and emerging technology, a fair assessment of customer satisfaction and customer needs, and a rather poor understanding of the remainder of these areas. Even if IT has a good grasp of business conditions and competitive pressures, it might have a less useful understanding of what to do with the information. The real test for IT is how well it takes this information and uses it to create service offerings targeted to the customer segments.

Establish SOM as the Key Contact Point for All IT Services   Shifting from being a technology product organization to a technology service organization is no small change. It will affect IT's strategy, plans, budgets, staffing, and perhaps most important, the way IT staff see themselves. However, the bigger risk is not being staggered by the enormity of the change, but by underestimating it. Experience indicates that many IT staff will not only have difficulty with the change, but some will openly oppose it. For them, IT is about technology, and technology is about hardware and software. As difficult as it might be to implement an IT strategy, or portfolio management, or even a customer management program, no change is as great an upheaval as the move to SOM. Even staff who understand and agree with the shift will find it difficult to follow in their day-to-day activities.

Fighting culture is a time-consuming and exhausting process and, when it is all said and done, usually results in limited success. Interestingly, as before, the solution to this conundrum is right under IT's nose. Although this problem might be new for IT, most vendor organizations have had to deal with it shortly after their first product shipped to their first customer. Many vendors found that the people who were so effective at building the products and services the company successfully sold were not the right people for designing and assessing those products and services. Vendors discovered that, to be successful, the enterprise had to encompass two different internal organizations, with two different missions, staffed by two different types of people, doing two very different jobs.

Traditional IT is an organization that is good at understanding technology, knowing the vendors who supply that technology, and, to a certain extent, how to turn that technology into IT services. These are all activities from the supply side of the value chain. Where IT struggles is in understanding customers and the services they need, which are all activities from the demand side of the value chain.

Vendors, rather than forcing staff who excel at the supply side to learn the demand side, have created a new demand-side organization. Marketing, sales, customer management, customer service, product managers, and similar functions are charged with figuring out what customers want and then designing the products and services that satisfy that want. IT can do the same.

Traditional IT works well as a factory turning out technology-based products and services. The majority of those who work there are happy with the idea that they are technology workers. For simplicity, we can call this group the *functional factory*.

There are others in IT, though usually a rather small minority, who enjoy working with customers, figuring out what they want, listening to their problems, and solving them where they can. We can call this organization the *front office*. In for-profit organizations, the front office is the home of the sales, marketing, and product management staff. It is where demand is measured, understood, and molded into products and services. The front office creates the service-offering designs and plans that the functional factory turns into reality (see Exhibit 7.9).

The account managers discussed in Chapter 5 are part of the front office. Their job is to represent all of the services IT offers to a subset of the IT customer base. As stated in Chapter 5, account managers do not define

Exhibit 7.9 Service-Offering Management and the Front Office

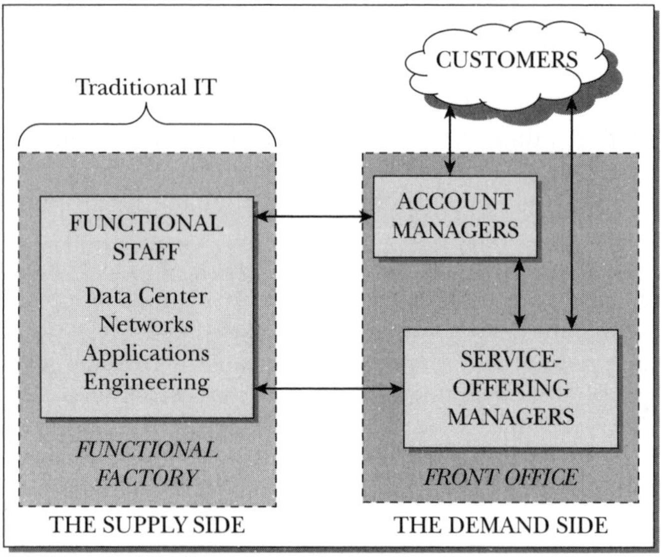

what those services should be. There needs to be another staff position in IT that is responsible for understanding customer demand and defining the solutions that satisfy that demand. A good name for this function is *service-offering management,* and the people who run it are *service-offering managers*.

Service-offering managers are responsible for:

- Segmenting the IT customer base

- Understanding what the segments need from IT to do their jobs

- Working with other IT staff from both the functional factory and the front office to define the service offerings and determine what they will cost

- Overseeing the supplier's job of turning the service-offering plans into real services

- Measuring the success of the service offering

The service-offering manager is responsible for the design, implementation, and post-implementation service of one or more service offerings. The service-offering manager, in essence, will own the service offering and hires someone else to source, build, and maintain it. To provide the best service at the best price, the service-offering manager could decide to hire the functional factory or an external vendor as the supplier. By doing this, the functional factory is forced to compete with outside vendors in the quality, functionality, and cost of the service offerings they can produce for the service-offering manager.

After the services are introduced, the service-offering managers are responsible for monitoring the success of the service offerings and making any needed changes. IT's service-offering manager is comparable to a vendor's product manager.

As can be seen in Exhibit 7.10, while account managers are responsible for all IT services offerings for a subset of IT's customer base, service-offering managers are responsible for a subset of the service offerings offered to IT's entire customer base.

Finding staff who can be successful in the service-offering management role will be difficult. A few IT staff might be interested, but it is doubtful that they will have the necessary skills. CIOs might find that, while they can train a few internal staff to be service-offering managers, they might also have to go outside for the skills. An excellent source would be successful vendor product managers.

A potential criticism of the front-office concept is that it adds a layer of staff between the customers and the people who provide the service. The concern is that this additional bureaucracy will slow service down, introduce

Exhibit 7.10   How Account Managers Differ from Service-Offering Managers

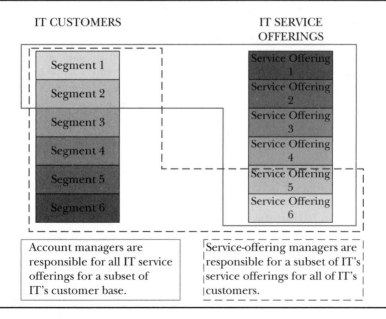

errors, and increase costs. However, vendors report that having customers work directly with functional factory staff was neither good for factory workers (their productivity fell) nor satisfying for customers (they felt their concerns were not well understood). More important, the services produced did not reflect either business needs or those needs championed by IT staff whose responsibility it is to understand customer needs.

SOME ADDITIONAL THOUGHTS

> *Service-offering management.* The organization and processes for overseeing the design, sourcing, procurement or creation, delivery, support, and performance of the services IT provides its customers. The service-offering manager not only decides which services to offer IT customers, but who will provide them (internal IT or an outside vendor), and how they will be offered and supported.

In his autobiography, Lee Iacocca, former president of the Ford Motor Company and CEO of the Chrysler Corporation, talks about the failure of the Edsel automobile and the development of the highly successful Mustang:

> The truth is you can only sell what people are willing to buy. . . . Our market researchers confirmed that the youthful image of the new decade had a firm basis in demographic reality. . . . There were equally interesting changes going on among older car buyers. . . . [who] . . . were beginning to look beyond the austere and the purely functional to consider more sporty and luxury models. . . . When we analyzed all this information, the conclusion was inescapable. Whereas the Edsel had been a car in search of a market it never found, *here was a market in search of a car* [italics added for emphasis]. The normal procedure in Detroit was to build a car and then try to identify its buyers. But we were in a position to move in the opposite direction—and tailor a new product for a hungry new market.[5]

It is a free market out there, even if the corporation has protected IT from it for years. The enterprise knows that it has to earn its way in the world, and to do that, it has to convince customers to buy its wares. Unless the company is part of the government or in some protected industry, customers have a choice to buy what it is selling or what a competitor is peddling. The goal is to be the customer's vendor of choice.

Many organizations are now putting pressure on IT. To survive, IT needs to be the company's technology vendor of choice, even if the choice is limited. To succeed in this market, IT needs to understand how the market works, how to use this knowledge to IT's advantage, and how to become

SERVICE-OFFERING MANAGEMENT	

DOs	DON'Ts
• Do define IT as a service organization, not as a technology product organization.	• Don't let technology or technology vendors decide what IT offers it customers.
• Do segment customers to determine what they need.	• Don't force *functional factory* staff to become *front-office* staff. They will not like it, and they will not do it properly.
• Do source all services with the best service component supplier.	• Don't be passive about IT's mission, services, or place in the enterprise.
• Do create a service-offering management position.	

the desired source for IT services. Service-offering management—the understanding of customer demand and how to satiate that demand—is an important component of IT's bid to survive in this brave new world.

Service-offering management can be summarized in the following five steps:

Step 1. IT must understand who its customers are. Customer segmentation divides the customer base into groups that share common needs.

Step 2. IT must understand the common needs of each segment and then define service offerings targeted to the segment needs. The offerings need to include not what vendors are pushing or what technology IT thinks is cool, but real solutions for real customers.

Step 3. IT must decide how to source the service offering. Should IT build the service offering, or should it buy it from an outside vendor? IT needs to understand its value added and costs, as well as the value added and costs of its suppliers and competitors (who might also be IT's suppliers). Three options can come from this analysis: (1) IT could decide to be the sole supplier (e.g., create and give a PC spreadsheet course); (2) IT could decide to be an integrator (e.g., purchase training books and videos and bundle them into an IT-developed training course); and (3) IT could contract with a vendor and pass through a vendor product or service (e.g., hire a training company to offer the course) as an IT course. The decision about which of the three options to choose should be driven by the value IT or others can add and the cost of that added value. The most important takeaway from this process is to be aware of what others could provide users; how what they do compares with what IT can do; and, if the others have a better solution, how IT can effectively compete with them.

Step 4. IT needs a way to measure the success (or lack of success) of the service-offering management efforts.

Step 5. To accomplish these steps, the organizational structure of IT will probably need to include staff whose training, experience, and interest centers on customers and service-offering development.

REFERENCES

The following are some literature, Web sites, and organizations that might be useful.

Some Representative Literature
Segmentation

Day, George. *The Market-Driven Organization*. Free Press, 1999.

Dragoon, Alice. "Give 'Em What They Do Not Know They Want." *CIO Magazine*, September 15, 2005.

Dragoon, Alice. "How To Do Customer Segmentation Right." *CIO Magazine*, October 1, 2005.

Driving an Operational Model That Integrates Customer Segmentation and Customer Management. IBM Institute for Business Value, IBM Corporation, 2003.

Hisrich, Robert D. *Marketing*. Barron's Educational Series, 1990.

Levinson, Meridith. "Slices of Life—Customer Segmentation." *CIO Magazine*, August 15, 2000.

McDonald, Malcolm, and Ian Dunbar. *Market Segmentation*. Elsevier, Butterworth-Heinemann, 2004.

User Segmentation. Intel Information Technology, Intel Corporation, March 2003.

Weinstein, Art. *Market Segmentation*, Revised Edition. Irwin Professional Books, 1994.

Product Development

Beckwith, Harry. *Selling the Invisible*. Warner Books, 1997.

Gorchels, Linda. *The Product Manager's Handbook*, 2nd Edition. NTC Business Books, 2000.

Lehmann, Donald R., and Russell S. Winer. *Product Management,* 3rd Edition. McGraw-Hill Irwin, 2002.

McGrath, Michael E. *Product Strategy for High-Tech Companies,* 2nd Edition. McGraw-Hill, 2001.

Mello, Sheila. *Customer-Centric Product Definition.* PDC Professional Publishing, 2002.

Whiteley, Richard C. *The Customer-Driven Company.* Addison Wesley, 1991.

NOTES

1. Sometimes customers are not part of any segment. This might be because they do not easily fall into a group or because the group they are part of is too small. A business might decide that, to be legitimate, a segment needs to have a minimum number of members. For example, an airline might decide that a segment can be no smaller than 10 percent of the potential market. Segments smaller than 10 percent would be excluded or folded into another segment.
2. Michael E. McGrath, *Product Strategy for High-Technology Companies,* 2nd Edition. (New York: McGraw-Hill, 2001), 93.
3. Core competencies will be examined in greater detail in Chapter 9, Organizational Competencies.
4. Michael E. Porter, *Competitive Advantage,* The Free Press, 1985.
5. Lee Iacocca and William Novak, *Iacocca: An Autobiography,* (New York: Bantam Books, 1984), 64–65.

8

Performance Management

When you can measure what you are speaking about,
and express it in numbers, you know something
about it; but when you cannot measure it, when you
cannot express it in numbers, your knowledge is of a
meager and unsatisfactory kind.

—*Lord Kelvin*

We're all entitled to our own opinions; we're not all
entitled to our own facts.

—*Phil Gramm*

One day a man announced that there was an elephant in the village. Six blind men, who had never experienced an elephant, rushed (as well as blind men can) to the animal and started exploring it with their hands.

The one who touched its head said that it was like a pot. Another held its tail and said it was like a rope. A third felt its leg and said it was like a pillar, while yet another held its trunk and said it was like a tree. The fifth touched its ear and said that the creature was like a fan, while the last embraced its side and said that it was like a wall.

They were arguing over who was right when a wise man approached and said that they were all right and yet all wrong. Insofar as they only experienced a part of the elephant, they were only able to accurately explain that part; but since they could not touch the whole creature, they were lost regarding its complete nature.

This story is attributed to the Chinese, and to both the Buddhists and Jains in India, and to the Muslims. It has been used to describe everything from epistemology and metaphysics to a defense of Christianity. It is believed to have originated as early as 220 B.C., yet it is included in many modern-day children's books.

One of the reasons for the story's popularity is the timelessness of its message: that truth can be colored by context. Each man was in possession of a fact. Where each went wrong was in believing that the truth held up beyond the narrow field of what he was experiencing. The trunk did feel like a tree, but if the man had raised his hand a little higher, he would have come across the ear that did feel like a fan. It was right to say that the trunk felt like a tree, but wrong to say that the elephant felt like a tree. The moral of the story, at least from IT's perspective, is to be careful about generalizing about the whole based on a truth about a small piece of that whole.

THE PROBLEM

One of the frustrations customers have with IT is reporting a problem with a service and then having IT argue with them. One can almost hear the following exchange:

Customer: "There is a problem with e-mail."

The help desk's dreaded response: "Sir, we show no problem with e-mail."

Customer: "I can't log on to e-mail; I can't even get the logon screen."

The implied "what is wrong with you" response: "Sir, we see nothing that should be causing that problem, and no one else has called in with a similar complaint."

Customer: "Are you saying I'm making this up?"

The "you're an idiot" coup de grace: "Sir, is your computer plugged in?"

Farfetched? Not really. Users routinely report outages before the help desk or the operations center are aware of them. Incredulity aside, customers feel frustrated when it seems that IT not only struggles to keep services available, but too often, IT is unaware when services are unavailable. Despite its technology, IT has a very poor understanding of exactly what the end user is experiencing.

THE IT SOLUTION

"You cannot manage what you cannot measure," was first said by more than two dozen pundits on numerous continents somewhere between 1600 and yesterday. Its questionable origin aside, the statement is quite true, which is probably why so many people were the first to say it, in the first place. When it comes to measuring things, IT takes a backseat to no one. Rarely has any organization collected more data about more things, events, and even nonevents. The average data center can tell you, in painful detail, how long spam sat in a gateway queue, the percentage of database page faults per I/O, how often cache is cleared, and so on—all, without a doubt, valuable information for somebody, somewhere.

So, after spending hundreds of thousands of dollars on monitoring software, why does a user find a service unavailable that IT cannot? The answer is that the user is wrong. E-mail was available; it was just a faulty router in Boring, Oregon, that caused the problem. The dumb user confused a router problem with an e-mail application problem. How stupid!

Actually, the user did a good job of pointing out the *sliced bread problem*. The sliced bread problem—it can be called SBP to keep technical credentials intact—is the difficulty one has of first slicing a loaf of bread and then reassembling the loaf without losing or misplacing any of the slices.

The Sliced Bread Problem

Useful work can be complicated. What the user considers a simple task, such as sending or receiving an e-mail message—call it a *simple business transaction*—can require many little things working together. Take a simple e-mail message sent from an employee staying at a hotel to a fellow employee at the office. The message will start on the sender's personal computer (PC), where it passes through one or more applications or perhaps a Web browser. It is then sent to the PC's network subsystem, where it is broken up into numerous packets. The packets are then passed to the hotel's local area network (LAN), potentially going through one or more routers, gateways, or switches, before they land on the hotel's server. From there the message is sent to the hotel's Internet Service Provider (ISP), where its destination address is checked against a domain name server. If all is okay, the packets go to an Internet gateway server to be passed on to the Internet.

On the Internet, the packets are handed off from message server to message server before arriving at the receiving company's ISP. The ISP then sends the packets to the receiving company's gateway. From there it will be sent over a LAN to an antivirus server. It will also probably be passed to an antispam server and then on to the wide area network (WAN), where it arrives at the e-mail server. The e-mail server's network subsystem reassembles the packets into the original e-mail message. It then sends the message to an e-mail application, which checks to see if the message is acceptable (i.e., is not junk mail or on a blocked senders list). If it is okay, the application forwards the message to the recipient's e-mail box.

When the recipient employee logs on to e-mail, the message is converted back into Ethernet packets. It is then sent over the WAN to the correct LAN, passing more routers, gateways, or switches until it winds up at the recipient's PC. On the PC, the packets are reassembled into an e-mail message and sent to the e-mail application. If the e-mail application filters detect no spam and the sender is not on the local PC's blocked senders list, the message is then made available to be read.

This example is not intended to describe everything that happens or how any particular e-mail system works. It simply gives an example of the myriad small activities that need to occur to complete a *simple business transaction*. Using the sliced bread analogy, every slice of bread represents an application server or a piece of a network. Business transactions enter at one end of the loaf and exit at the other end. In between, they pass from server to network, then to another server and to another network, on and on.

The majority of IT monitoring and diagnostic tools take a magnifying glass to a small component of the overall system, such as looking at how the PC communicates with the LAN. Perhaps a magnifying glass is the wrong analogy. A microscope might be more accurate, because current tools can look at an individual packet of data and tell you every stop it made along the information superhighway, as well as any side trips the packet made along proprietary back roads. The data is then stored in the tool's database for future analysis or display. Some tools could fill a notebook on the history of a single packet. All the technician has to do is sit at a PC and call up the data on network traffic between two time stamps, say one-tenth of a second apart. Technicians can also observe the length of a queue, where a message is sitting, or the number of times a database management system had to go to network storage to retrieve data for a single transaction. Going back to our analogy, tools tend to specialize, reporting on a single slice of bread.

Telling the Slice from the Loaf

Monitoring tools provide an accurate and detailed picture of a slice of the business transaction. The problem is not looking at the slice—current tools do that pretty well—but at the entire loaf. Information about the entire business transaction—what the end user experiences—resides in numerous, perhaps proprietary, databases that can only be understood by multiple applications, most likely from multiple vendors. Vendors do a very good job of carving the loaf into slices but, because no vendor offer tools that focus on every slice, they have trouble reassembling the loaf.

Why should anyone care? Because, although these tools have an uncanny ability to tell a technician exactly where a packet is or how long it sat on server xyz, they are not very good at telling the technician why a particular user cannot log on to e-mail. Information about the loaf—what the end user experiences—is hard to come by.

By and large, technicians need tools that look at slices cut more thinly than ever. But sometimes they need to see the big picture—the business transaction. When a user calls the help desk to report that e-mail is down, looking just at the systems that monitor the e-mail application is not enough. Unbeknownst to the user, he has misspoken. The problem is not that e-mail is *down*, but that the application is *unavailable*, and it might be unavailable because a switch or a router is malfunctioning. Technicians need to see the big picture before looking at the more detailed one. Just as a spotting scope is used to point the larger telescope in the right direction, the help desk needs to be pointed in the general direction of the problem before the big lens can focus on the exact cause.

Senior IT managers' needs are quite different from those of the technician. Occasionally they need to see the slices, but senior managers usually need loaf information, not slice information. Senior managers do not need diagnostic tools; they need to know if IT is, in fact, offering the services it has promised its customers. They need to know whether the total end-user experience is positive. Obtaining the information they need requires looking at the whole loaf and perhaps looking at the entire bakery.

Vendors are beginning to understand this, and they are starting to create more holistic pictures of IT's performance. Some are trying to pull together detailed data, whereas others are ignoring the detailed information already collected and trying to gather broader information afresh.

An Inexpensive Way of Measuring One Type of End-User Performance

How good are monitoring tools at measuring the end-user experience? If one adds up all of the pieces of the business transaction, reported by all of the various business tools, do they result in a good representation of what the end user experiences?

One company wanted to know, so it built an inexpensive system to test its performance tools. The test subject was e-mail. The company took a number of old, retired laptops and distributed them in closets (e.g., telephone, server, cable, etc.) in offices around the world. Each laptop was given its own e-mail account. A script was written to have the personal computers (PCs) send an e-mail message, with a 1-megabyte attachment, every 15 minutes, to another e-mail account in the home office. The body of the e-mail contained the exact time it was sent. The home office PC would read the e-mail message containing the time it was sent and calculate how long it took the message to get to the recipient PC. It then recorded this information in a database in the home office. Once a day, a PC in the home office read the database entries and created a report of end-user e-mail performance. The report gave information on the time it took each e-mail message, coming from offices all over the world, to reach the home office e-mail account.

The results were surprising. Transactions between offices that were critical to the business, and were thought to have the best IT resources, sometimes had the worst performance. When the technicians went to their expensive performance tools, they could find the cause of the poor performance only about half the time. The retired laptops were better at reporting the end-user experience, at least for e-mail, than all of the expensive tools combined.

The results of the experiment were threefold: (1) some new tools were acquired or existing products retooled to monitor blind spots; (2) some tools were retired as useless or redundant; and (3) the management team realized that it would need to rethink the entire concept of measuring the end-user experience.

Some IT organizations are taking the problem into their own hands and moving monitoring tool-generated information from vendor proprietary databases into integrated, IT-created ones. By amassing the data from numerous tools, sold by multiple vendors, they hope to leverage the detailed information they already collect to provide the broader information IT senior management needs. Unfortunately, they are still coming up short; IT still does not have an effective way to measure the end-user experience, other than to ask the end user.

WHAT THE FOR-PROFITS CAN TEACH IT

Picture a Wall Street trader surrounded by a half-dozen computer monitors, holding three phones, and shouting to someone across the room to buy or sell at seven-eighths. The image is certainly dynamic, and one can understand Hollywood's fascination with this scene. Currency traders buy and sell money. All day long, they buy dollars and sell pounds, buy yen and sell euros, hoping to pick up a fraction of a cent on each note sold. The trick is knowing when a currency is overvalued or undervalued against another. If yen are undervalued against the dollar, then buy yen and sell dollars.

But how do you know whether yen are undervalued? The Bank of Japan has an opinion on the value of the yen versus the dollar, as does the U.S. Federal Reserve Bank, the Bank of England, and many more. However, other sources might be just as useful as the Fed.

In 1986, *The Economist* printed a tongue-in-cheek article stating that the value of a currency could be determined, and its rise or fall predicted, by looking at how much a McDonald's Big Mac costs in that country.[1] For example, if a Big Mac costs $2.70 in the United States but, at the current exchange rate, it costs $2.58 in Great Britain, then the British pound was considered to be undervalued against the dollar by around 4.65 percent.

The Big Mac index, as it came to be called, is based on a principle economists call purchasing power parity (PPP). PPP assumes that, over time, the value of a currency adjusts to reflect what it can buy. For example, imagine that goods and services that cost $100 in the United States, at the current exchange rate, cost $95 in Europe. According to PPP, the price of the two currencies will adjust over time until they reach an equilibrium where the real cost of the goods and services will be the same.

How good is the Big Mac index? What started out as a joke has now been published every year in *The Economist* since 1986 and, while not all economists are enthralled with it, its accuracy is still actively debated in the economic trade press.

A few years later, Hollywood got into the game when researchers discovered that the number of per capita McDonald's restaurants in a foreign country could predict the success of U.S. movies in that country. The more

McDonald's restaurants (per capita), the better Hollywood movies would do in that country.[2]

Economists and Hollywood discovered two very important principles that would be of use to IT. The first principle is that nonfinancial metrics are often effective leading indicators of financial performance. Sometimes buying a hamburger is a good way of calculating your future bank account balance. The second principle is that you might need to uncover some surrogate data in order to understand the primary data. The film industry discovered that if you want an effective way of predicting box office sales, you might have to count fast-food restaurants. This message conveyed by these two principles became very real and very popular with senior business managers with the introduction of the Balanced Scorecard.

Robert S. Kaplan and David P. Norton introduced the Balanced Scorecard in 1992.[3] Like many great ideas, there was little new in what they said, yet their paper was one of the most significant business messages of the 1990s. Kaplan and Norton collected some good thinking that had been out there for a few years, added some new ideas and twists to it, and packaged it into a single concept.

You Want History with That?

The history is telling. Understanding business performance took a giant step forward in the mid-nineteenth century with the introduction of standardized financial reporting. Until then, business reported how it was doing however it liked. Stockholders and potential investors had little objective information to gauge company performance. As more standardized financial reporting was introduced, stockholders gained a more effective way of measuring success and worth. From then until the 1990s, financial reporting became *the* way to measure company performance—not just for stockholders, but for managers as well.

Kaplan and Norton rocked the boat by saying (if not first, certainly louder than others) that financial performance is just one measure of company success, and not necessarily the best one. Other *operational measures* are needed to balance the perception of a company's performance. The operational measures cited by Kaplan and Norton were the *customer perspective* (how customers see the company), the *internal perspective* (the internal processes at which the company must excel), and the *innovation and learning perspective* (the new products, or improvements to existing products, that create new value).

The problem with the *financial perspective* (how shareholders see the company) is that, for management, it is an after-the-fact measure. Financial reports do not tell management what it needs to do; rather, they just indicate whether management failed or succeeded at doing what it did in the previous period. Financial measures are a lagging indicator of enterprise success. Operational measures can be more useful to management because they are actionable (e.g., reduce order-to-cash time by 30 percent) and more forward-looking (e.g., by reducing cost to serve, revenue will increase). Operational measures can be leading indicators of enterprise success.

Successful operational measures need to be *strategic, decomposable, quantifiable, actionable,* and *limited*. The BSC, as disciples like to call the balanced scorecard, should be tied to the company's strategic goals. If a *strategic* goal is to improve customer service, then customer service ought to be featured prominently on the scorecard. The same is true for cost reduction, product innovation, or any other strategic goal.

The scorecard's goals and measures should also be *decomposable* to all levels of management. A business's strategic goals are not just for the CEO. All levels of management should be working toward their achievement. However, sometimes, to make the goals more relevant and actionable for a management level, or even for an individual manager, the goals need to be broken down or reformatted to reflect the context in which they are to be applied. Useful scorecard goals and measures are those that can be decomposed to be relevant for every manager in the organization. Kaplan and Norton use the example of breaking down the *customer perspective* into the main customer concerns: *time, quality, performance and service,* and *cost*. Each of these, in turn, could be further decomposed.

The measures, particularly those that have been decomposed, need to be *quantifiable*. Numeric values are needed to be able to measure progress and success. As discussed earlier, the measures need to be *actionable*. The purpose of the BSC is to generate activity toward the accomplishment of the strategic goals. To do that, managers need to know what they have to do. Unactionable items on a scorecard are no more than window dressing.

The number of items on the scorecard needs to be *limited* to just a few measures. Kaplan and Norton chose just four measures because they felt that it was important to free managers from the blitz of information with which they are routinely bombarded. Keeping the list short allows the managers to truly focus on those items, rather than reading reams of paper from which they absorb little. The ideal scorecard should fit on one page.

Kaplan and Norton's four perspectives were developed with the help of 12 companies that had a decidedly manufacturing bent. However, one is not limited to Kaplan's particular perspectives or to just four. Other authors have recommended other measures. Sink and Tuttle, in 1989, recommended that a company follow seven distinct measures: *efficiency, effectiveness, productivity, profitability, quality, innovation,* and one they call *quality of work life*.[4] In 1994, Thor recommended five measures: *profitability, productivity, external quality, internal quality,* and *other quality*.[5] Jack Welch, former CEO of General Electric, has said that he only needs three measures to manage a company: *cash flow, customer satisfaction,* and *employee satisfaction*.[6]

Many, if not most, organizations have come up with their own measures, sometimes shoehorning them into the Kaplan framework and sometimes not. Most BSC aficionados feel that it is more important to develop measures significant for the organization than to follow what someone else has done.

That said, what exactly makes a scorecard a balanced scorecard? Regardless of the exact construct, for IT's purposes, a scorecard can be called a BSC if it follows five simple rules:

1. It measures nonfinancial (operational) as well as financial performance.

2. The measures are strategic, decomposable, quantifiable, and actionable.

3. There are a limited number of measures—ideally seven or fewer. [7]

4. It marshals staff to action consistent with corporate strategy.

5. It measures the success of the action.

If the scorecard does all of these things, then most people (perhaps even Kaplan and Norton) would be comfortable calling it a balanced scorecard.

By now, it should be obvious that the BSC is not just a performance measurement tool, but also a progress measurement tool. Kaplan and Norton see the BSC as a way of measuring the progress the enterprise is making in achieving its strategic goals. Unfortunately, recognizing and following through on the progress aspect of the BSC is probably the major failing of most scorecard implementations. Poorly stated goals, inadequately defined measures, lack of will, or simply a misunderstanding of the purpose of the BSC have made many scorecards no more than just another fancy report.

Kaplan and Norton were writing for the CEO and presenting a way of measuring performance for an entire enterprise. However, the BSC can be useful for IT as well. The decomposition of the BSC raises an interesting issue. If the CEO's scorecard needs to be decomposable into action items for his subordinates, then couldn't the decomposable measures form a scorecard for those managers? The answer, luckily, is yes. This brings us to the CIO. If the CEO's scorecard is decomposable to the CIO, then does this form the basis for a CIO scorecard? Moreover, if decomposition works for the CIO, why not for the data center director, and so on, down to the first-line managers?

Even though Kaplan and Norton were creating a scorecard for the entire enterprise, its fundamental principles work equally well for components of the enterprise. Done properly, not only could the CIO create an IT Scorecard, but the successful implementation of the IT Scorecard should be an important contribution to the CEO's enterprise scorecard.

Measuring IT Performance

Too often, IT reporting is at too low a level, or important information is lost in a sea of useless data. Even if this information is of some value for IT—which is questionable—sharing it with senior business managers reinforces the old stereotype that IT cannot communicate with business-people. Most IT shops could use a good information housecleaning, throwing out useless numbers, metrics, and indicators and restocking their repositories with more practical information.

The Law of Information Utility states that useful information serves only one of two purposes: (1) it indicates whether a decision is needed, and (2), if a decision is needed, it helps in making the decision. The law reinforces the notion that information needs to be clear, useful, and actionable. The IT Scorecard can help IT achieve the necessary information housecleaning.

IT needs a credible reporting tool that lays out, for the CEO down to first-line IT supervisors, how well IT is performing its mission. While IT staff need to know the status of the technology components that make up the service offerings, senior business and senior IT managers want to know if end users are getting what they need and what they are paying for. If end users are not getting what they need, then the report needs to go into the reasons why and what IT is doing about it.

The following sections present one way IT could capitalize on the work of the for-profits. It is only one interpretation, and possibly not the best, but it does marry the successes of the BSC with IT's objectives and the needs of IT's customers.

A successful IT Scorecard should incorporate the BSC's five rules. However, there are six IT-centric rules that should be added to the five BSC rules to create a more useful IT Scorecard. The IT rules to add are (1) *IT strategy*, (2) *cascading measures*, (3) *multiple presentation formats*, (4) the use of *key performance indicators* and *performance measures*, (5) a report on the *end-user experience*, and (6) *indexing*.

IT Strategy   The BSC uses the business strategy as its centerpiece. The IT Scorecard does not change this, but it does add the IT strategy to the business strategy. The two strategies should fit together well. If there are conflicts or some other disconnects between the two strategies, then there is probably something wrong with the IT strategy.

Cascading Measures   The IT Scorecard should be limited to the handful of measures that are most critical to the CIO and senior business managers. However, IT can go further and use the one-page scorecard as the framework for a single report targeted at all IT managers and external constituents (such as senior business managers), generated from a common data source.

The BSC consists of one page with up to seven measures on the page. The top level of the IT Scorecard is the same, a single page displaying up to seven measures. For example, Ship Bottom Boat Works' IT Scorecard has five measures on one page: *service-offering performance, service-offering development, customer satisfaction, employee satisfaction,* and *financial status*.

However, the IT Scorecard can go further than the BSC. Instead of stopping with the seven most important measures, the IT Scorecard can have additional levels, each containing additional derivative measures of greater granularity and detail than the previous level. The top level could cascade into a second level containing more detail about the information presented on the top level. Keeping the one-page metaphor, there would be one page for the top level (call it level one). However, the second level would consist of one page for each measure listed on the top page. The top page (level one) for Ship Bottom consists of five measures. Level two would consist of five pages, one page for each level-one measure.

For example, one of the level-one Ship Bottom measures, *service-offering performance*, would become a full page at level two. This page would contain up to seven more detailed and granular metrics providing additional information about *service-offering performance*. For Ship Bottom's scorecard, that would mean that the level-one measure *service-offering performance* would cascade into Ship Bottom's six service offerings: *collaboration, application support, computing support, personal computing services, risk mitigation,* and *voice communications*. All six would be on a single level-two page.

Level three could go into greater detail about each of the measures presented at level two. For example, there would be a single page for *application support* that would contain items for *payroll, supply chain management, order entry*, and so on, while the level-three page for *computing support* would include information about *help-desk calls, desk-side support*, and so forth.

The final result is an *n*-level report, with the most general information at the top and increasing detail at each lower level. Exhibit 8.1 gives an example of a multilevel IT scorecard. The top page would be most useful for the senior business managers and the CIO, while the second level would be more useful to the CIO's direct reports. First-line managers might find the information on the third, fourth, or fifth levels more useful for them.

This approach lends itself to easily drilling down from a higher level to a lower level, gaining detail as one descends. For example, the CIO might read only the top level for *employee satisfaction* if its marks were high, but might decide to drill down to a lower level if the top-level indicators showed some disturbing news about *customer satisfaction*.

Why have a cascading scorecard? There are several good reasons:

- *Eliminates inconsistent reporting.* A cascading scorecard shows that all levels of management reporting, from the CEO down to an operations shift supervisor, use the same data. Using the same data reduces, if not eliminates, the conflicting and contradictory information that can result when reports to various managers come from different sources.

- *Allows focusing on important issues.* Managers can quickly scan over what is working well and focus on what is not. Seeing a red flag, managers can quickly drill down to gain more detailed information about what is truly important in understanding the problem.

Exhibit 8.1   Cascading IT Scorecard

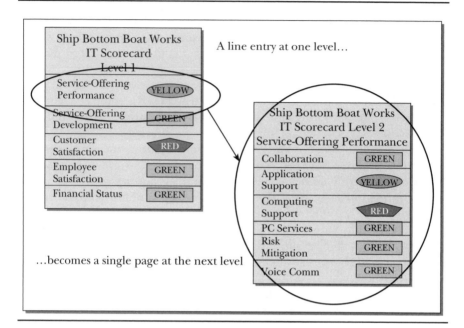

- *Increases credibility.* Senior managers are more comfortable knowing that the information they see comes from the same source as the information used by front-line managers. A single source of information will help some managers overcome any lingering fears that someone might be altering the data. Others will be more comfortable knowing that they could drill down to more detail if they wanted to, even though they might never do so.

Multiple Presentation Formats   Presentation is an important scorecard consideration. Already mentioned is the importance of limiting the number of indicators so that the top level of the scorecard can fit on a single page. A second challenge is interpretation. If the scorecard lists service-offering performance as 72, should the CIO be pleased or concerned? It depends on what 72 means. A number alone is not useful, because it also needs an interpretation. Placing a scale next to the indicator that defines 1 to 50 as poor, 51 to 80 as acceptable, and 81 to 100 as good would be better. To understand if service-offering performance is acceptable, the CIO only needs to read the number and look at the scale.

A better solution is to color code the entry green, yellow, or red, for good, acceptable, or poor. Often called the stoplight metaphor, this mechanism allows the CIO to simply scan the scorecard to see what is going well and what is not. However, there is a problem with the stoplight metaphor. It does not give answers to why the performance is good or bad, it can only pique interest. What do you do when you see something red and your interest has been piqued?

Imagine that the *customer satisfaction* metric on the Ship Bottom scorecard is red. The manager can narrow down the cause by looking at the second level of the scorecard, under *customer satisfaction* where all of the indicators are green except for the bright red *availability*. As good as this information is, it is still not actionable. The stoplight metaphor is only useful for gaining attention. For true information about a problem, you still need, in most cases, numbers.

The various cascading levels allow IT to capitalize on the stoplight metaphor without leaving the manager with an information gap. IT can use the green, yellow, red metaphor for information at the top level(s) of the cascading scorecard, but switch to numbers for the lower levels. While a scorecard with all numbers can be difficult to interpret, having a scorecard of just symbols is an even greater mistake. The best balance is to use symbols, such as colors, for the top level(s), but switch to numbers for lower levels.

Take the example of e-mail uptime. For Ship Bottom, e-mail is part of the *collaboration* service offering, so it would appear on level three. If *e-mail* is red at level three, and we want to know why, we can go to level four and see that e-mail was available only 94 percent of the time. The report would also tell us that, to be green, e-mail must be available more than 98 percent of the time, while availability between 95 and 98 percent is yellow. Certainly, the stoplight metaphor works for the top level, and also probably for level two, and maybe even level three, but for lower levels, numbers are more appropriate.

Key Performance Indicators and Performance Measures   Schneiderman[8] reports that one of the major reasons why scorecards fail is that the measures used are poorly defined. Companies often have inconsistent data definitions without ever knowing it. It is not uncommon for each business unit to define information, such as headcount or backlog, quite differently. Surprisingly, financial data is not immune from this inconsistency in definition. Discrepancies are also routine for common and critical information such as revenue, sales, and expenses.

The most difficult and time-consuming part of developing a useful and credible scorecard is data definition. What does it mean to say an application is available? Does uptime include planned maintenance? Does project effort include training and administrative time? How many hours are in a man-year? Data definition is not only the most time-consuming scorecard development task, but it is also ongoing.

Why ongoing? Aside from business or regulatory changes—and ignoring, for the moment, business acquisitions and new application packages containing their own definitions—an important analysis and decision process is needed to determine what data to use. In short, there is the data we want and the data we have, and they are not always the same.

Up to this point, the words *metric, measure,* and *indicator* have been used interchangeably. Although this is consistent with most scorecard authors, it will eventually lead to confusion. For this book, a *metric* will be the generic term for the item on a line of a scorecard, such as *customer satisfaction* or *revenue.* Metrics can be of two types: *key performance indicators* (KPIs) or *performance measures* (PMs). Information that is wanted, such as customer satisfaction, is a *KPI.*[9] KPIs provide the critical or key information that managers need to run their business, whether it's Jack Welch at GE or the CIO in IT. That's the easy part.

The hard part is where does one get the data for the KPI *customer satisfaction?* There are customer surveys, customer complaints, feedback from sales and support staff, and so forth. Although all give a taste of customer satisfaction, all are fallible (i.e., don't survey all customers, contain poorly constructed questions, include compliments exaggerated by sales staff, underreport complaints, etc.). Unfortunately, despite their fallibility, these sources might be the best IT is going to get. Managers are left with the reality that a *KPI* is the metric they want, but a PM is the metric they have to live with. A corollary is that the more accurate the PM, the more useful the *KPI.* The U.S. film industry found that the *number of foreign McDonald's restaurants (per capita)* was a surprising PM for the *KPI, projected film industry revenue (per country).* In short, a *KPI* is the metric that sits next to a line item on a scorecard, while the value of that *KPI* is a PM. Look at it this way: A KPI raises a question (how satisfied are our customers?). A PM answers the question (78 percent say they are pleased with IT's performance).

KPIs and PMs did not start with automation. For example, decades ago, before automation, managers wanted to know how long it took to enter

---

Key Performance Indicators, Performance Measures, and Division of Labor

Although key performance indicators (KPIs) and performance measures (PMs) have a very close relationship on the scorecard, their genealogy is quite different. KPIs are what we want to know about information technology (IT), be it strategic information such as *customer satisfaction* or the tactical *mean time between failures.* The creation of KPIs is often a senior management responsibility.

PMs, however, are the realm of the line supervisors and technical experts, whose job is to find the data that can answer the question raised by the KPI. These supervisors and experts will need to comb the data IT already collects, looking for a good fit with the KPI, or determine how a new PM might be found or constructed to fill that role.

an order (the KPI *time to enter an order*). Supervisors would stand behind clerks with stopwatches to time how long it took them to complete a business transaction. After computerization, IT was able to use a more accurate and less intrusive performance measure for the KPI, *time to enter an order*.

When Ship Bottom Boat Works first created its IT Scorecard, it wanted to measure the KPI *customer satisfaction*. The first approach was to count the number of complaint calls made to IT's help desk in a month. *Number of help-desk phone calls per month* became its first *customer satisfaction* PM. IT abandoned this PM when it discovered that 90 percent of the calls to the help desk were not complaints, but password resets or questions about using an application.

Instead, Ship Bottom IT switched how it processed help-desk calls. The call ticket was modified to include a box for the help-desk analyst to check if, at the analyst's discretion, he or she thought the call was a complaint. For example, an employee calling to say that e-mail was down was a complaint, whereas a password reset request was not. This new PM, *number of help-desk complaints per month*, was better than the old PM *number of help-desk phone calls per month*, but it still had problems. The problem was that when a widely used application was down, such as e-mail, the complaint numbers were higher than when a more critical application, such as a manufacturing system, was unavailable. The reason was that the number of e-mail users was larger than the number of manufacturing system users, so it was not surprising that the number of complaints about the less important e-mail application would routinely exceed the number of complaints about the more critical manufacturing system.

Ship Bottom finally settled on a customer satisfaction survey. Each month, 8.33 percent of IT's technology consumers were surveyed (so, over one year, every employee would be surveyed once). They were asked to indicate their satisfaction with each IT service offering on a scale of one to five, with five being exceptionally satisfied and one being not satisfied at all.

Throughout this time, Ship Bottom had the same KPI, *customer satisfaction*, but three different PMs (*number of help-desk phone calls per month, number of help-desk complaints per month,* and *customer survey satisfaction rating*). As the IT Scorecard matured, IT's PMs matured, with each successive generation of PMs giving a more accurate and less subjective answer.

As one would imagine, KPIs have a longer life than PMs do, because it is likely that the KPI will be supported by multiple PMs over time. IT should periodically review its PMs to see whether new, more accurate ones, that better reflect the KPIs, are available.

It is important for IT to recognize that the purpose of the scorecard is to report on KPIs, not PMs. Some IT shops can become enamored with a PM and keep it long after a better PM is available for that KPI. This is sometimes seen in chargeback systems where, in days past, IT struggled to find a PM that reflected the KPI *customer computer usage*. Lacking good PMs, some bad ones were adopted. End users sometimes received IT bills

---

Performance Measures Are Not Just Data

The Key Performance Indicator (KPI) *customer satisfaction* is a datum. It consists of a value and the interpretation (definition) of the metric. Like a KPI, a Performance Measure (PM) is a datum with a value and an interpretation, but it also has a genealogy or history.

One of the most important differences between KPIs and PMs is that PMs stand for KPIs. The idealized KPI *customer satisfaction* needs real-world information to make it meaningful, and that real-world information is the flawed, and all too real, PM. While the KPI *customer satisfaction* will probably have a life as long as IT exists, PMs come and go as the technologies, or processes to obtain them, improve or become less costly.

To gauge the veracity as well as the cost of a PM, IT must know where it came from, how it was obtained (extracted, calculated, purchased, etc.), and the costs of doing so.

---

indicating how many logical I/Os, physical I/Os, page faults, EXCPs, or whatever was countable, that the customer used that period. Some organizations continue to use these poor PMs, long after better PMs become available. This is unfortunate because only when IT adopts meaningful PMs will users start to believe that they are paying IT for what they really consume.

End-User Experience   Senior business management wants to know about the service IT is, or should be, providing them. If staff members in the Stinking Bay, Arkansas, office could not access the order entry system on Thursday, they want to know why. If the disaster recovery site will be down for two days, they want to know about it. If the network team is reassigning some IP addresses, they couldn't care less—unless it means Stinking Bay, Arkansas, will be down again. They want to know about serious events that affect the company. They also want to believe what IT has to say about these activities. Therein is the trap for IT. Remember the e-mail user who could not access his e-mail because a local router was down? If that user and others like him complain to their boss, and she complains to her boss, and that boss does not see on the IT Scorecard that there was an e-mail problem, they all might very well conclude that IT is hiding the facts.

Reporting on service offerings can be dangerous if the audience does not understand the definition of what they are seeing. From the end-user perspective, e-mail was down; from IT's perspective, e-mail was fine, but a router was down. Who is correct? Both. From a service perspective, e-mail was unavailable, but from a technology perspective, the e-mail server was fine. However, there was a network problem with a router that disrupted service, including the e-mail service for some users. Which issue should IT report? Both. End users need to see that IT is aware of the problems they encounter and honestly reports those problems. Meanwhile, IT staff need to know that a router failed in Boring, Oregon. How do you report both on one IT Scorecard? Use the levels.

The higher levels of the scorecard should report on the *end-user experience*. In the case of the router problem, the higher level of the scorecard would report problems with the collaboration e-mail service. Why? Because there *was* a problem with the e-mail service—users could not use it. However, as you go down the levels of the scorecard, the service offerings at the top are replaced by the technology components that, when put together, make up the service offerings. On the second or third level, managers see that the e-mail service had problems, while at the fifth or sixth level, technical staff can see that the e-mail application was fine but there was a router problem in Oregon (see Exhibit 8.2).

The source data for these two views is the same—a router problem. However, this datum provided two distinct views. The first is an end users' view of their service-offering experience with IT, and the second is a technician's view of the technology components that make up IT's infrastructure.

The value of the technical view is obvious; managers need to know that there was a router failure. If it is a lone incident, then the technical staff can take care of it. If it is a pattern, then management might need to get involved.

The end-user view of the data, which is centered on the services provided to users, is useful for both senior business and senior IT management. It tells managers how well IT is doing in providing the services users think are important. It also strengthens IT's credibility, because bad customer experiences are openly reported for all to see.

Exhibit 8.2   IT Scorecard Levels

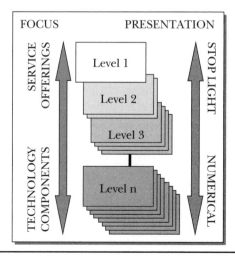

Indexing One of Ship Bottom's service offerings is collaboration, which includes e-mail. E-mail scorecard performance is derived from three components: *availability, virus and spam interception,* and *disk usage.* Availability is defined as the percentage of the time the application is up and running. Using the stoplight metaphor, availability is green if the service is available at least 98 percent of the time; yellow if it is available at least 95 percent of the time; and red if it is below 95 percent. Ship Bottom has three e-mail servers: A, B, and C. A was available 98 percent during the period, B was 99 percent available, and C was 94 percent available. What is Ship Bottom's e-mail availability? Ninety-seven percent (yellow) is the straight average, and that might be a good answer. But suppose that server C handles twice the e-mail accounts and twice the number of messages as the other two. Should IT take that into account? Probably.

The point is clear, even if the mathematics is not. It is not always easy to come up with a single number or symbol (green, yellow, red) from multiple data points. Furthermore, suppose IT concludes that the average for availability is yellow. What does IT do if the virus and spam interception and the disk storage metrics are green? What is the average for e-mail? Green, because two out of three of the metrics are green? Yellow, because the most important one is yellow?

Coming up with a single value to represent multiple data points is sometimes an inexact science. It is made even more complicated if the data points are symbols and not numbers, or if the numbers represent different domains. (A domain is the set of possible values for a variable. The acceptable values for revenue come from the domain *currency,* while response time uses the domain *time.* Domain problems can occur when operations are attempted across domains as in adding dollars to seconds.) Deriving a single value to represent multiple data points is sometimes called *indexing.* Indexing is no more than defining and publishing a formula for how to derive a single value from multiple data sources. Different weights could be placed on the different data sources reflecting the importance of those sources.

Indexing is controversial because it can imply a level of accuracy and precision that does not exist. Critics point out that the formulas used to index can be arbitrary and even misleading. It is the arbitrariness that leads to the *accuracy* problem. It can usually be corrected by establishing, publishing, and enforcing the standards (definitions, formulas, etc.) used to define the index. The *precision* problem is a little different, as can be demonstrated by looking at Ship Bottom Boat Works again.

Ship Bottom publishes its IT Scorecard monthly. The five items at level one can expand to hundreds at level five. Senior business management would like to know how IT is doing relative to last month, and the month before that, and last year. There is no practical way for IT to precisely calculate IT performance for March versus February given the hundreds of data points, their various definitions, and the different domains from which they are drawn. However, relative performance is possible if it is well defined. Relative precision (better than, worse than) for the entire IT organization can be conveyed by reducing the entire scorecard to a single value. That value can then be compared with other periods.

Ship Bottom's IT staff developed a way to convert the top-level stoplight colors to numbers (green is four, yellow is two, and red is zero) and then assign a weight to each level-one item (service-offering performance has a weight of four, service-offering development a weight of two, customer satisfaction a five, employee satisfaction a three, and financial status a weight of one).

Exhibit 8.3 shows that multiplying the numbers by the weight and averaging the total gives a single IT Scorecard Index of 2.13. This number can be compared with previous months, or it can be used to see whether there is a trend.

The source values for the index need not be limited to level one of the scorecard. Level two, or level three, or a combination of levels, or just selected metrics could be used to define the index. What is important is that the definitions and formulas used to create the index should be standardized, published, and followed.

The precision problem can be resolved if the index is used solely for directionality. While it is not accurate to say that IT was twice as good in March, when its overall score was 3, as it was in February, when its overall score was 1.5; it is acceptable to say that IT in March was better than IT in February. Indices can be useful for pointing out if an organization is improving or getting worse.

Indices can be useful, but they can also be dangerous. Measuring what is not important, or drawing conclusions from slight variations, can be problematic. However, indices can also give IT a useful tool for internal team building and for developing external goodwill. But beware: No IT shop should jump into a scorecard lightly, and indexing should be adopted with extreme caution.

Exhibit 8.3   IT Scorecard Index

Ship Bottom Boat Works IT Scorecard Index				
Values: Green = 4 Yellow = 2 Red = 0		STOPLIGHT	CALCULATED	
VALUE AREA	WEIGHT	VALUE	VALUE	
Service-Offering Performance	4	2	8	
Service-Offering Development	2	4	8	
Customer Satisfaction	5	0	0	
Employee Satisfaction	3	4	12	Scorecard
Financial Status	1	4	4	Index
	15		32	Value
	Points		Total	2.13

Putting It All Together   What started out as a simple one-page scorecard report has grown into a book the size of the Manhattan phone directory. Or maybe not. It depends on how the program is implemented. Here are a few important takeaways:

- *Follow the rules.* Scorecard success has been elusive for some companies. The primary reason is that they were more interested in *having a scorecard* than in *gaining the information* a scorecard can provide. Following a simple set of rules, such as those in Exhibit 8.4, can mean the difference between failure and success.

- *Communicate.* If IT wants to stay in business, it needs to communicate with its customer base. Customers want to know what is going on, that they can rely on needed services, and whether they are getting their money's worth. This information can only come from IT.

Exhibit 8.4   Combined IT Scorecard Rules

RULES FROM KAPLAN AND NORTON AND THIS CHAPTER

1. Create metrics that are nonfinancial (operational) as well as financial.

2. Ensure that the metrics are strategic, decomposable, quantifiable, and actionable.

3. Limit the number of metrics—seven or fewer—and fit them on one page.

4. Ensure that the scorecard marshals staff to action consistent with the corporate strategy.

5. Measure the successes of the actions.

6. Add the IT strategy to the business strategy.

7. Cascade metrics down to actionable items for all levels of management.

8. Provide multiple presentation formats or views for different constituents.

9. Define and collect both key performance indicators and performance measures.

10. Report on the customer (end-user) experience.

11. Provide indices to gauge aggregate and time-series performance.

- *Maintain a service focus.* Both IT senior management and business senior management need to know what the customer is experiencing. This is more of a challenge for IT than the business. As was stated earlier, left to its own devices, IT would sell technology, but users buy service. IT needs to keep the service focus in the forefront, resisting the sirens of technology.

- *Use a single source of data.* It makes sense that the information reported to the CEO has the same pedigree as the information used by the first-level technicians. This does not mean that they see the same numbers or reports, but that there is the minimum likelihood of errors (one system saying everything is fine while another reports a problem) if there is a single source for all reporting data. It is also most likely cheaper, at least in the long run. Using one set of tools to collect data for the CEO and another set of tools for IT technical staff will likely be more expensive.

- *Employ multiple presentation formats.* Although the source of the data for the technicians and the CEO should be the same, the view of that data needs to be quite different. The CEO does not have to hear about dynamic host configuration protocol (DHCP) problems, but he or she probably wants to know how well IT is serving the business. How that data is presented is also probably different. While the stoplight metaphor is popular with the senior business management crowd, it is less useful for technical staff.

- *Use distinct levels of detail.* The structure or views of the reports for the various audiences will need to differ. While telecommunications managers need many pages of reports to see latency figures in every office worldwide, the business unit heads do not. The top two or three levels of the scorecard might be sufficient for them. Technical staff members will find the more detailed information, available in the lower levels of the scorecard, more useful for their jobs. Senior business managers should be told that more detailed information is available, if they want to see it. One of the primary purposes of the scorecard is to provide transparency, a virtue not achievable if information is kept secret. Some business managers might want to see the more detailed information for a short period, but if the scorecard is successful, and if IT's credibility grows, most will be willing to leave the more detailed data untouched.

- *Launch and learn.* There are four challenges to starting a good scorecard. The first is developing the definitions for the information reported (the KPIs). The second is finding the measures (the PMs) that are sufficiently close to, and can stand in for, the KPIs. The third is developing acceptable indices to display the data. The fourth is starting with the right audience. This will be a trial-and-error process.

- *Start slow, but with continual progress.* Develop just a few (KPIs) and collect the data (PMs) for them. Display those few metrics on the first scorecard for a selected audience, perhaps only the CIO. Then, for the next month, develop a few more KPIs and PMs, and maybe an index or two. Expand the scorecard audience to include senior IT managers. The following month, add a few more metrics and find a friendly senior business manager who is willing to receive a test or pilot report. Get feedback and modify the process as necessary. Never let a reporting cycle pass without some improvement. If the scorecard looks the same on day 180 as it did on day 1, then IT is either exceptional or kidding itself.

- *Keep it simple.* Be wary of slick, high-tech presentation formats. A poor scorecard can be excused as a trial or experiment if it looks handmade. Businesspeople know what it is to try out something new and untested, so make the scorecard look like a trial run, not a slick, finished product. It can always be spiffed up later after it is a recognized success. IT people can become enamored with technology far more than end users, paying too little attention to the guts of a thing while the skin looks professional.

SOME ADDITIONAL THOUGHTS

> *Performance management.*   The function of quantifying, analyzing, and communicating the efficiency and effectiveness of IT services from the technical, functional, financial, business, and individual customer perspectives.

One would assume that performance management and reporting would be easy for IT. After all, IT is awash in data. Performance monitoring tools, operating systems, and systems and application software packages generate megabytes of performance data. IT management should only have to select information from this mass of manufactured data to create useful reports.

Unfortunately, much of the data produced by the myriad of hardware and software tools is of questionable managerial value. IT's task becomes a laborious bottom-up search for data that is at least marginally relevant for its reporting audience. This quest can be summed up by the interrogatory, "what have I got, and how can I use it?"

This chapter presents a top-down, performance management and reporting approach that asks a very different question, "what do I need, and how do I get it?" Both approaches (bottom-up and top-down) can be resource intensive, but only the latter can provide management with the information it needs to do its job.

Earlier in the chapter, the Law of Information Utility was cited, which states that useful information either warns that a decision is needed or helps in making the decision. PMs conform to this law nicely. Customer performance reporting gives senior management a picture of exactly what its customer base is experiencing. Talk to any marketing expert or sales-person, and he or she will say that the most important information source is a window into the customer experience. It gives the vendor an unprec-edented picture of what works and what does not. Like your grandfather, twisting the rabbit-ear antenna on top of his TV set until the picture was just right, customer experience reporting can be a real-time monitor so a vendor, or IT, can tweak and adjust its service offerings to best suit the user. In the language of the Law of Information Utility, customer performance reporting tells the vendor, or IT, when a change to a product or service is needed, or it helps make the change. Yet surprisingly, most IT organiza-tions either do not have a picture of the end-user experience at all, or if they do, the image is spotty and incomplete.

Customer performance reporting can add a third role for informa-tion beyond the two stated in the Law of Information Utility. It can provide senior business management with the information they need to feel com-fortable that those in charge of IT are safe hands. Customer performance reporting gives IT a chance to toot its own horn in a language that senior business management understands. Even the most supportive non-IT sen-ior executives sometimes harbor doubt when they see the IT budget. Many feel uncomfortable knowing so little about an area that costs so much. They wonder if the money is being spent wisely. Lastly, they are frustrated when IT either does not communicate with them or, when IT does, the message is incomprehensible.

A customer-focused IT Scorecard gives IT an opportunity to inform senior business managers, in a way they can understand, about how IT is per-forming. The good and the bad are presented in a clear and transparent way that is as meaningful as can be for even the most techno-phobic executive.

Key Performance Indicators, Performance measures, and Market Intelligence

Although most information technology (IT) professionals at other organiza-tions will not have heard of the key performance indicator/performance meas-ure (KPI/PM) distinction, nonetheless, they probably use both types of data.

If the CIO wants senior IT managers to participate in the market intel-ligence program (see Chapter 6), then uncovering the reporting data used by other companies would be a useful task. Metrics that meet IT's standards, and that are also meaningful for senior business management, are rare and should be treated as treasures.

While the senior IT managers are hunting down KPIs, junior managers and technical experts should be interviewing their counterparts for useful PMs.

PERFORMANCE MANAGEMENT

DOs	DON'Ts
• Do strive to understand and measure the customer experience.	• Don't create just another management report.
• Do create a communications vehicle for senior business management, laying out, in business terms, how well IT is performing its mission.	• Don't allow disconnects, or even apparent disconnects, to occur between IT reports and end-user reality.
• Do take the time to get the data definitions right.	• Don't move too quickly (the area is complex and will need considerable tweaking), but do not let this be an excuse for a lack of progress.

Like much of market-driven management, the end-user performance reporting philosophy, approach, and end game might seem counterintuitive to some in IT. Like a five-year-old coming home from school with his first hand-drawn picture of an airplane, some in IT want attention paid to their personal or team successes. Not mentioning in the CIO's report to the CEO that all application servers were backed up to tape in a record 4 hours and 23 minutes last Monday is like not having that airplane picture on the refrigerator. IT management needs to encourage IT staff, keep them engaged, keep their morale high, and keep their technical edge sharp. Any CIO worth his or her salt has programs in place to do this. However, the CIO must also keep senior business management engaged, and keep their support for IT high and their understanding of IT on point. The two jobs are equally important for the CIO.

As was mentioned in Chapter 1, more than anything else, IT's customers are looking to IT for transparency and safe hands—transparency in how IT conducts its business and safe hands in how IT can be trusted to do the right thing for the enterprise. Performance management is part of how IT demonstrates both transparency and safe hands. Infallibility is not required, but honesty is. A good performance management program will show that IT is flawed, that it makes mistakes, but also that it is willing to admit its mistakes and work to eliminate them. More important, it shows that IT is working to provide customers with what they need to do their jobs. The existence of an open and honest performance-reporting program shows that IT is working to fulfill its mission and strategic promises to the business.

REFERENCES

The following are some literature, Web sites, and organizations that might be useful:

Some Representative Literature

Berkman, Eric. "How to Use the Balanced Scorecard." *CIO Magazine*, May 15, 2002.

Frost, Bob. *Measuring Performance*. Measurement International, 2000.

Hoffman, Thomas. "Measuring Up: Meaningful Metrics." Computerworld, July 31, 2006. www.computerworld.com/action/article.do?command=viewArticleBasic&articleId=112519&source=NLT_AM&nlid=1

Horvath, Peter, and Ralf Sauter. "Why Budgeting Fails: One Management System is Not Enough." *Balanced Scorecard Report*, Harvard Business School Publishing, September-October 2004.

Kaplan, Robert S., and David P. Norton. "The Balanced Scorecard—Measures that Drive Performance."*Harvard Business Review*, January-February 1992.

Kaplan, Robert S., and David Norton. "Using Balanced Scorecard as a Strategic Management System." *Harvard Business Review*, January-February 1992.

Kaplan, Robert S., and David Norton. *Balanced Scorecard*. Harvard Business School Press, 1996.

Koch, Christopher. "The Metrics Trap. . .And How to Avoid It."*CIO Magazine*, April 1, 2006.

Mayor, Tracy. "Red Light, Green Light." *CIO Magazine*, October 1, 2001.

Rohm, Howard. "A Balancing Act." *Perform*, Vol. 2, Issue 2.

Rohm, Howard, and Larry Halbach. "A Balancing Act: Sustaining New Directions." *Perform*, Vol. 3, Issue 2.

Schneiderman, Arthur M. "Why Balanced Scorecards Fail." *Journal of Strategic Performance Management*, January 1999, Special Edition, p. 6.

Schneiderman, Arthur M., Jeffrey W. Bennett, Steven B. Hedlund, and George Yep. "Time to Unbalance Your Scorecard." *Strategy + Business*, Issue 24, Third Quarter 2001, p. 12.

Sink, D. S., and T. C. Tuttle. *Planning and Measurement in Your Organization of the Future*. Industrial Engineering and Management Press, 1989.

Thor, C. G. *The Measures of Success: Creating a High Performance Organization*. Oliver Wright Publications, 1994.

Tillmann, George. "A CIO's View of the Balanced Scorecard." *Strategy + Business*, Issue 34, Spring 2004, pp. 16–21.

Some Helpful Organizations and Web Sites
Balanced Scorecard Institute, www.balancedscorecard.org U.S. Foundation for Performance Measurement, www.netmain.com/usfpm/

NOTES

1. "Fast Food and Strong Currencies: The Economist Big Mac Index," *The Economist*, 76, June 9, 2005.
2. C. Samuel Craig, William H. Greene, Susan P. Douglas, "Culture Matters: Consumer Acceptance of U.S. Films in Foreign Markets," *Journal of International Marketing*, Vol. 13, No. 4, Winter 2005, pp. 80–103.
3. Robert S. Kaplan and David P. Norton, "The Balanced Scorecard—Measures That Drive Performance," *Harvard Business Review*, January-February 1992.
4. D. S. Sink and T. C. Tuttle, *Planning and Measurement in Your Organization of the Future*, Industrial Engineering and Management Press, 1989.
5. C. G. Thor, *The Measures of Success: Creating a High-Performance Organization*, Oliver Wright Publications, Inc., 1994.
6. At a Computerworld conference in Scottsdale, Arizona, in early 2003, Warren Bennis, author and professor at the University of Southern California, showed a video of his interview with Jack Welch, CEO of General Electric, made some years earlier. In the video, Bennis asked about the management measures Welch and his team used and the technology created to produce them. Welch interrupted Bennis to say that all he really needed to run a company were three measures: cash flow, customer satisfaction, and employee satisfaction.
7. Arthur M. Schneiderman, "Why Balanced Scorecards Fail," *Journal of Strategic Performance Management*, January 1999, Special Edition, p. 6.
8. *Ibid.*
9. For some authors, a Key Performance Indicator (KPI) is used only to track a strategic objective. They would object to a KPI being applied for nonstrategic information, such as *help-desk call resolution time*. However, this author believes that the definitions presented in this book, for both a KPI and a performance measure (PM), are more relevant and functional for IT than definitions embraced by other authors.

PART THREE
PUSHING THE ENVELOPE

9

Organizational Competencies

I believe the true road to preeminent success in any
line is to make yourself master in that line. I have no
faith in the policy of scattering one's resources.
—*Andrew Carnegie*

We should be careful to get out of an experience only
the wisdom that is in it—and stop there.
—*Mark Twain*

In some ways, the 1970s were the heyday of the programmer. Vendors,
particularly hardware vendors, wrote systems software, such as operating
systems, file and database management systems, and teleprocessing monitors, but rarely delved into application software. The same was true for
third-party software vendors, who focused on systems software and a few
application development tools. Applications were written by in-house staff,
who cranked out the proprietary payroll, accounts payable, and order entry
systems the company needed to run its business.

THE PROBLEM

The heyday was short-lived. By the late 1970s and early 1980s, the number
of cost overruns, missed deadlines, missing or inaccurate functionality, and
project failures had become an epidemic. The problem was twofold. First,
information technology (IT) as a service provider, particularly of internally
developed computer-based applications, was showing cracks. The need
for larger, complex, and integrated applications was too much for what
was largely an organization based on individual programmer skills. Late,
inadequate, and expensive projects were the result of, at least according to
the business, a lack of organizational professionalism. There was a general

217

consensus among business managers that the cowboy programmer was destined for that ride into the sunset. If IT could not provide a more professional approach, then the enterprise would do business with the growing number of new third-party application software developers. The message was clear: IT had to straighten up and become more business-like, or its function would be outsourced.

Second, IT was fighting an identity crisis; some might even say an inferiority complex. Its cowboy self-image was maligned by its overhead status. IT was a new science, a new component of the business enterprise, and, in IT's mind at least, the future of—everything. How could IT be viewed as just a support organization, and a poor one at that? It is hard to be meek when you know you are destined for greatness. After all, IT was not like the submissive and longanimous accountants, who were long ago beaten into corporate submission (conveniently forgetting, of course, that many of those same acquiescent accountants are now running those corporations). IT had something to prove to the parvenu now occupying corner offices throughout the enterprise. IT would become more business-like. IT would become a business.

THE IT SOLUTION

And so it came to be. In 1979, Saint Jude Airlines had just completed its new payroll system for the staggering sum of $100,000. Although it functioned well, the cost nearly threw the chief financial officer (CFO) and chief executive officer (CEO) into convulsions. Then the chief information officer (CIO) had an idea. He knew the CIO at Ship Bottom Boat Works and that Ship Bottom was thinking about rewriting its payroll system. What if the airline could sell its new payroll system to Ship Bottom? Say for $50,000? It would be win-win. Saint Jude would recover half of its payroll investment, and Ship Bottom would get a new payroll system for half of what a new one would cost. And if Saint Jude could find a second customer, then it could recover the total cost of the application. A third customer would put the company in the black and change IT from a stodgy old cost center into a bona fide profit center.

Saint Jude was not alone. The late 1970s, and especially the early 1980s, saw many companies entering the application package market. Why build when you can buy? If you build, why not sell it to others and make a buck or two from all that work? Soon, everybody who was anybody was trying to sell something. Like an insecure child trying to gain approval from an emotionally distant father, IT struggled for recognition as an equal with line management by showing that it too could generate revenue. But it was not to be.

Much to Saint Jude's chagrin, its new payroll customers were not satisfied to purchase their software and then go away. They wanted support.

Ship Bottom, and the others who bought the payroll package, wanted the bugs fixed and better documentation. They needed training classes and help-desk support. They wanted new releases as tax laws changed and additional options for benefits and deductions. That quick $50,000 became a sinkhole of new and ongoing costs.

Saint Jude, Ship Bottom, and others learned a valuable lesson: It takes more than good software to be a software vendor. It takes *being* a vendor. Being a successful vendor is more than writing good code; it is even more than having 24-hour support. Being a successful vendor requires the culture, training, motivation, and desire to be a vendor—something most internal IT organizations did not want any part of. A considerable number of skills, processes, and motivations are needed to be an internal systems provider. These are neither more, nor less, difficult or complex than the skills, processes, and motivations needed to be a vendor—but they are different.

The "be more like a business" message, combined with IT's desire to prove itself, made IT sticking its toe in the for-profit waters irresistible. IT almost had it right. Looking to the for-profits for guidance about how to survive in the corporate world was the right approach; IT just went about it the wrong way. IT's method of acting more business-like and proving its value to the enterprise left it open to new criticisms.

Not many things have changed in the last 30 years. IT organizations are still being told that they have to be more business-like. The new millennium is filled with stories and testimonials on every newsstand about *running IT like a business* (RITLAB). Add a book about market-driven management, that touts IT copying what technology vendors do right, and is this another potential disaster? Maybe.

Despite encouragement from the business, IT's decision to become a profit center was a self-inflicted wound. The real takeaway from RITLAB, market-driven management, and all the other IT self-help techniques is not to become a vendor, but to take from vendors, and elsewhere, the techniques and tips that work for a support organization. It is not *imitation* of the for-profits that is needed, but *selective emulation*.

WHAT THE FOR-PROFITS CAN TEACH IT

Saint Jude did not fail in its for-profit software venture because it did not have the intelligence or stamina, but because it was an airline. One of the important lessons businesses learned in the late 1970s and early 1980s—which had nothing to do with IT, but everything to do with being a successful business—is to stick with what you do best. Find your competencies and focus on them. What should an organization do about the remainder of what has to be done? Hire someone whose competencies are more in line with what is needed. Need a payroll package? Hire a company that specializes in payroll packages; or better yet, hire a company that is an expert in doing payrolls.

A Cautionary Tale

As mentioned in Chapter 7, the 1960s was the age of the conglomerate, when the best and the brightest believed that economies of scale and good, solid, if only general, management skills were all a company needed to excel. Large conglomerates, supported by armies of MBAs, entered industries formerly dominated by small to mid-sized companies. The result was some rather strange bedfellows. For example, ITT, originally named the International Telephone and Telegraph Company, bought more than 300 businesses during the 1960s, including a bakery, a car rental company, a hotel chain, an auto parts supplier, and a cosmetics company. Litton Industries, originally a manufacturer of navigation equipment, bought furniture makers, a cash register company, and appliance manufacturers. Textron, a yarn manufacturer, bought companies that produced radar antennas, chainsaws, plywood, cruise ships, helicopters, photocopy paper, and pharmaceuticals. Gulf and Western started out as a stamping and plating company but later bought a movie studio, a publishing house, and the Miss Universe contest, among other properties.

Some companies, like General Electric (GE), did it right, but most lost considerable sums of money when the economy turned sour during the late 1960s and early 1970s. The lesson learned from the era of the conglomerates is that size and raw brainpower are not enough; you also have to know what you are doing. Expertise, be it in the manufacture, sales, or support of a product, is needed to be successful.

Formalizing this sound advice would have to wait until the 1990s, when Prahalad and Hamel probably coined, but certainly popularized, the phrase *core competency*.[1] They argued that corporations could not do everything well. Rather, a company should focus on what it does best, where its skills are unique, and where it can beat its competitors. They called this sweet spot the core competence, the place where senior management should put all of its energies.

Core Competencies

A core competency is (1) attractive to a sufficiently large market, (2) perceived by customers as generating products or services that provide a significant benefit, and (3) not easily imitated by competitors.

Prahalad and Hamel gave two examples in their 1990 paper, one of doing it right and one of doing it wrong. NEC, the Japanese technology giant, worked to "exploit the convergence" of the communications and computer technologies. It recognized its core competence, communications, melded well with the emerging semiconductor market and would provide a powerful combination that had market potential, could generate great products, and that competitors would find hard to copy. NEC is still a worldwide technology player with 2006 revenue of about $40 billion.

Prahalad and Hamel also cited the larger GTE, the U.S. communications giant, that had, according to them, lacked "clarity" in its strategic goals. GTE did not adequately identify and exploit its core competencies. Some years after the publication of Prahalad and Hamel's article, GTE was acquired by Verizon.

Core Competency Versus Individual Competency

The word *competency* can be confusing. In its most popular uses, the word is applied not to an organization, but to an individual, where it usually refers to a personal skill. Prahalad and Hamel apply the word to an organization. They reserve *core competence* for skills that are pervasive throughout the organization, can produce multiple products or services that are needed by a number of markets, and are not easily found in competitors.

Recent usage has applied the phrase *core competency* to individuals as well. For example, the American Institute of Certified Public Accountants (AICPA) has developed what it calls a set of skills-based competencies needed by all students entering the accounting profession.

The same is true for the Association of Schools of Public Health (ASPH), which has its own set of core competencies for public health experts.

It is important for the reader to remember that for Prahalad and Hamel, a core competency is a property of an organization and not an individual.

Source: AICPA Web site http://ceae.aicpa.org/Resources/Education+and+ Curriculum+Development/Core+Competency+Framework+and+ Educational+Competency+Assessment+Web+Site/. ASPH Web site http://www.asph.org/document.cfm?page=851.

As Prahalad and Hamel saw it, the problem in the West was the dominant management style of holding a diversified portfolio of businesses. Large Western corporations were organized and run as federations of separate businesses, with each business unit having a significant level of autonomy. Assets, such as staff, were viewed as owned by the business unit, rather than by the corporation. Cooperation among business units was minimal, formal, and transactional.

The problems in the West went further. Price and performance dominated the Western management style. When a product line or a business unit could no longer maintain its level of profitability, it was broken up or sold. In the former case, partners were found to provide the least profitable product components. Consumer products companies looked to Asia to provide cheap components for radios, TVs, and computers. Eventually the entire product was manufactured by overseas companies, which gained the competency for producing these products.

Asian companies, or at least the good ones, looked at the landscape differently, through the following approaches:

- *Identify core competencies.* Asian companies identified, not core markets, not core businesses, but core competencies as their most important assets.

- *Target the intersection of competencies.* The winning companies targeted areas where competencies merged or intersected. For example, Sony's core competencies are in electronics and miniaturization, while Canon has competencies in optics, imaging, and microprocessor controls. Sony built the Walkman, small TVs, and miniature camcorders. Canon used its competencies to build cameras, copiers, laser printers, and image scanners. Both companies are market leaders, major players in some markets and dominant in others. Focusing on core competencies can bring about significant revolutionary products from simple synergies between competencies. In essence, companies like these spawned a product revolution through competency evolution.

- *Require that every business unit use and contribute competencies.* Successful companies are organized so that every business contributes to the corporate competencies and is expected to exploit them. Competencies are owned not by business units, but by the corporation. Staff with core competency skills can be moved anywhere within the corporation at the corporation's discretion. Sony ensures that its miniaturization experts work with its electronics experts. For Canon, core competent staff are routinely moved back and forth between the camera and copier divisions.

- *Ensure that management focuses on competency development.* Senior management's role is quite different in Asia, where it focuses on competency development and nourishment. Managers are expected to:

    - *Identify future core competencies.* Competencies have a long life, probably in the range of a decade or more, spanning the life cycles of multiple product lines. However, they will not last forever, and because it might take a decade to develop a competency, the corporation has to be constantly on the lookout for new ones.

    - *Build needed competencies and maintain those that are strong.* By moving staff with core competency skills around the corporation, knowledge is spread and new core competency–based products, called core products, can be developed across the company.

    - *Reward staff and businesses for developing and using the competencies.* Recognition and rewards for gaining and exploiting core competencies need to be corporate-wide, not just within a business unit.

Look at Ship Bottom Boat Works: For years, Ship Bottom was known for its molded wood hulls. It invented a precise and complex process of steaming three different types of wood, treating the layers with an internally developed adhesive, and compressing them together under considerable pressure. The resulting boat hull was strong, flexible, and lightweight; yet it still held all the beauty of natural wood. The process also allowed the wood to be molded into shapes that were useful for the interior of the boat or on the deck. Ship Bottom's decorative shelving and cabinets, as well as the sturdy, yet stunning, deck combings and wood fittings, were well known in boating circles. However, labor costs were placing significant pressures on the company. Ship Bottom had to reduce costs if it was to keep its traditional margins.

When Is a Competency a Core Competency?

Having information technology (IT) staff with sufficient identical, similar, or related skills organized in such a way that the skilled staff can constructively work together constitutes a competency.

Discovering that all of the data center staff members are expert tap dancers means that they are skilled individuals, but it does not necessarily mean that the skills constitute an organizational competency. However, if the dancers can work together to produce a tap dance extravaganza, or even just a small demonstration, then they probably have a competency. But is this competency a core competency? To answer this question, one must look at Prahalad and Hamel's three rules:

Rule 1: Is the competency something that a large number of IT's customers could benefit from?

Rule 2: Does (can) the competency contribute to products or services that provide significant benefit to IT's customers?

Rule 3: Is the competency difficult for competitors to imitate?

If the answer to the three questions is Yes, then the competency is a core competency, and the products or services this competency produces are core products or core services. If the answer to any of them is No, then the competency is not a core competency, and products or services produced from it are not core products or core services.

The owners of Ship Bottom decided to take action. They would outsource the production of the brass and chrome deck fittings to a company in Mexico and the cabinetry to a company in Taiwan. The results were positive. After a learning period, both the plant in Mexico and the one in Taiwan were producing deck fittings and cabinets in quantity, of acceptable quality, and at reduced cost. Two years into the change, Ship Bottom had Taiwan producing some of the more expensive, but complex, hull moldings as well. Ship Bottom managers thought this was a good idea, because now the company had two sources for its molded wood products. If there was a problem at one plant, such as a strike or a fire, the slack could be taken up by the other one.

Over the next five years, things did not go as well. The number of people in the Ship Bottom, New Jersey, plant who knew how to produce the signature molded-wood products decreased, and the average age of those who remained increased, getting close to retirement. Worse, the Taiwan company was taken over by a Japanese boat-building conglomerate that could easily compete with Ship Bottom using Ship Bottom's homegrown technology.

Outsourcing the deck fixtures to Mexico was a good idea. Ship Bottom had no distinctive or unique ability in making deck fittings. These fittings were commodity items, produced by dozens of factories world-wide (see Exhibit 9.1). The wood moldings were another story. It was Ship Bottom's core product, and the manufacturing process was its core competency. Rather than protect that competency, Ship Bottom gave it away to an eventual competitor. Worse, in having someone else produce its core products, Ship Bottom reduced its own competence in making them.

The moral of the story is clear: Identify, protect, and grow core competencies. Produce core products that rely on the core competencies. Identify end products that do not rely on core competencies or can be produced easily by competitors. Consider outsourcing, subcontracting, or

Exhibit 9.1   Core Competencies and Core Services

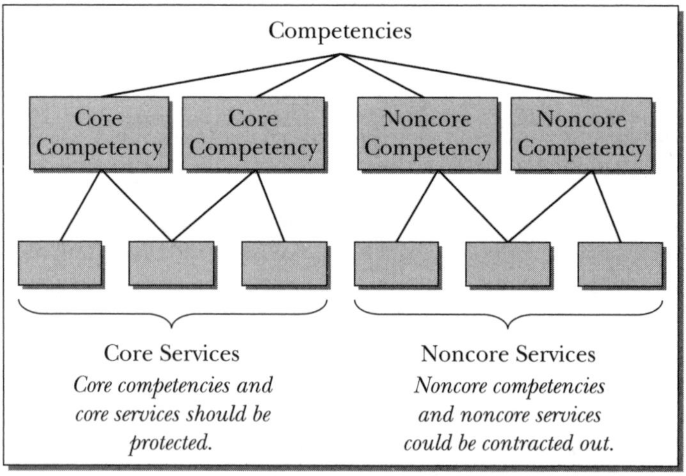

divesting the production of these noncore competency end products or components. Never, never let others produce your core products.

Porter, Prahalad, and Hamel, Oh My!

In science, as in business, a new good idea becomes a great idea when it fits in nicely with other good ideas. Physicists tell us that Einstein's Special Theory of Relativity completed the work of Faraday and Maxwell on electromagnetic radiation. Likewise, his General Theory of Relativity completed the circle started by Galileo's and then Newton's well-used, but less understood, laws of gravity. For the rest of us, what would Baskin be without Robbins? Prahalad and Hamel's core competency concept fits in nicely with Michael Porter's competitive advantage (see Chapter 7). While Porter said that a company should focus where it had a competitive advantage, he provided little information on how to identify or acquire such an advantage. Prahalad and Hamel completed the work of Porter by showing that a company can identify or acquire a competitive advantage by focusing on its core competencies.

Saint Jude Airlines entered the application package industry before Porter, Prahalad, and Hamel published their respective works. Had IT waited until 1990 to start its venture, things might have been different. Saint Jude would have recognized that its core competency was in shipping people and freight around the country by airplane, not in developing, marketing, selling, and supporting application packages. It would have seen that it had no core competency in being a technology vendor, and that it held no competitive advantage over anyone else on the planet with a working payroll system.

Veni, Vidi, Vendor

Market-driven management techniques, such as strategy, governance, portfolio management, customer management, market intelligence, service-offering management, and performance management, are all business concepts in which the best businesses excel. Even so, neither market-driven management nor RITLAB, taken by themselves or together, make a vendor, but they can do a good job of making a first-rate IT organization.

Some technical staff want to work for a technology vendor and some want to work for an internal service organization. Assuming these people have an inkling of what they are doing, then IT would be wise to take these staff decisions as sound judgment. Without stating it, these technogentsia know the difference between the two professions, know that they require different skills, different temperaments, and even different cultures, and that their career choice is the one that best suits them.

IT management needs to do the same. It needs to decide whether it wants to be a vendor or an internal service organization. This is not a snap decision, but should involve an examination of IT's mission, culture, competencies, and any competitive advantage it might have.

Exhibit 9.2 applies the work of Porter, Prahalad, and Hamel to a profile of a typical IT organization. The results are quite interesting, although not surprising.

To be a successful vendor of a product or service that passes the Porter, Prahalad, Hamel screen would be difficult and a rare exception for an internal service provider. IT would need to develop a unique solution for its internal clients that also fulfilled the needs of some external organizations—needs that were not already being filled by external vendors.

Exhibit 9.2 Applying Porter, Prahalad, and Hamel to Most IT Organizations

IT's potential core competencies	1. Knowledge of some technology products in a number of different technology areas. Proficient in most, expert in few to none. 2. Extensive knowledge of the parent organization's business. 3. Excellent knowledge of the business processes, the people who run and maintain the business, and the technology they need.
Attractive to a sufficiently large market?	1. No 2. Only the business 3. Only the business
Customers perceive the benefit of the competency?	1. No 2. Yes 3. Yes
The core competencies are something competitors cannot easily imitate?	1. IT's knowledge of technology is easily replicated. 2. IT's knowledge of the business is not easily replicated. 3. IT's ability to automate the business is not easily replicated.
Competitive advantage?	1. No 2. Yes 3. Yes
Which potential core competencies pass the screen?	2. Extensive knowledge of the parent organization's business. 3. Excellent knowledge of the business processes, the people who run and maintain the business, and the technology they need.

This has happened in the past, but in almost every case, it turned out to be an unexpected result. American Airlines' internal Sabre reservation system became a popular package used by several other airlines. The World Wide Web started out as an internal filing and file-sharing system for the Conseil Européen pour la Recherche Nucléaire, or European Council for Nuclear Research (CERN) in Switzerland. In both cases, there was no original plan to market or make the system available outside of the organization. In both cases, the decision to let the system expand beyond its internal base was made after the system was internally installed, used, and deemed very successful. Then, and only then, was there speculation about its external potential.

Even so, the decisions both organizations made were to keep their internal IT organization the same and far away from functioning as an external vendor. CERN made the specifications for the World Wide Web public, thus essentially washing its hands of it. American Airlines eventually set up a separate organization to market, sell, and support the airline reservation system. Both organizations knew that it was folly to have the internal IT support organization also function as an external vendor.

This makes sense. What CEO is going to let an internal IT organization spend money developing products or services for noncompany use? Virtually every product or service developed for internal use that became a successful external product or service was unplanned. Moreover, in virtually every case, the new external product was turned over to an external organization to peddle it.

Applying Porter, Prahalad, and Hamel to IT

While Porter, Prahalad, and Hamel might have dashed IT's hopes of being the next Google, they can still help an IT organization be successful in its critical, though perhaps less glamorous, internal support role. These authors were writing for CEOs of large enterprises and not for CIOs. Some of their concepts do not exactly fit, and sometimes the language is not on point, but there is sufficient meat left on the bones to make a satisfying meal for IT.

It should now be clear that most IT shops have a set of competencies that allow them to compete with, and beat, almost every other technology organization on Earth, if they use them correctly. First, IT knows the business better than any other technology organization. It has worked with the same business managers and staff for decades. It is familiar with the corporation's culture, its tolerance for risk, what the business's customers want, and how it generates revenue. Second, IT has decades of knowledge applying technology to the business. It knows what has worked in the past, what has not worked, and what will likely please its users.

Understanding its core competencies completes the picture. IT can now appreciate what it does better than anyone else. It can understand its competitive advantage and how it can compete with even the most aggressive competitor. Lastly, it can now provide its customers with the services they want and need.

Any outside vendor would love to have these competencies. With them, it could probably push IT aside and deal directly with corporate or the business units. IT would be totally disintermediated. But outside vendors do not have these competencies. Their only hope of supplanting IT is if IT does not exploit its competencies with efficient and effective core services.

Not Just Surviving, but Thriving

IT can exploit the work of Porter, Prahalad, and Hamel by following three simple steps. The CIO and the IT management should:

1. *Identify IT's core competencies.* IT should list all of its competencies, such as application development, network design and management, the help desk, and so forth. From this list, IT should identify its *core* competencies (i.e., the competencies that are critical to the enterprise and fundamental to IT). The list might look something like: (1) knowledge of how to apply technology to the parent organization's businesses and (2) having a relationship with technology consumers in order to understand their needs and to develop and deliver the technology to support their work.

2. *Identify IT's core service offerings.* IT should list all of its service offerings, such as collaboration, desk-side support, report distribution, PC training, and so forth. Then IT management should study the list and identify the *core service offerings* that are derived from their core competencies.

   Understanding core competencies and core products and services is not always black and white. Sony might make the Walkman, but another company makes the plastic that goes into the Walkman case. Canon might make the camera, but it does not manufacture the wires that connect the electronic components. Even core products have components that are commodity items. Judgment will be needed to decide if service X, which relies on core competency Y, is a core service or not. Take the example of help-desk support. While the IT organization might have a core competency in understanding the business, and that competency might be critical to answering user questions about a manufacturing system, they might not be critical when answering questions about a PC operating system or word processing application.

   Exactly where the tipping point is, from being a core service dependent on a core competency to being a noncore service that has some reliance on core competency will require some sound insight and judgment.

3. *Answer some soul-searching questions about IT's competencies and services.* IT management should ask itself the following questions:

- Do the core service offerings flow from the core competencies?

  If the answer is No, then there is a disconnect. Either IT does not know what its core competencies are, or it does not know what its core service offerings are, or IT has no core competence in the production of its core services.

- Does IT have the right core competencies?

  If not, how does IT plan to acquire them?

- Is IT providing the right core service offerings given its core competencies?

  What other services should IT be providing that could emanate from its core competencies? What core services might derive from the intersection of its core competencies?

- What are IT's noncore services? Should IT be providing these noncore services or should IT obtain a better service elsewhere? At a better price?

  The noncore services are candidates for subcontracting or outsourcing. Some organizations prefer not to be too heavily involved in noncore services, but would rather have the organization focus all of its energies on core services.

- Would subcontracting or outsourcing noncore services allow IT to focus additional resources on core competencies and core services?

  This can be an IT Rubicon, because, as Prahalad and Hamel point out, once a competency (core or noncore) is given away, it is very difficult to retrieve. However, it is very attractive to allow IT to place all of its energies where it can make the most difference.

Contracting, Outsourcing, and Offshoring

These three steps might shed a completely new light on what IT functions are candidates for subcontracting and when IT should consider outsourcing them.

Recognizing the role core competencies and competitive advantage should play in IT, if IT plans to outsource a service, that service should never be in *control* of a core service or a process that is a core competency. Noncore services or services not derived from a core competency could be outsourced, if the outsourcing would allow IT to better focus on its core competencies and services. For example, Ship Bottom could outsource the production of deck fittings if that would allow the company to better focus on its core wood moldings. However, Ship Bottom should not outsource a core product (its wood moldings) or its core competency (the production process for creating the wood moldings) if it wants to remain a major player in that market.

Note the reference is to *control* of a core service and not *production*. It might be that certain components of a core service could, and perhaps should, be produced by an outside supplier, as discussed in Chapter 7. Even Sony and NEC had outside suppliers, but they always understood what they would let the outside supplier contribute and what they would never let anyone else contribute. In the Ship Bottom example, no one is suggesting that the company buy timberland in the Amazon or acquire a sawmill to provide the wood it needs for its signature wood moldings.

What is surprising is how many companies do outsource core competencies. Prahalad and Hamel give the example of Chrysler purchasing engines from Japan; something, they believe, one would never see a Japanese automaker do. Many IT organizations have been known to outsource core services as well, a serious mistake according to Prahalad and Hamel.

The exception for not outsourcing a core service might be an unhealthy company needing cash or a very poorly managed core competency. IT could be the unfortunate victim of outsourcing if a parent company desperately needs short-term cash to stave off creditors, or if senior business management is so mistrustful of IT that it would rather pass the headache on to someone else. Other than these situations, management, business, or IT ought to use Porter, Prahalad, and Hamel to understand IT's core contributions before signing away core services and their related core competencies. They might not be able to retrieve them if they later change their mind.

SOME ADDITIONAL THOUGHTS

Looking to the for-profits for guidance in running an internal support organization such as IT can have an unfortunate consequence. It can seduce management into thinking that the desired state, or final goal, for IT is to be a for-profit organization. In 99.99 percent of the cases, that is not the right course for IT. The experience of others, the inclinations of IT's own staff, and the analysis of some heavy thinkers, show that IT's destiny is in supporting its internal technology consumers. The lesson of the for-profits is to add the techniques to IT's arsenal that it needs for fulfilling its mission—not for changing its mission.

One of the for-profit techniques IT can use is to assess its own core competencies and the core services they produce. In the final analysis, many IT shops will discover that they have two core competencies:[2]

1. *IT knows the business.* The first IT competency is that IT knows the business of the enterprise better than any outsider does. IT might not know it as well as the people in the business units, but outside of them, no one knows more about how the company operates, its culture, its people, its do's, and its don'ts. IT holds a competence that virtually no other technology organization on the planet can come close to.

2. *IT knows how to apply technology to the business.* IT's second competency is that it has the potential, even if it has not successfully fulfilled it, to do what no other technology organization can do—provide technology support customized for the business. In Chapter 7 it was stated that the major disconnect between IT and its users is that *IT sells technology, but users buy service.* The internal customer community can buy technology from the same vendors IT buys it from. It might even get a better price. What it cannot buy elsewhere is the knowledge of the business, a familiarity with company culture, or decades of experience in knowing what technology works and does not work in that organization's unique environment.

IT holds in its hand a set of core competencies and the potential for the core services that no one else in the world can provide.

Whatever IT's core competencies are, they are its most valued assets, its crown jewels, and need to be treated appropriately.

ORGANIZATIONAL COMPETENCIES

DOs	DON'Ts
• Do uncover IT's core competencies.	• Don't draw the wrong conclusions from being told to act more like a business.
• Do work to maintain current core competencies and build new ones.	• Don't divert energies from core competencies and core services to noncore competencies and noncore services.
• Do understand IT's competitive advantage.	• Don't let others take control of IT's core competencies or its core services.
• Do identify IT's core services	
• Do consider outsourcing noncore services in order to focus all resources on core services.	

REFERENCES

The following are some literature, Web sites, and organizations that might be useful:

Some Representative Literature
Core Competence

Kak, Anjana. "Sustainable Competitive Advantage with Core Competence: A Review." *Global Journal of Flexible Systems Management*. December 2002.

Prahalad, C. K., and Gary Hamel. "The Core Competence of the Corporation." *Harvard Business Review*, Vol. 68, No. 3, May-June 1990, pp. 79–93.

Prahalad, C. K., and Gary Hamel. *Competing for the Future*. Harvard Business School Press, 1994.

Knowledge Management

(While the subject of the following books is knowledge management, both deal with how to acquire, maintain, and expand core competence.)

Leonard-Barton, Dorothy. *Wellsprings of Knowledge: Building and Sustaining the Source of Innovation*. Harvard Business School Press, 1995.

Nonaka, Ikujiro, and Hirotaka Takeuchi. *The Knowledge-Creating Company*. Oxford University Press, 1994.

Competitive Advantage

Porter, Michael E. *Competitive Advantage: Creating and Sustaining Superior Performance*. The Free Press, 1985.

Porter, Michael E. *Competitive Strategy*. The Free Press, 1980.

NOTES

1. C.K. Prahalad and Gary Hamel, "The Core Competence of the Corporation," *Harvard Business Review*, Vol. 68, No. 3, May-June 1990, pp. 79–93.
2. Two core competencies are about right for most IT organizations. Prahalad and Hamel say that the average conglomerate probably has no more than five or six core competencies. If a company reports it has 20 or 30 competencies, it is probably counting capabilities, which are a far cry from core competencies. Therefore, two or three core competencies, at most, sounds right for IT.

10

In Search of Customer Service

There is no such thing as service industries.
There are only industries whose service components
are greater or less than those of other industries.
Everybody is in service.
—*Theodore Levitt*

I find it rather easy to portray a businessman.
Being bland, rather cruel, and incompetent comes
naturally to me.
—*John Cleese*

A businessperson was planning to fly from London to New York on Virgin Atlantic Airlines. The plane had mechanical trouble, so the flight was cancelled. Virgin Atlantic then booked its stranded passengers on a British Air flight leaving shortly after the scheduled Virgin Atlantic flight. The lines for the British Air ticket counters were extremely long, this being a Friday evening, so even though British Air was in a different terminal, a Virgin Atlantic agent stood on line for each Virgin Atlantic business-class passenger. When the agent was next in line, the Virgin Atlantic customer was fetched and took his or her place as next to be served by the British Air ticket agent.

Virgin Atlantic offered free limo service to and from the airport for business-class passengers. Because he was no longer flying Virgin Atlantic, the businessperson thought that he would have to rent a car at New York's JFK airport. However, upon arrival in New York, a Virgin Atlantic agent met the businessperson in the British Air terminal. Standing next to her was a limo driver to take him home. That incident took place more than 15 years ago, but he still tells his friends about it. The businessperson was the author of this book. The cost to Virgin Atlantic, with the possible exception of the limo, was minimal. The benefit? The customer remembers the interaction almost two decades later.

This Virgin Atlantic story is a good example of how an organization can benefit from the services it provides to its customers. Virgin Atlantic's reputation grew on a day when it had to cancel a flight—very unusual for an airline. However, as good as this service was, exactly what one would call it is not as clear. It was probably not part of any service offering or the service component of a service offering. It is doubtful that there is a Virgin Atlantic manual somewhere laying out the steps this team followed when the flight was cancelled. What they did was probably beyond what is routinely called for. This was a type of service rarely mentioned by businesses, examined by academics, or experienced by customers. We do not even have a very good word for this type of behavior.

DO WHAT I SAY, NOT WHAT I DO

A premise of this book has been that to find out what information technology (IT) should do, first figure out what the successful for-profits do, particularly technology vendors, and then follow their lead. The assumption is that the successful for-profits know what they are doing. In many cases this is a safe bet. The for-profits have been at it for a long time, with many of their businesses thriving, so they must be doing something right. True as this might be, it does not mean that the for-profits are doing everything right.

There is growing evidence, mostly anecdotal, that, at least in the United States, customer service is declining and sinking rapidly. Americans, and many Europeans, feel that service is a casualty of the cost-cutting wars. Articles in newspapers and journals point to this loss of service.[1] The evidence is compelling. Gone are the gas stations where uniformed attendants rushed to fill your tank, wash your windshield, and check your oil. Gone are humans answering phones or your cashed paper checks returned by the bank. Gone are doctor house calls, free delivery of medicine by drugstores, and twice-a-day mail service. The airlines? What can one possibly say about the airlines!

By some estimates, service peaked around 1990 at the height of the quality era when Western firms invented or adopted several quality programs, such as Total Quality Management (TQM), ISO 9000, and Six Sigma. Quality and service became inextricably linked together, because researchers used customer service as a measure of quality.[2] The higher the perceived customer service, the better the quality of the vendor's products and services. At least, that was the theory. Since the early 1990s, however, cost cutting, and not service, has driven Western business.[3]

These findings are at odds with the data reported by the American Customer Satisfaction Index (ACSI), which indicates that customer

Exhibit 10.1   ACS Index Results

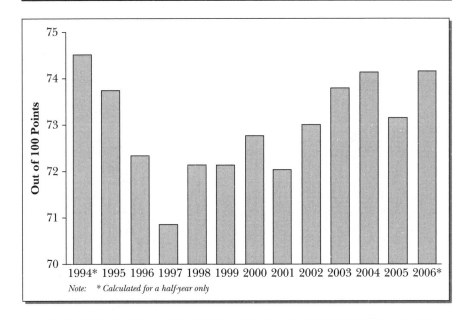

Note: * Calculated for a half-year only

Source: The American Customer Satisfaction Index (ACSI). www.theacsi.org

satisfaction, since 1994, when the ACSI was founded, bottomed out in 1997 (Exhibit 10.1). Since that low, ACSI has reported that customer satisfaction is once again rising, almost to its all-time 1994 high.[4] Why the discrepancy between the ACSI and anecdotal reports?

Is service better or worse? The problem is how do you measure service? It seems you cannot. If one looks at the literature, no one tries to measure customer service anymore; instead they measure customer satisfaction. If customer satisfaction is high, then service is presumed to be good; and if customer satisfaction is low, then service is presumed to be poor. How well service and satisfaction correlate is unknown, but rather assumed. Luckily, there are several ways of measuring customer satisfaction. The simplest way to understand how satisfied a customer is with a product or service is to ask him or her.

If the assumed linkage between customer satisfaction and service is correct, then there still needs to be an explanation of the discrepancy between the ACSI and anecdotal reports. The problem, it turns out, might still be with the definitions. ACSI says it measures customer satisfaction, but the bent of the index is still toward rating product quality and how satisfied customers are with the products they purchased. If customers rate a product, brand, or company high, then ACSI theorizes that the customer is satisfied with the product and the service that surrounds that product. This is

---

Exhibit 10.2   American Customer Satisfaction Index Definition

"The American Customer Satisfaction Index (ACSI) is an economic indicator [of customer satisfaction] based on modeling of customer evaluations of the quality of goods and services purchased in the United States and produced by both domestic and foreign firms with substantial U.S. market share."

Source: The American Customer Satisfaction Index (ACSI). http://www.theacsi.org/

---

good news for vendors, because there is a common belief that a satisfied customer is likely to buy that product again in the future. Given its definition (Exhibit 10.2), ACSI is probably right; the quality of some products has increased. In the 1960s, the life expectancy of an American car was about 60,000 miles. Now that number has more than doubled.

However, there are two complications with IT using customer satisfaction as a stand-in for customer service. The first complication is that customer satisfaction might not be as telling an indicator of how pleased the customer is after all. Klein and Einstein point out that there is a fundamental difference between customer satisfaction and customer loyalty.[5] Customer satisfaction, they say, is a measure of the customer's most recent transaction with the business, while loyalty is an indication of future behavior. According to Klein and Einstein, statistics show that satisfied customers do not always translate into return customers. Revenues, they say, are generated by loyal, not satisfied, customers. If Klein and Einstein, are right, then ACSI's definition of customer satisfaction might be a bit hollow and telling of little.

The second complication with IT using customer satisfaction as a stand-in for customer service is the definition of customer satisfaction. As was stated in earlier chapters, IT's value added to the products and services the business needs and uses, is service—more specifically, IT provides a service component to the service offering. Outside suppliers are better at building hardware and creating most software, but they do not know IT's customers. IT is best positioned to understand how the enterprise staff use hardware and software, how corporate and local business decisions are made, and how the business wants to grow. Only IT understands the problems employees face every day in trying to do their jobs. The most significant value IT can add, and its core competency, is providing the services customers need to maximize the benefits of the hardware and software IT purchases for them. IT's *raison d'être* is service.

ACSI's definition of customer satisfaction consists of a combination of the quality of the product and the service that accompanies that product. Service alone (a service component) is not measured. However, this definition is inconsistent with the common notion of a service as "a nonmaterial equivalent of a good"[6] (see Chapter 7), or even the way some academics use the term, for example, Quinn and Gagnon's use of service as a "primary output [that] is neither a product nor a construction."[7]

In 1990, Christian Gronroos published a work[8] saying that there were two different kinds of service, *technical service* and *functional service*. *Technical service* is the type of service one experiences when one calls a help desk or has the corner garage fix the brakes on the car. Gronroos calls it the "What?" since it answers the question of what the customer gets from the vendor. Technical service is usually customer-initiated—the customer usually takes the first step by calling or visiting the vendor.

The second kind of service is *functional service*, which answers the question "How?" It relates to how the service was delivered. Functional service is usually vendor-initiated. For example, the garage might have done a good job fixing the brakes on the car (technical service), but its mechanics were discourteous and abrupt (functional service). The advice one receives from the help desk is an example of technical service, while the personal service function of account management,[9] discussed in Chapter 5, would be an example of functional service.

A NEW LOOK AT SERVICE

There just might be hope for service. IBM and a few universities, such as North Carolina State University and the University of California at Berkeley, are working to create service as an area of academic study. The goal is to get academics and students interested in the scientific study of service.

Services Sciences, Management, and Engineering (SSME), as the area is currently called, is a response to the shift away from manufacturing and toward a service economy. IBM and its partners want the same attention

---

Services Sciences, Management, and Engineering

Service Science, Management, and Engineering (SSME) is a term introduced by IBM to describe Services Sciences, an interdisciplinary approach to the study, design, and implementation of services systems – complex systems in which specific arrangements of people and technologies take actions that provide value for others. More precisely, SSME has been defined as the application of science, management, and engineering disciplines to tasks that one organization beneficially performs for and with another.

Source: Wikipedia http://en.wikipedia.org/wiki/
Service_Science%2C_Management_and_Engineering

given to services as is currently paid to manufacturing. The reason for this, according to IBM's Web site, is that 75 percent of the labor force in the United States and the United Kingdom works in services.[10] IBM is undergoing a shift from being a manufacturer to being a service provider; service now generates more than two-thirds of IBM's revenue.[11]

Some believe that IBM is trailing others who have been working on this problem for more than two decades.[12] Arizona State University houses the Center for Service Leadership and is a forerunner in the service sciences. It, and some other institutions, such as the Marketing Science Institute and the American Marketing Association, started work in the field 20 years ago, trying to define and measure service. For obvious reasons, the original focus was heavily marketing-oriented (customer satisfaction and loyalty, service encounters, etc.). Vanderbilt University founded the Center for Services Marketing in 1990, and Vanderbilt's Owen Graduate School of Management offers a strong customer service and service quality curriculum.

Other schools, such as Wisconsin and Victoria in Canada, have added courses and even degrees in service science. The focus has also changed, with current topics centering on the impact of technology on the service encounter. Self-service technologies, which make you scan your own purchases, pump your own gas, and make your own reservations, are current hot topics. Two steps forward and one step back, some might think, but at least the subject is service. IBM's SSME adds large-scale engineering to the work Arizona State and the others have started.

The relevance of service science, or SSME, to IT is, as yet, unknown. It is encouraging to see service thought of as a science rather than just a minimum-wage job. However, IBM's software development and outsourcing-based interest in service is probably quite different from IT's. Which brings us back to the question, is anybody working to improve or measure the pure service IT provides? Certainly not IBM, or other organizations, whose definition of service as a provider-client interaction that creates value,[13] is sufficiently broad to include the sale of kangaroo steaks and cruise ships. No one, it seems, is working on service simply as the "nonmaterial equivalent of a good."

SERVICE ECONOMY VERSUS SERVICE MENTALITY

The poor state of reported service in the United States points out an obvious problem. Either American businesses do not care about providing service, or they incorrectly think that being part of a service economy means that they automatically have a service mentality. IBM might be correct that 75 percent of U.S. and British workers labor in the service economy, but that does not mean that they have a service mentality.

The problem, it seems, is that the word *service* can be used in three very different ways:

1. *Professional services.* Service can be a purchased item. For example, one can purchase a product, such as a personal computer (PC), or one can purchase a service, such as lawn care. In both cases, a customer acquires from a vendor something they want and for which they are willing to exchange money. Accounting firms, consultants, and fortune tellers have been successfully providing this type of service for years.

2. *Customer support.* Service can mean support. The purchaser of an item might expect that the purchase includes some service as well. The PC customer might expect that the computer vendor will provide a help line, spare parts, or a repair service. Likewise, the purchaser of the lawn care service might receive some additional support, such as online bill payment or e-mail notification of visits. Support for consumer items is usually added into the price of the item and is not charged for separately. Support is bundled into the original purchase price of the product because the vendor believes that the purchaser will not fully benefit from the item without it. Further, without the bundled support, customer satisfaction and customer loyalty could suffer and potential future business with it.

3. *Customer courtesy.* Service can be an intangible benefit provided to a customer, or prospective customer, in support of some customer need for which there is no direct or linked product offering or service offering, purchase or payment. This is the service you get from a smiling counterperson in a diner, a helpful customer service rep in a car dealership, or even the blanket and pillow you get on an airplane. This type of service makes the interaction between a vendor and a customer just a bit more enjoyable or, at least, less painful.

One of the problems with having three different, but not well-articulated, meanings for service is that it fosters equivocation and inconsistent usage. The reports of customer satisfaction improvement reported by the ACSI were probably referring to *customer support*, whereas the anecdotal reports of poor customer service reported in the popular and trade press could be any of the three, although most likely *customer courtesy*. We do not know for sure, because neither group adequately defines what it means by service.

An interesting question is which type of service, *professional, support,* or *courtesy*, provides the most material benefit to the vendor? Which type is the basis for customer satisfaction? Which type is the reason for repeat business?

Customer satisfaction with *professional services* should probably be measured the same way you measure customer satisfaction with a product—the revenue they generate or by asking the customer. Some surveys of professional services exist, but the most common source is word of mouth. Who is the best lawyer in town, the best dentist, or the best lawn care service is probably answered by asking one's neighbors. Their answers will probably focus on the professional skills of the vendor.

Measuring customer satisfaction for *customer support* is more problematic, because it is difficult for many customers to separate the product or professional service from its support. For example, is it possible to like the automaker's support when one hates the car? But, there are exceptions. For example, it is not unreasonable for a friend, who praises her new computer printer, to complain about being placed on hold for two hours when she calls the support hotline.

Customer courtesy is perhaps the most difficult to differentiate from the other two. There are two challenges in measuring customer courtesy. The first is how do you separate it from the product or professional service rendered? Customer reaction to a purchase (how good or bad it is) would seem to overshadow customer courtesy in all but the most extreme cases. For example, some patients might prefer to go to the grumpy and abrupt dentist whose fillings stay in, rather than to go to the friendly and courteous dentist across the street whose fillings fall out. Here professional service proves far more important than customer courtesy.

Second, customer courtesy seems to be more obvious when it is missing than when it is present. People remember poor customer courtesy far more than they remember good customer courtesy, unless it is unusual like the Virgin Atlantic example that began this chapter. However, as that example shows, this does not mean that good customer courtesy is not effective, just that it might be more difficult to measure.

Courtesy can be thought of as a service not directly related to a product offering or a service offering. Rather, it is usually more closely associated with the company, or the brand, than with any of the company's products or services. When it is part of a product offering or a service-offering transaction (a customer event), customers usually view it as beyond basic support.

Customer courtesy might be the most difficult to measure, but there are two qualities about it that should be easy to recognize. First, it is generally inexpensive to provide. Having staff act courteously toward customers costs little. The cost of coffee in a car dealership is insignificant. Not having customers on hold for 20 minutes might only require process changes, in which case it costs little.

The second quality of customer courtesy is that it is probably the most memorable part of the transaction for the customer. Customers usually remember good treatment by vendor staff and rarely forget poor treatment. Have a bad experience with an airline, and it will be remembered for years.

These service distinctions fit in nicely with the different usages of service presented in this book. A *service offering* is the same as a *professional service*. Customer service, in the popular sense, is probably a combination of *customer support* and *customer courtesy*. For Gronroos, customer

Exhibit 10.3 Comparative Customer Service Definitions: A Best Guess

	ACSI	Gronroos	Klein and Einstein	Anecdotal Press Reports	Market-Driven Management
Professional Services	Customer Satisfaction				Service Offering
Customer Support	Customer Satisfaction	Technical Service	Customer Service?		Service Component
Customer Courtesy		Functional Service	Customer Loyalty?	Customer Service	Personal Service

support would seem to line up with technical service. In this book, *customer support* is a *service component*.

Customer courtesy is probably close to Gronroos's functional service. Klein and Einstein's concepts are a little more difficult to categorize. At least on the surface, it would seem that their customer satisfaction is closer to customer support, while their customer loyalty at least partially lines up with customer courtesy (although there is probably a large customer support component in it). As discussed in Chapter 5, the concept of *customer courtesy* would align with the account manager's *personal service*.

Exhibit 10.3 is an attempt to categorize the various usages of customer service and its derivative phrases. Unfortunately, with apologies to the various authors, this is mostly conjecture, because exact and comparable definitions are still difficult to obtain. One thing is clear: The service landscape is still in the process of being formed.

What is interesting about Exhibit 10.3 is that, even with its faults, it does explain the disconnect between the ACSI data that suggests that service is improving and the anecdotal reports of decreasing service in the press. It would seem that ACSI was reporting on the product offering or the service offering and its associated customer support (Gronroos's technical service), while the anecdotal reports in the press are lamenting the lack of customer courtesy (Gronroos's functional service). Both ACSI and the press might be right. While the customer service associated with supporting the products and services vendors offer is improving, the customer service we associate with common courtesy is declining.

If customer courtesy is not a revenue generator, then this is good news for businesses that provide adequate customer support, even if they do not provide acceptable customer courtesy. However, if courtesy does play a role in revenue generation, as the work of Klein and Einstein seems to suggest, then business might be missing a significant opportunity.

How much does customer support cost? How much does customer courtesy cost? Published numbers are sketchy to nonexistent, but common sense would indicate that courtesy is usually considerably less expensive than support. Support involves training related to continually changing short-lived products and services and might require expensive tools and techniques. Courtesy, however, requires some training that will likely have a long life and rarely requires expensive tools or techniques, although there might be increased labor costs. Even so, it is probably safe to say that, in most situations, courtesy is considerably cheaper than support.

DO YOU WANT COURTESY WITH THAT?

According to many business leaders, the level of support or courtesy associated with a product offering or service offering will depend on the consumer, who will ultimately decide the proper trade-off between cost and the level of service. The U.S. airline industry says that the main reason airline service is so poor is that customers are not willing to pay for it. The average consumer would rather have as little service as possible, if that reduction in service translates into consumer cost savings. The result is smaller seats, less legroom, long lines, fees for checked baggage, and stale sandwiches.

Is this the right strategy, and have the airlines found the right formula? As stated in previous chapters, Henry Ford, Akio Morita, and others have shown that customers do not always know what they want. Should a business leader always follow the noise of the crowd, or (like Ford and Morita) should they sometimes lead the crowd? Perhaps the terrible reputation the airlines have is because they are listening too literally to their customers. Maybe the airlines do not understand the distinction between support and courtesy, or that the latter costs considerably less than the former. Maybe the airline customers would be happier paying just a dollar or two more for a little better service, without jeopardizing cheap fares.

For the time being, it is very difficult to say what role courtesy plays in a customer's feeling toward a service provider. It might play a minor role or, then again, it might play a very significant one. What is known is that, in at least most circumstances, courtesy is much cheaper than product or service support. The combination of cheap to provide and potentially significant returns makes customer courtesy a very difficult area to ignore.

Does the airline situation portend a Hobson's choice facing IT? While IT's clients (senior business management) are very cost-conscious, IT's consumers (end users) are not. The IT consumer might want and expect a level of service that the IT client is not willing to pay for. Should IT work to please the clients and disappoint the consumer, or the reverse? The answer is neither. The challenge for IT, and the true meaning of a service mentality, is looking for ways to provide exceptional service at reasonable cost. The answer is not always support. Sometimes courtesy is all that is needed. Separating customer support that might be expensive from the cheaper customer courtesy might yield the right blend of service at reasonable cost—exactly what Chapter 1 said market-driven management is all about.

This was also the message in Chapter 4. IT might not be able to give each customer—whether that customer is a business unit head or an order entry clerk—what he or she wants from IT. The money, the priorities, even the corporate will might not support their request. Most workers understand this. They know they will not always get what they want. What they do always want is to be listened to, taken seriously, treated fairly, and informed, in a timely manner, of the status and disposition of their request. An important part of a successful portfolio management program is the fairness and courtesy extended to all constituents.

While the academics and for-profits have done an excellent job pointing out the importance of customer service, the academics have not done a very good job improving it, nor have the for-profits done a very good job providing it. They are even struggling to define it. If service is actually declining, then what kind of a role model are the for-profits for IT? Where does this leave IT? Recognizing the importance of service in the for-profit world cannot be underestimated. IT should thank the for-profits for that. But exactly how to improve and measure service must be left to IT. IT has to be careful in following even successful businesses when it comes to service. Improving IT service to match that of the for-profits might not be good enough. Maybe this will be an area where IT can teach the profit centers a thing or two.

REFERENCES

The following are some literature, Web sites, and organizations that might be useful:

Some Helpful Organizations and Web Sites
  American Customer Satisfaction Index (ACSI). ACSI reports customer satisfaction for 10 U.S. economic sectors, 43 industries, and more than 200 companies, as well as local and federal government agencies. www.theacsi.org.

  American Marketing Association. A large organization with more than 38,000 members, it strives to be a leading source of marketing information and knowledge sharing. www.marketingpower.com.

  Center for Services Leadership. The CSL is a part of Arizona State University and works to bring together the business community and the global academic community. CSL also offers executive program advanced degrees (MBA and Ph.D.) in service science. http://wpcarey. asu.edu/csl/.

  Marketing Science Institute. Established in 1961, the Marketing Science Institute works to bring together both academics at more than

100 universities and business leaders. Its mission is to support academic research that can help businesses succeed. http:www.msi.org/.

NOTES

1. Stephen Koepp, "Pul-eeze! Will Somebody Help Me? Frustrated American Consumers Wonder Where the Service Went," *Time Magazine*, February 2, 1987, Vol. 129, No. 5; Daniel Pedersen, "Why the Service Is Missing from America's Service Economy," *Newsweek*, June 23, 1997; Darren McDermott, "Customer Satisfaction: Quality, Service Barely Pass Muster With Consumer," *Wall Street Journal*, August 16, 1999, p. A2; and Miss Manners (Judith Martin), "Will Service Still Stink?" *Time Magazine*, May 22, 2000.
2. Donald R. Lehmann and Russell S. Winer, *Product Management*, 3rd Edition, New York: McGraw-Hill Irwin, 2002).
3. Art Kleiner, "Beware the Product Death Cycle," *Strategy + Business*, Spring 2005, Issue 38.
4. The American Customer Satisfaction Index (ACSI), www.theacsi.org.
5. Mark Klein and Arthur Einstein, "The Myth of Customer Satisfaction," *Strategy + Business*, Spring 2003, Issue 30, pp. 1–2.
6. Wikipedia, http://en.wikipedia.org/wiki/Service.
7. James Brian Quinn and Christopher E. Gagnon, "Will Services Follow Manufacturing into Decline?" *Harvard Business Review*, November-December 1986, p. 95.
8. Christian Gronroos, *Service Management and Marketing: Managing the Moment of Truth in Service Competition*, Lexington Books, 1990.
9. Donald R. Lehmann and Russell S. Winer, *Product Management*, 3rd Edition, (New York: McGraw-Hill Irwin, 2002).
10. IBM SSME, www.research.ibm.com/ssme/.
11. C. P. Chandrasekhar and Jayati Ghosh, "The Global Diffusion of IT Supply," *BusinessLine*, October 10, 2006, www.thehindubusinessline.com/2006/10/17/stories/2006101700431100.htm.
12. Mary Jo Bitner and Stephen W. Brown, "The Evolution and Discovery of Service Science in Business Schools," *Communications of the ACM*, July 2006, Vol. 49, No. 7, pp. 33–34, 73–78.
13. IBM SSME, www.research.ibm.com/ssme/services.shtml.

11

Local Heroes

The reason progress is slow is that we always expect
other men to be the heroes and to live the heroic
lives. But we all have hero stuff in us.
—*Wilfred A. Peterson*

It is surmounting difficulties that makes heroes.
—*Louis Pasteur*

An American purchased an expensive watch from a first-rate jewelry store
in Tokyo. The paper bag containing the watch was of the finest quality,
with the name of the store in green letters on a pale yellow background.
Below the store name, printed in English, were the words, "The worlds most
beautifully." Why was the tag line for a Japanese jewelry store in English,
and why did a first-rate store have a tag line that did not make sense?

To understand the reasons for the wording on the bag, one has to look
a little closer at Japanese culture. Like most of the world, Japan is enamored with Western pop culture. Travel to Moscow, Bangkok, or Hong Kong
and you will experience large numbers of the locals, particularly the young,
wearing blue jeans, listening to Western music, and watching Western
movies. Japan is no different. Spend a Saturday in one of Tokyo's parks, or
visit any of its many shopping areas, and one will see UCLA T-shirts and
New York Yankees baseball caps among a sea of other Western iconic names
splashed across shirts, coats, and hats. Japan's acceptance of foreign ideas
has led to the popular Western belief that Japan just copies others, particularly the West. This is reinforced by the electronics and computer industries, among others, where Japan has done well copying what was created
in the United States and Europe.

But this is only a half-truth. Japan does copy good ideas from the
West, or wherever it finds them, but then the Japanese take those ideas
and modify and improve them to gain the best from them. Japan inherited

the videocassette recorder (VCR) from the United States, but it took the American design and increased its reliability while reducing its costs. Germany might claim the invention of the automobile, but the Japanese made it both dependable and affordable. The Japanese do not suffer from the "not invented here" (NIH) syndrome that is so prevalent in the West. They take what they like, but then they make it uniquely Japanese. Yes they copy, but then they improve it and make it theirs.

"The worlds most beautifully," called Jinglish by Westerners living in Japan, is neither English nor a mistake, but it is uniquely Japanese. Many Japanese companies like to use Western words in their names and tag lines, similar to the way many American perfume companies like to use French words. However, the Japanese are more interested in the symmetry of the words than their meaning. "The worlds most beautifully" was used because it appeared aesthetic to the storeowner. It is no more English, nor was it meant to be, than *eau de cologne*.

The lesson from the Japanese is to take what is good, no matter who came up with the idea first, and then mold and craft it to make it better fit the situation. This is also the philosophy behind market-driven management. IT managers can improve their organizations by looking around, learning what works, taking those ideas, and molding them to their environment. Some of these ideas will come from other IT organizations, others will come from outside of IT, even from the for-profits.

The premise is not new. *Running IT like a business* (RITLAB), the most popular do-it-yourself advice for IT for the last decade, centers on just that. IT, it says, should learn from the big businesses how to get along with senior business management. The advice is quite simple: Look like a business, act like a business, talk like a business, hang out with businesspeople, and you will be thought of as a businessperson. This is not a case of the business is smart and IT is dumb. It is just that the business world has a couple of thousand years head start on IT.

Not surprisingly, RITLAB focuses on two areas. The first RITLAB focal point is *aligning IT with the business* (an unfortunate choice of words because it implies that IT is *not* part of the business), an amalgam of IT strategy, governance, and reporting to senior management in a way it can understand. *Cost management* is the second RITLAB focal area. As this book has stated time and again, these are all laudable ideas. The problem with RITLAB is not what it contains, but what it does not.

CIO Magazine has been one of the most active advocates of RITLAB. It has not only published numerous articles on the subject, but it dedicated its May 1, 2004 issue to this topic.[1] *CIO* surveyed more than 100 IT executives. They asked them for their opinion of the RITLAB practices they tried— both the benefits they derived from them and the difficulties they experienced implementing them. The IT executives were asked to choose from a list of more than 40 practices. The practices were programs such as, "conduct regular strategic planning meetings to achieve alignment," and "compensate/reward IT employees/managers based on the performance of the IT organization." What is interesting is that, by the author's estimate, 89 percent of the practices were for the direct benefit of senior business management—what market-driven management calls IT's clients. Only 11 percent of the RITLAB practices were for the direct benefit of IT's technology consumers, the staff who use IT's services every day. Of the 10 practices deemed "most effective,"[2] *all of them,* by the author's estimate, were skewed toward the IT client (see Exhibit 11.1).

Granted, consumers would gain indirect benefit from some of the practices aimed at IT's clients, just as IT's clients would be pleased by the positive results of the practices directly aimed at IT's consumers. It is also sometimes difficult to judge, from a simple phrase, with no accompanying definition, whether "publish catalog of services/standards" is aimed more at IT's senior business management clients or technology consumers. Saying that only 11 percent of the practices are aimed directly at technology consumers might be too conservative a number. However, whether the number is 11 percent, or double or triple that, it still shows RITLAB's bias toward senior business management at the expense of the technology consumer.

Market-driven management (MDM) tries to correct RITLAB's deficiency, but without going too far in the opposite direction. Not wanting to "throw the baby out with the bathwater," MDM tries not to replace RITLAB, but to build on it. RITLAB's failing is not one of commission, but omission—it simply left the little people, slugging it out in the corporate trenches, out of the equation.

Exhibit 11.1   Who Benefits from Running IT Like a Business?

CIO Magazine's 10 Most Effective Practices	Primary Beneficiary
Regularly use portfolio management or other project prioritization methodology.	IT Client
Employ an IT-dedicated financial officer.	IT Client
Position the CIO as a member of the corporate board or executive committee.	IT Client
Employ IT dedicated CFO, COO, HR, marketing positions	IT Client
Win and showcase IT awards.	IT Client
Regularly use project management methodologies.	IT Client
Employ internal relationship managers/account executives to work with the business.	IT Client
Conduct regular strategic planning meetings to achieve alignment.	IT Client
Perform audits.	IT Client
Use leadership development programs.	IT Client

Some might suggest that MDM's swing toward the consumer is modest—maybe even too modest. IT governance, strategy and planning, portfolio management, and market intelligence are more likely to bring a satisfying smile to the faces of senior business managers than to consumers. However, if run correctly, the foot soldiers of the organization should have a hand in IT governance, strategy and planning, and portfolio management through their inclusion on the IT Steering Committee's councils and special interest groups.

Consumers could also gain from the market intelligence IT collects. They could be the recipients of improved service as a result of what IT learns from interviewing staff in other IT shops. Of course, market intelligence could just as easily show IT how to further reduce costs or curtail service to be more in line with competitors, proving market intelligence can be a double-edged sword for IT's consumers.

Customer management, service-offering management, and, arguably, the majority of performance management are aimed squarely at the technology consumer. Some organizations see customer management as reaching out to business managers on major IT–business issues (as seen in the wording of one of *CIO Magazine's* top-ten most utilized practices: "Employ internal relationship managers/account executives *to work with the business* [italics added for emphasis]."[3] MDM also believes that customer management should serve IT's clients, but the function should not end with just supporting clients. Customer management also entails working closely with IT's consumers. In fact, it would seem unlikely that an account manager could be effective working with clients if he or she does not have a good understanding of the plight of the consumer. This is a case where both types of customers benefit from IT working closely with the other.

Service-offering management (SOM) is an obvious homerun for the technology consumer. SOM's mission is to understand what the technology consumer needs and to fulfill that need to the best of IT's ability. There is a benefit for clients as well. When consumers are working at peak effectiveness, they are in the best position to generate the revenue that benefits all.

Performance management is a more complex area. Clients are certainly an important, and maybe the first, target for IT sharing its wins and losses. However, studies, as well as anecdotal evidence, show that informed consumers are more satisfied with the service they receive than their counterparts who are not well informed. The consumer is also the winner if IT can finally understand, objectively report, and, therefore, improve the customer experience. Although not perfect, MDM does a better job of satisfying customer demand than just using RITLAB alone.

However, pointing out the similarities or differences among different improvement programs is missing the point. IT does not have to choose. The good news is that IT is a guest at an intellectual smorgasbord. IT is free to pick and choose among the different options spread out before it. Like the Japanese in the story at the beginning of this chapter, IT should examine all of these programs, pick them up, turn them over, and take a little taste. Is this one better than that one? Try them all, or just try a few. Find the ones that fit the organization the best. The only mistake IT can make is not to join in the meal.

ACHIEVING MARKET-DRIVEN MANAGEMENT

As was stated in Chapter 1, what the business is looking for from IT is efficiency, effectiveness, transparency, and safe hands. Of these four business objectives for IT, the last two, transparency and safe hands, are the most important. Even if IT cannot achieve efficiency and effectiveness on its own, if the business views IT's processes as transparent and IT's staff as safe hands, then the business can help IT achieve the missing two business objectives.

MDM is a collection of business techniques and tools to help IT achieve the four business objectives for IT. Some MDM techniques focus more on one objective than another. For example, governance and strategy are heavily skewed toward transparency and effectiveness, while customer management is more aligned with safe hands. However, there is a little bit of each of the four objectives in every MDM component. The MDM techniques discussed in this book are important additions to the IT arsenal. With them, IT can achieve the four business objectives for IT.

That is the good news. The not-so-good news is that implementing the MDM techniques will not be easy. IT managers, who successfully implemented some or all of the MDM techniques, have tales of successes and failures, of do's and don'ts. The most important lessons learned and recommendations from the battle-scarred can be summarized into the following short set of rules:

- *Ensure that the basic blocking and tackling is in place.* IT needs to get its house in order. The infrastructure has to be there, and the fundamental services at least need to be available for IT's customers before any RITLAB or MDM approaches can be undertaken.

  When critical systems are failing every day, senior business management will not be receptive to IT ignoring daily operating problems to work on longer-range issues. Anything other than fixing immediate problems will be viewed by the business as a distraction at best and a smoke screen at worst.

- *Energize the clients.* Senior business managers need to see IT as safe hands and its processes as transparent. They need to feel that IT, perhaps with their help, is capable of providing services when and where they are needed by the enterprise, at an acceptable price. IT needs to be viewed as an active force and not as a passive service station. IT cannot do it alone and should not be perceived as doing it alone.

IT governance, IT strategy and planning, and portfolio management are proven techniques IT can use to both engage and energize its clients.

- *Energize the consumers.* Consumers need to know that IT listens to them and is on their side. They need to feel that they count, that their ideas, as well as their needs, are taken seriously and acted upon. IT should work to get consumers involved in the technology and service selection processes either actively, through the use of the councils and special interest groups of the IT Steering Committee, or passively, through interviews, focus groups, or just talking with them in hallways. It would be very difficult and extraordinary to over-communicate with this group. IT governance, strategy and planning, customer management, and service-offering management are all aimed at helping energize consumers.

- *Energize the IT staff.* Senior IT management faces two significant IT staff issues. The first is disassociation. While some IT staff will understand the changes involved with MDM, they will perplex others. It is hard for someone who works in a data center or network operations center to relate to the problems facing an account manager in Odd, West Virginia. They see IT as about hardware and software and not about complaining users. Being demand-driven (providing customers with what they need) rather than supply-driven (providing what is widely available) can ring hollow for these IT workers. For them, the energies expended on RITLAB or MDM are a waste of resources.

  However, most staff will come around if the plan for changing IT includes a program for educating IT staff. Seeing progress is important. Performance management that measures not just technology, or even services, but customer satisfaction becomes critical because it allows staff to see the effects of their efforts.

  The second issue is culture. There is perhaps no greater force working within an organization than culture. Management can change the organizational strategy, the operational procedures, even the reward system, and still find that fundamental change is elusive. No carrot and no stick can easily ensnare this force. Time, immersion, and repetition, taken together, form one of the few weapons that can alter culture. The new message needs to be absorbed into all parts of the organization and repeated again and again for, perhaps, years.

  A nonexclusive alternative is to not fight the tide. Rather than relying solely on changing the current culture in the organization, IT management can set up a separate organization, within IT, with the desired culture built in. This is the plan behind dividing IT into a functional factory and a front office. The front office will be the new organization with a new customer-focused culture.

  For many, the best solution is to do both: Work to change the overall culture of IT while establishing organizational pockets of progressive thought. IT governance, in which the IT staff participates in the councils and special interest groups of the IT Steering Committee, will help engage IT staff in the new culture. Customer management and service-offering management can help establish a new IT front-office organization that supports the new culture.

- *Create the products and services the business really needs and can afford.* Engage customers in product/service definition, procurement, and delivery. Focus on IT's core competencies while relying on others' core competencies (suppliers, partners, outsourcers) to supplement IT's. Provide the best possible services consumers want and need. Measure performance from a customer perspective. Service-offering management, market intelligence, and performance management are designed to help in this area.

- *Tell it like it is.* Ensure that clients, consumers, and IT staff understand IT's plans, processes, services, performance, accomplishments, and failures. Make all processes and procedures as transparent as possible. Tout successes, but be willing to confess mistakes and missteps. Be credible. IT governance, IT strategy and planning, customer management, and performance management will help.

FIRST STEPS FIRST

Step one (basic blocking and tackling) is what most IT organizations are currently doing fairly well. It is also an assumption of MDM, which focuses on the remaining five steps. Although step one needs to be completed first, the remaining steps are not sequential and can be completed in any sequence, or even simultaneously, if all of the necessary resources are available.

Most senior business managers will applaud IT's RITLAB or MDM or similar initiatives if the basics are in place. However, if fundamental services are missing, then initiatives such as RITLAB and MDM will be dismissed. IT's customers will probably not take kindly to IT working on a three-year strategic plan when IT cannot keep the network up for more than a few hours at a time. Instead, it might be seen as IT overreaching its ability, unrealistic in its expectations, or simply out of control. IT attempting to impress senior business management with advanced business initiatives before all necessary and basic services are in place is like a diamond in a plastic tiara. The sparkle is there, but who cares.

A FINAL THOUGHT

RITLAB, MDM, research firms, lessons from IT managers who have been through it already, the IT press with its management flavor of the month, your Uncle Harold who recently retired from the shoe business—all have something valuable to say about running IT, yet none has all of the answers. Follow the Japanese model: Study them all, adapt them all, and adopt what makes sense. This is not dogma. Even the for-profit heroes do not have all of the answers for themselves, much less for the cost centers of the world. Each IT organization, each CIO, each IT manager needs to select what is right for him or her and for his or her organization. Overhead heroes, it turns out, exist, but they are local heroes, running local support organizations.

REFERENCES

The following are some Web sites and organizations that might be useful:

Baseline magazine. Focuses on IT tactics through case studies, practical tips, and IT-relevant materials, such as return on investment (ROI) and total cost of ownership (TCO) workbooks. www.baselinemag.com/.

CIO Decisions. Presents itself as the magazine for the small to medium-sized company, although the articles are often relevant for any size organization. http://searchcio.techtarget.com/.

CIO Insight. Focuses on IT strategy with trends, stories, research, and interviews with leading thinkers. www.cioinsight.com/.

CIO Magazine. Features articles on many aspects of running an IT organization from both academics and practitioners. www.cio.com/(Note the special section on Running IT Like a Business: www.cio.com/ritlab/).

NOTES

1. "Special Report: How to Run I.T. Like a Business," *CIO Magazine*, May 1, 2004, pp. 48–83.
2. "Running IT Like a Business," *CIO Magazine*, http://www2.cio.com/research/surveyreport.cfm?id=71.
3. "Special Report: How to Run I.T. Like a Business," *CIO Magazine*, May 1, 2004, pp. 48–83.

Index

IT is under pressure to change the way it functions within a corporation. Some senior business managers recognize IT as a critical business enabler, but for others, IT is too unreliable and too untrustworthy to play a critical business role. To better position IT to realize its full potential as an equal business partner, IT needs to be viewed by the business as safe hands—providing IT services efficiently and effectively with transparent processes and procedures.

The Business-Oriented CIO: A Guide to Market-Driven Management equips CIOs with the same or similar tools used by for-profits to create real business value. It brings together the best of the best in IT best practices, programs, techniques, and experiences of CIOs and senior IT managers. Using an approach called Market-Driven Management to adopt for-profit techniques for the cost center, this practical book reveals the winning formula necessary to run an IT business, including:

- Understanding internal customer needs by applying for-profit customer segmentation techniques

- Adopting board of director methods to enhance IT governance

- Creating an IT strategy that actually aligns with the business

- Using portfolio management to ensure that all IT constituencies are fairly represented